Bowling
STEPS TO SUCCESS

Doug Wiedman
Purdue University

Human Kinetics

Library of Congress Cataloging-in-Publication Data

Wiedman, Doug, 1964-
  Bowling : steps to success / Doug Wiedman.
    p. cm.
  ISBN 0-7360-5528-2 (soft cover)
  1. Bowling--Study and teaching. I. Title.
  GV903.W48 2006
  794.6--dc22   2005014087

ISBN-10: 0-7360-5528-2
ISBN-13: 978-0-7360-5528-4

The Web addresses cited in this text were current as of 10/17/2005 unless otherwise noted.

Acquisitions Editor: Jana Hunter
Developmental Editor: Cynthia McEntire
Assistant Editor: Scott Hawkins
Copyeditor: Patricia MacDonald
Proofreader: Sue Fetters
Permission Manager: Carly Breeding
Graphic Designer: Nancy Rasmus
Graphic Artist: Kim McFarland
Cover Designer: Keith Blomberg
Photographer (cover): Tom Roberts
Art Manager: Kareema McLendon
Illustrator: Roberto Sabas
Printer: Versa Press

Human Kinetics books are available at special discounts for bulk purchase. Special editions or book excerpts can also be created to specification. For details, contact the Special Sales Manager at Human Kinetics.

Printed in the United States of America   10 9 8 7 6 5 4 3

Web site: www.HumanKinetics.com

Human Kinetics
P.O. Box 5076
Champaign, IL 61825-5076

e-mail: humank@hkusa.com

Human Kinetics
475 Devonshire Road, Unit 100
Windsor, ON N8Y 2L5
800-465-7301 (in Canada only)
e-mail: orders@hkcanada.com

Europe: Human Kinetics
107 Bradford Road
Stanningley
Leeds LS28 6AT, United Kingdom
+44 (0)113 255 5665
e-mail: hk@hkeurope.com

Australia: Human Kinetics
57A Price Avenue
Lower Mitcham, South Australia 5062
08 8372 0999
e-mail: info@hkaustralia.com

New Zealand: Human Kinetics
Division of Sports Distributors NZ Ltd.
P.O. Box 300 226 Albany
North Shore City, Auckland
0064 9 448 1207
e-mail: info@humankinetics.co.nz

This book is dedicated to the thousands of students
who have taken my course at Purdue University.
Thank you for your patience and effort.
My greatest hope is that you have found as much joy
in learning the game as I have in teaching it.

To my wife, Beverly, and our children, Kellie, Kyle, and Kristin.
Thank you not just for tolerating my passion for the game
but also for sharing it with me.

 Contents

Climbing the Steps to Bowling Success

Over the years, bowling has been one of the world's most popular forms of recreation. In the United States, it is estimated that 40 to 50 million people bowl at least once a year. Worldwide, yearly participation approaches 100 million. Bowling is one of only five activities recognized by the President's Council on Physical Fitness and Sports for its lifelong promotion of physical activity.

One of the reasons for bowling's popularity is its accessibility. Bowling presents opportunities for participation to all players regardless of age, gender, or physical condition. The equipment required to begin to bowl is not expensive. In fact, almost every bowling center has an assortment of balls and shoes available on site. Participants can try out the sport without incurring much initial expense.

More-committed bowlers, those who bowl weekly, are usually members of one of the sport's sanctioning organizations. The combined membership of the four major organizations—the American Bowling Congress (ABC), the Women's International Bowling Congress (WIBC), the Young American Bowling Alliance (YABA), and the United States Bowling Congress (USBC)—is nearly 3.25 million men, women, and youths. These organizations are among the world's largest sports organizations.

But there is a problem with the popularity of bowling. As a social activity, bowling lends itself to a fun and relaxed atmosphere. Unfortunately, many critics of the game see only this social aspect and do not look carefully at the sport's athletic demands. Many regular participants, some of whom started to bowl at a young age, are also guilty of taking the athletic aspects of the game for granted. After all, a few pins can be knocked down many different ways. The perception that anything goes leads many bowlers to establish poor motor habits, which inevitably leads to poor performance. Surprisingly, there are very few ways to knock down all the pins consistently.

The goal of *Bowling: Steps to Success* is to give bowlers the opportunity to learn the sport aspects of the game so they will develop not only a new respect for bowling but also the skills required to participate successfully. Through knowledge and skill development, bowlers can find a deeper level of appreciation for the challenges of the game. If doing something is fun, then doing it well is more than fun—it is satisfying. Increased scoring potential and the achievement of personal goals drive the bowler to pursue even higher levels of performance. Successful implementation of the concepts discussed in this book will give the reader this opportunity.

Do not accept the status quo. Do not doubt your ability to improve. No athlete should quit or accept a level of mediocrity because the game is no longer satisfying.

Many bowling proprietors, using the guidelines established by the USBC, are working to promote the sporting aspect of bowling. The various levels of coaching endorsements, Team USA, Junior Gold, and the "sport-shot" lane condition program are some of the important developments that have come from this effort. Because of their efforts, a new emphasis on the sporting aspects of the game is emerging. Opportunities to learn the game from trained, qualified coaches are on the rise. Business owners and leadership figures are recognizing the needs and preferences of the committed participant.

Just by reading this book, you are demonstrating your willingness to accept the challenges of the game. Knowledge is the first step toward surmounting challenges. *Bowling: Steps to Success* provides the information you need to achieve your bowling goals. The ultimate goal of this book is to provide the *why* as well as the *how* for the sport of bowling. This will promote a greater appreciation for the game and facilitate skill development throughout a lifelong involvement in bowling.

Bowling: Steps to Success is written to suit the needs of all bowlers at all levels. Those new to the sport will benefit from the systematic instruction, which can be adjusted to suit each bowler's rate of development or level of interest. More-experienced players will find that each step isolates a particular element of the game, helping troubleshoot weak spots that may have developed and guiding the bowler to more-advanced techniques. Instructors will find the basic concepts around which a course may be developed.

In *Bowling: Steps to Success*, you will follow a specific developmental process. First you will learn basic information about the game and its physical facilities. You will discover how to establish a proper learning mind-set and how to

select the proper equipment. Subsequent steps lead you through the series of skills essential for bowling success. Each of these steps includes a brief discussion of the physical principles that influence the nature of the movement, followed by a description of the sport-specific movement. Progressive practice drills are included. Drills allow for the proper development of specific motor habits. The illustrations, charts, and checklists enhance the text to provide a fuller understanding of the game.

Later steps discuss more-advanced aspects of bowling, such as spare-shooting strategies, recognizing and adapting to lane conditions, and developing physical versatility, which allows the athlete to cope with a wide range of performance demands.

Bowling: Steps to Success provides a systematic approach to playing and teaching bowling. Follow the same sequence as you work your way through each step:

1. Read the explanation of what is covered in the step, why the step is important, and how to execute or perform the step.

2. Follow the illustrations.

3. Review the missteps, which note common errors and corrections.

4. Perform the drills. Drills improve skills through repetition and purposeful practice. Read the directions and record your score. Drills appear near the skill instructions so you can refer to the instructions easily if you have trouble with the drill.

Competence breeds confidence. With *Bowling: Steps to Success* as your guide, every time you step into a bowling center presents another chance to develop your skills and increase your enjoyment of the sport. This book will help you conquer the challenges of bowling. The goal is to make every bowling outing a pleasurable and satisfying experience. With patience, diligence, and an open mind, you will embark on an athletic journey that will satisfy for a lifetime.

■ Acknowledgments

In life's journey, many sources of information and inspiration contribute to success. Here is a sampling of these influences in my life. In particular, I wish to acknowledge the help and support of the following friends and colleagues in making this book a reality:

• Grant Chleborad, student, teammate, and bowling buddy. After telling me you had listed my name on a coaching Web site, you said, "You never know what might come from it." This book is what came from it. Thank you for your respect and your friendship.

• Dr. Donald Corrigan and Dr. Thomas Templin, heads of the department of health and kinesiology at Purdue University. You have given me the opportunity to make a vocation out of my avocation. I consider myself among the lucky few who wake every morning looking forward to the day ahead.

• Tom Taylor, operator of the Triple Crown Pro Shop. For more than 10 years, you have demonstrated endless patience when answering ball-drilling questions. You have also given invaluable help to my family and me concerning bowling equipment, allowing all of us to enjoy a measure of success at this game. In addition, thank you for providing outstanding service to the hundreds of my students who have come looking for advice and bowling balls. Your dedi-cation to the game, your respect for the bowler and customer, and your commitment to the trade are greatly appreciated.

• Terry Clayton, assistant director of the Purdue Memorial Union. In the winter of 1993, a chance luncheon meeting at a Fred Borden instructional clinic led to the creation of the bowling course. You recognized an opportunity others had turned their backs on. Every year since then, we have shown just how shortsighted they were. Thank you for your confidence.

• Holly and Rich Conrad, owners of Star Lanes in Lafayette, Indiana. Your support of the high school program has given me an opportunity to coach not just at another venue but also at another level. I cannot express how satisfying it is to help in the development of young players. Your generosity deserves greater recognition.

• *Bowlers Journal International.* As a history major, I appreciate your effort to preserve the legacy of the sport of bowling. Many of your articles provide excellent reading, highlighting the history and development of the game that is still going on.

• Scott Savage, manager of the PMU Recreation Center. I am looking forward to working with you in the development of new bowling programs and to the continued success of the intercollegiate bowling team. Go Purdue!

The Sport of Bowling

Bowling has a long and diverse history. Bowling-type games have been played throughout the world in many different cultures. Evidence of these games has been discovered in some of the world's most ancient cultures. For many years, it was thought that a bowling game existed in ancient Egypt from about 5200 b.c., although this is no longer believed to be completely accurate. Bowling artifacts found in a child's tomb turned out to be not as old as previously thought. However, even after knocking off a few thousand years, this evidence still proves that bowling is an ancient game. Bowling was played in the Polynesian islands as well, on a course very similar to the 60-foot distance used in today's game. Bowling on the green has existed for centuries in England. Bocce, an Italian bowling game, has been around for more than a thousand years and is still played today.

Bowling at pins most likely originated in Germany. In fact, to this day bowlers can be referred to as keglers, from the German word *kegeln,* to bowl. The Germans took the game very seriously. During the Middle Ages, bowling took on a religious significance as part of the church service. A pin was set up to represent the pagans; the ability to knock the pin down was a testament to a person's godliness. It's tough enough bowling with a few dollars on the line; imagine bowling for the sanctity of your soul!

Martin Luther himself was reputed to be an avid bowler.

One medieval king was known to have banned the game because his soldiers were spending too much time bowling and not enough time practicing their archery. Apparently, his highness had a problem with recreation getting in the way of the defense of the realm. Francis Drake, when notified of the approaching Spanish Armada in 1588, was rumored to have commented, "I have time to finish my game of bowles [sic] and defeat the Spanish Armada."

The Dutch brought the game to the New World, and you can still find many areas of the country that bear the name Bowling Green. Early bowling in America frequently featured only nine pins. The pins were set up in the shape of a diamond, like the billiard game 9 ball today. The goal was to knock down all the pins except the middle pin, referred to as the kingpin. The 5 pin in the modern triangular setup is still called the kingpin even though the intent of knocking down all the pins has changed from the original game. One of the earliest references to bowling appears in Washington Irving's early 1800s story "Rip Van Winkle."

Variations of the game were as diverse as the culture and circumstances of the participants. There is little doubt that a tenpin version was played even while ninepins was popular. Some believe tenpin bowling officially originated over a legal matter. Because bowling was so strongly associated with drinking and gambling, a Connecticut law was passed in the early 1800s banning the game of ninepins. An enterprising individual is reputed to have added a 10th pin (probably after learning of tenpin bowling in other locales) to circumvent the legal restriction. The shape of the setup was changed from a diamond to a triangle. Eventually clubs developed in many larger cities. Various attempts, most unsuccessful, were made to organize the sport, but the game remained without codified standards for a number of years. Balls and pins varied greatly in both size and weight, according to local customs and resources, as did the width and length of the lane. A consistent method for keeping score was not even in use.

The first successful national organization was the American Bowling Congress (ABC), founded in 1895. The ABC standardized the basic rules and equipment for the first time in the game's long history. Factors such as lane dimension, ball weight and size, pin weight and size, scorekeeping, and even the spacing between the pins in the setup were established through the early efforts of the ABC. The ABC's first national tournament was held in 1901.

The early part of the 20th century was the era of individual match play. The local hotshot of one city would challenge the hotshot of another city in home-against-home matches. These matches would involve 20, 30, or even 40 games of competition in each bowler's home bowling center. As with many activities in which civic or personal pride is at stake, considerable quantities of action- and side-wager money changed hands.

One of the more colorful characters at this time was a Bavarian named Count Gengler. A man of imposing stature, Gengler often came to matches fully decked out in top hat and cane. This image undoubtedly added an aura to his performances as well as an intimidation factor. Psyching out the opponent has a long history. Gengler developed a one-step approach while bowling on the rugged alleys of his home country. This one-step technique was so precise he could throw strikes in the dark. During these demonstrations, he would get himself ready on the approach and then ask that the bowling

center lights be shut off. After everyone heard the ball roll down the lane and the pins crash, the house lights would be turned on again. All the pins would be cleared off the deck! In one memorable exhibition, he was reputed to have thrown a perfect game (12 consecutive strikes) without ever seeing the pins. The Count's reputation was built on his money matches. When asked why he was called the Count, his manager (or bankroller) responded, "Because when the bowling is done he's the one *counting* all the money." The early leadership of the ABC frowned on this professionalism. Despite his skills, Count Gengler was never elected to the ABC Hall of Fame.

Jimmy Smith, another legend of bowling's early years, was known for his match-play success. Smith, one of the sport's early national champions, did have one memorable losing match, however. In 1927, Smith played against a relatively unknown bowler named Floretta McCutcheon. Soon after the founding of the Women's International Bowling Congress (WIBC) in 1916, women began demonstrating their skills on the lanes. Jimmy Smith found himself a victim of this newfound prowess. When talking about the match, Smith said, "I have just met the world's finest bowler, and she is a woman." After the match, "Mrs. Mac" went on an exhibition tour and became a noted instructor, introducing the game to thousands of women. Slowly but surely, women began to assert their influence and skill on the game, which lent a new respectability to the sport. As women became increasingly involved, bowling alleys cleaned up to become the modern, family-oriented recreational facilities found today.

The end of prohibition saw the growth of team play. Many of the most successful teams, usually composed of the bowling stars of the day, were sponsored by breweries such as Stroh's or Pabst Blue Ribbon. One team, Herman's Undertakers, had a formidable match-play reputation and set many of the early team scoring records. The most famous team of this era was Budweiser's. All five players in the lineup during the 1950s were future hall-of-famers. The team's top players were Don Carter and Dick Weber, generally recognized as two of the finest bowlers of all time.

The team era started to wane with the formation of the Professional Bowlers Association

The Best Pro Ever

Earl Anthony is considered, by most, to be the greatest professional bowler ever. In approximately 275 tournaments during his 14-year career, he won 41 national titles and finished second 42 times. He was the first PBA player to earn $100,000 in tournament winnings in a year and the first to reach $1,000,000 in a career. Anthony retired in 1984. His record of 41 titles has yet to be broken.

In recent years, Walter Ray Williams has placed himself among the greatest bowlers of all time. As of the 2004 season, he was within striking distance of Anthony's national title record, with 39 titles of his own.

(PBA) tour in 1958. The monetary incentive drew most of the best players onto the professional tour. For example, in 1961 Don Carter became the first professional athlete from any sport to sign a million-dollar endorsement contract. Lending his name to bowling equipment was worth $100,000 per year for 10 years. In the early 1960s, Don Carter was one of the world's highest-paid athletes; his combined earnings from endorsement deals, public-relation events, and tournament winnings totaled nearly $200,000 per year. As the financial incentive grew stronger, the emphasis of the sport increasingly leaned toward individual effort.

Even as late as the mid-1970s, the prize money earned by the top professional bowlers compared favorably with the salaries of other professional athletes. Before the era of free agency, when the average salary for a professional baseball player was about $75,000, the top bowler on the tour earned more than $100,000.

In the early 1960s, the PBA signed a contract with the ABC television network, a relationship that lasted 34 years. Athletes such as Billy Welu, Don Johnson, Johnny Petraglia, Marshall Holman, and Mark Roth became household names as their matches were broadcast into millions of homes every week. The ABC network's Saturday afternoon lineup of *American Sportsman,* the PBA tour telecast, and *Wide World of Sports* was one of television's most popular. The ratings for the PBA's Saturday telecast consistently beat all other sports televised in that time slot.

Membership in the national organizations peaked in the late 1970s when both the ABC and WIBC had more than four million members each. Junior bowlers were represented by the American Junior Bowling Congress (AJBC, now called the Young American Bowling Alliance). Its membership also peaked at this time at about 850,000. They were (and still are) the world's largest sport sanctioning organizations.

Throughout bowling's modern era, controversies have arisen. Many purists claim that easy lane conditions and technological intrusions (in particular, the materials and dynamics of the ball) have chipped away at the sporting aspect of the game. They cite this as the reason for the considerable drop in ABC and WIBC membership over the last 25 years. (As of 2004, ABC membership is about 1.6 million, while the WIBC has about 1.2 million members.) In recent years, more than 40,000 perfect games (score of 300) were bowled in sanctioned competitions each season, along with thousands of honor scores for individual games and series. Many question the integrity of a sport in which more than 10 times as many sanctioned honor scores are bowled as there used to be even though there are fewer than half as many members of the sanctioning organizations as there were just 25 years ago. These perceptions, combined with changes in society's recreational outlets, have eroded membership.

Efforts to reverse this decline are being made:

1. The Team USA coaching program was reorganized to combine all aspects of instruction into one coherent program. The new USBC coaching program allows athletes to receive a consistent program of instruction from the time they first take up bowling as youths until they reach the highest levels of the game.

2. Sport bowling competitions are being sanctioned. The most important aspect of sport bowling is the use of challenging lane conditions. Lane condition patterns are

dictated by the sanctioning body's sport bowling program. For a sport bowling competition to be sanctioned, a bowling center must be verified as being in compliance with the conditions established by the sanctioning body. Special awards and recognition are granted to bowlers who choose to play as sport bowlers.

3. Delegates of the three sanctioning organizations—ABC, WIBC, and YABA—voted to combine all membership under one organization. For the first time in the sport's history, one organization represents competitive bowling in the United States. In the spring of 2004, the United States Bowling Congress (USBC) was created. Its goal is to speak with one voice for bowlers of all ages and skill levels in the promotion and development of the game.

BOWLING LANE AND EQUIPMENT

The rules, equipment specifications, and scoring system of tenpin bowling are standardized worldwide.

Pins are 15 inches tall, with a diameter at the widest point of about 4 3/4 inches. They measure 1 1/2 inches at the narrowest part of the neck and stand on a flat base 2 1/2 inches wide. Pins weigh 3 pounds 6 ounces to 3 pounds 10 ounces.

Pins are arranged in an equilateral triangle, with the top of the triangle pointing toward the bowler (figure 1). There is a distance of 12 inches between the center of one pin and any other pin next to it. The entire arrangement makes a triangle 3 feet on each side.

The bowling lane (figure 2) is made of wood or very hard synthetic material. The lane must be flat to a tolerance of 40/1,000ths of an inch, as measured across the entire width of the lane. The surface the bowler walks on (the approach) measures 16 to 17 feet from the beginning of the approach to the foul line. From the foul line to the center of the front (head) pin is 60 feet. The lane is 41 to 42 inches across. The depressions on either side of the lane (called the *gutters* or *channels)* are about 10 inches wide and 3 1/2 inches deep.

The bowling ball is 27 inches in circumference. Balls must be made out of solid, nonmetallic material. The maximum weight of a bowling ball is 16 pounds. After the finger holes are drilled into a ball, it is weighed on a dodo scale to highlight any imbalances. A ball cannot have a difference of more than 3 ounces between the top and bottom halves (figure 3). The maximum imbalance allowed between the left and right halves or the front and back halves is only 1 ounce.

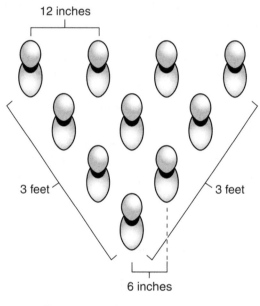

Figure 1 Tenpin triangular setup.

Besides the bowling ball, a few other pieces of equipment are particular to bowling. Well-made shoes promote a smooth approach and a balanced finish while generating power. High-quality bowling shoes have a different sole on either shoe. The sole of the shoe used for sliding is made of smooth leather; the other shoe, used in the power step, has a nonmarking, rubberized surface for traction. Rental shoes have a slide sole on both shoes so they can be used by both left- and right-handed bowlers. The poor traction of rental shoes has a negative influence on the development of sound footwork and balance. House shoes are not designed to provide good support or a consistent slide. Explore the possibility of acquiring your own bowling shoes.

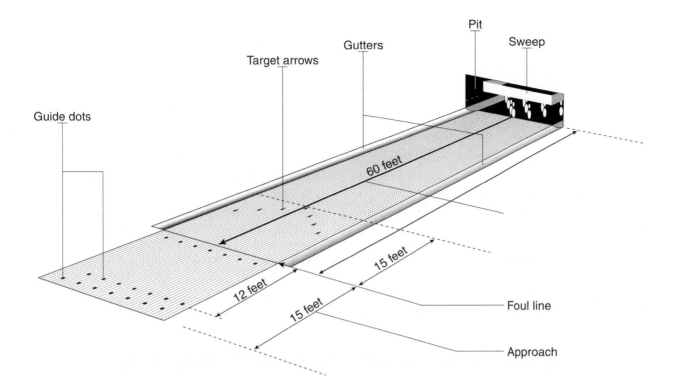

Figure 2 The bowling lane.

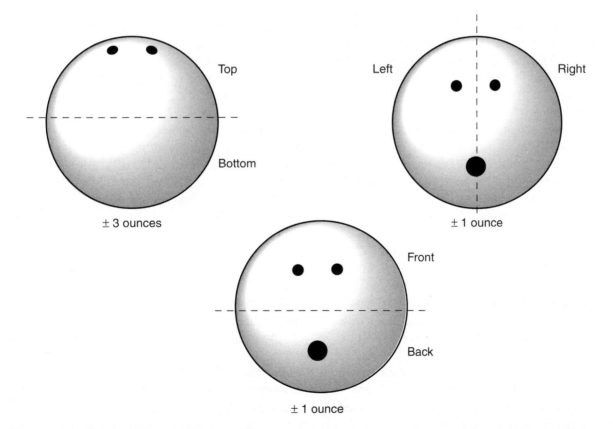

Figure 3 The bowling ball split along three different axes. Imbalance between the top and bottom halves can be no more than 3 ounces. Imbalance between the left and right halves and the front and back halves can be no more than 1 ounce.

Although bowling centers do not generally enforce dress codes, bowlers should use common sense when making clothing choices. Wear loose, comfortable clothing. Avoid clothing that is so tight it restricts movement, but do not wear items that are so baggy they get in the way. Bowling is an athletic activity; this is not the time to make a fashion statement. Bowling does not require a lot of intense physical activity, but it does require a large range of motion. Choose clothing that allows you to bend at the knees and make a long, fluid swing.

Bowling gloves are also available, and many different types are on the market. Some gloves have a textured or tacky surface, providing a better grip on the ball. Other types of gloves contain hard support pieces to help the bowler maintain proper wrist position. Some gloves support just the wrist, but others support all the way up the hand to the fingers. Certain glove styles allow the bowler to adjust the position of the support for more comfort.

The problem with bowling gloves is that they limit a bowler's range of motion. They act as a crutch; the bowler never develops the wrist and hand strength needed to perform without the help of a mechanical aid. Use wrist support only if absolutely necessary. If weakness or injury prevents the development of proper release technique, then use a wrist support. For the majority of bowlers, though, it is better to develop wrist strength and release versatility without an artificial support.

RULES OF PLAY AND ETIQUETTE

The basic rules of play are simple, and everyone, even the youngest bowlers, should follow them.

A player is allowed up to two throws of the ball with each turn, called a *frame*. The score for each throw is recorded on the scorecard. The goal is to knock down as many pins as possible. If all 10 pins are knocked down on the first throw of the frame, no more throws are needed. This is called a *strike*. If fewer than 10 pins are knocked down on the first throw, the bowler makes a *spare attempt*. If all the remaining pins are knocked down on the second throw, it is referred to as a *spare*. If any pins remain standing after the second throw, the bowler is said to have an *open frame*. The bowler is not allowed any more throws in that frame. The mechanical sweep will remove any remaining pins.

The end of the approach is indicated by the *foul line*. No part of the bowler's body may touch any part of the building or lane past the foul line. If contact past the foul line is made, that throw counts as zero. If a foul occurs on the first throw of a frame, the bowler is permitted the second throw of that frame. All bowling centers have a device (usually a light beam) that indicates when a bowler has fouled. This device is usually turned off during open play, but it must be activated during sanctioned competition.

If the ball falls into the gutter, it is considered a dead ball. A zero is scored for any gutter ball. If the ball bounces back up from the gutter and onto the lane, knocking over pins, those pins are not scored. If this happens on the first throw, the machine must be cycled to a full set of pins before the second throw is taken. At bowling centers that use automatic scoring, the score must be changed using the score correction feature because the scorekeeping device cannot tell if pins have been knocked down legitimately or not.

Pins that have fallen over but are not removed by the sweep are considered *dead wood*. Do not play the dead wood. All fallen pins must be cleared off the lane and out of the gutters. A ball that touches any dead wood, whether the pin is on the lane or in the gutter, is a dead ball. The throw counts but is scored a zero because it touched the dead wood. In some instances, a lane attendant must be asked to remove pins that are outside the reach of the sweep.

Pins knocked over by the pinsetter must be reset. If the machine happens to knock over a pin, the pin must be reset at its original position. Even if it appears that the pin would have fallen on its own, if the pin falls as a result of the pinsetter, the pin must be reset before any subsequent throws. A pin standing out of position (referred to as *off spot* or *out of range*) must be played where it is standing. Only pins inadvertently knocked over must be reset.

Bowling Lingo

In an effort to promote the game in a more positive manner, some have tried to remove words with particularly negative connotations. For instance, participants do not bowl in an *alley;* they bowl *on the lanes* inside a *recreation facility* or *bowling center.* Another example is the use of the word *channel* instead of *gutter.*

Although the first effort is worthy from a public perception point of view, the second has never really caught on. The vast majority of bowlers are comfortable with the term *gutter.* Personally, the closest I ever come to throwing a ball into a channel is after a particularly bad outing, when I seriously consider throwing my bowling equipment off the nearest bridge!

No substance may be put on the ball or the shoes that will possibly alter any playing surface—the ball, the approach, or the lane. Any substance that mars the surface of the ball or lane or that leaves a residue behind on the approach is not permitted. Altering the ball's surface (e.g., by sanding or refinishing) is allowed before the ball is first used in competition. Once a ball has been thrown during competition, no further alterations are permitted until competition is completed. The ball may be wiped clean during competition, though. Balls thrown during the practice time before the start of a competition may be altered. Many serious bowlers have more than one ball. No matter how many balls you bring, once competition has started no ball's surface (even one that has not yet been used in competition) may be altered. Because of the wide variety of cleaning chemicals on the market, some of which alter the ball surface chemically rather than with abrasives, it is becoming very difficult for tournament officials to police the cleaning of balls. To avoid any impropriety some tournaments are allowing only the use of a clean, dry towel for the purpose of wiping off the ball between shots. Make sure you know the tournament's rules before you start bowling.

It is considered good etiquette to stand off the end of the lane while waiting your turn. When getting ready, a bowler should first look at the lanes to the immediate left and right before stepping onto the approach. This prevents the bowler from disturbing anyone who may be getting ready to bowl on an adjacent lane. Loud talk and obnoxious behavior that may disrupt another bowler's game have no place in the bowling center.

Do not use somebody else's ball without asking permission first. A ball in use, even a house ball, is considered a bowler's private property.

Courtesy dictates cleaning up the bowling area when all players are finished. Return house balls to the ball rack, and bring rental shoes to the control desk. This prevents clutter and makes it easier for bowlers who use the lanes next.

SCOREKEEPING

A scorecard is used to keep track of the scores during a game. Many bowling centers now use automatic scoring, but old-fashioned paper scorecards can also be used. See figure 4 for an example of a scorecard.

Each individual game has 10 frames. When all pins are knocked down in a frame, whether with one or two throws, it is called a *mark.* A mark rather than a number is used to indicate the throw on the scorecard. Knocking down all 10 pins on the first throw, a strike, is indicated by an X in the upper right corner of the frame. Knocking down all 10 pins with two throws is a spare. The number of pins knocked over on the first throw is written in the upper left corner of the frame on the scorecard. In the upper right corner of the frame, a diagonal line (/) indicates the successful conversion of the spare. For individual throws, the number of pins knocked over on the first throw is written in the upper left corner of the frame, and the number of pins knocked over on the second throw is written in the upper right corner of the frame. The cumulative score of the two throws is recorded in the frame underneath the individual scores.

1	2	3	4	5	6	7	8	9	10
9 /	8 /	5 4	X 7 2	X	X 7 2	9 /	8 /	8
18	33	42	61	70	97	116	125	143	161

Figure 4 Sample scorecard showing open frames, strikes, and spares.

A bonus is awarded for frames that have marks:

- For a strike, the bowler receives 10 for the frame plus the scores for the next two throws.
- For a spare, the bowler receives 10 for the frame plus the score for the next single throw.

In an open frame, no bonus is awarded. The bowler scores only the pin count for the two throws of that frame.

The last frame is the only frame in which a third throw is possible. A bowler who gets a spare in the 10th frame is given one extra throw. A bowler who gets a strike in the 10th frame is given two extra throws.

SAFETY IN THE BOWLING CENTER

Although bowling is not a contact sport, bowlers need to keep safety in mind to prevent injuring themselves or others in the bowling center.

First, select a suitable bowling ball. Having the right ball not only promotes better performance but also ensures physical well-being. Choose a ball of an appropriate weight with finger holes the right size. In step 1, we further discuss proper grip choices.

There is no exact formula for determining the proper weight of a ball. Younger bowlers may want to go with a ball that is 10 percent of their body weight. Another method for a young bowler is to choose a ball with a weight in pounds equal to his or her age. For older bowlers, these methods are less applicable. What it comes down to is comfort. An older bowler's maturity and muscular development may allow for a greater strength-to-weight relationship. Also, sound mechanics such as a fluid swing, evenly paced footwork, and good balance will allow a bowler to throw a heavier ball. Essentially the ball swings itself, like the pendulum on a grandfather clock, and the bowler merely walks along with the swing.

Remember, these methods are only guidelines. I remember one young bowler who, though small for his age and barely 115 pounds, had no trouble using a 14-pound ball. At the age of 15, he was already averaging in the 190s and had a high game of 278 and a high three-game series of 769. On the other hand, bowlers have injured themselves or others because of the untimely and misdirected release of a poorly fitting ball.

Performance inconsistency and its negative impact on scoring aside, the poor fit of a ball is one of the major causes of discomfort and outright injury in bowling. In particular, a poorly fitting ball affects the hand, wrist, elbow, and shoulder of the throwing arm.

A quick practice drill to test ball fit and weight allows bowlers, and their instructors, to judge their grip strength endurance and control of the ball during the arc of the swing. Begin by standing in a relaxed finish position, with the slide foot forward and the back leg behind (figure 5a). The upper body should tilt slightly forward. Let the ball hang at your side, with the palm facing forward. Gently swing the ball back and forth, gradually increasing the size of the swing arc (figure 5b). You should be able to perform three or four full swings. If it feels as if you could swing the ball indefinitely, the ball is probably too light. If you struggle to control your grip on the ball after just a couple of swings, the ball is either too heavy or doesn't fit correctly.

Another important aspect of safety is cleanliness. Moisture is the number one enemy of

Figure 5 Practice-swing test. *(a)* Stand in finish position with ball hanging at your side. *(b)* Swing the ball in a short arc, gradually increasing the length of the swing.

safety. Be very careful where drinks are set down. Pay close attention to where you walk, particularly when you make trips to the food service areas or restrooms. Any moisture on a bowling shoe's sliding sole will cause an abrupt stick on the approach. This is very dangerous. Poor footing while bowling has the potential to cause serious injury to the knees or lower back. Falling onto a slippery, oily lane (possibly while still holding the ball) will undoubtedly ruin a bowler's day. Have a lane attendant clean up any spilled drinks or dropped food immediately. Bowlers should be considerate about keeping all food items away from the bowling area.

Never go past the foul line. The lane is coated with a very thin film of oil that is nearly invisible. Stepping past the foul line is very hazardous. Bowlers who step past the foul line onto the lane frequently slip and fall.

Wipe the ball and your hands clean with a towel after every throw. This will help you maintain a firm grip on the ball both during the swing and when preparing to bowl. Be careful when picking up the ball from the ball return. Place your hands on the sides of the ball, not the front and back, to prevent an incoming ball from crushing a finger. When picking up the ball, use both hands and bend at the knees (figure 6). Do not insert your fingers into the holes when lifting the ball from the ball return. Placing the fingers in the holes should be one of the last items of a preshot routine.

Keep movements, gestures, and body English to your own lane. Avoid stepping onto another lane after your throw. Stepping in front of another bowler is not only distracting and rude but also unsafe—a collision between two bowlers can be very dangerous. As soon as your ball hits the pins, walk straight back to the end of your own lane.

Clothing is also a safety concern. Tight outfits restrict movement; baggy clothes get in the way. Recent fashion trends toward excessively baggy pants create a particular hazard. The long, wide cuffs of the pant legs dragging along the floor easily get under the slide foot. Many bowlers have taken serious spills because of baggy pants. These types of pants also pick up considerable dirt and moisture, especially when worn in inclement weather, creating both a mess and a hazard on the lanes.

Figure 6 Pick up the ball from the ball return using both hands and bending at the knees. Place hands on the sides of the ball when removing the ball from the ball return.

PREPARING FOR ATHLETIC ACTIVITY

Many people are surprised by how physically stressful bowling is, and many participants (even serious bowlers) fail to prepare for the athletic demands of the sport. This oversight invariably leads to both acute and chronic injuries. Bowling performance has numerous imbalance characteristics. For instance, all of the swing weight is on one side of the body. In addition, the approach is finished on one foot. The body's need to accommodate for the force and counterforce elements of the game, as well as the range of motion of various joints, makes preparation imperative. An overall fitness regimen and a specific warm-up routine are as important for bowling as they are for any other athletic activity.

Begin with a good all-around stretching regimen. Make sure the stretching routine emphasizes the lower back and legs because much of the power aspect of bowling is generated through the leg drive. Be sure to perform calf and hamstring stretches. Groin stretches are also recommended.

A good range of motion in the swing shoulder is helpful. The longer and more fluid the swing, the less likely muscular tension will pull the swing off target. Stretch out the shoulder over a full range of motion in all directions of movement. Gentle stretching exercises for the wrist and hand prepare the forearm and hand for the stress of the grip and release motions.

Weight training is not a priority. Excessive muscle development often restricts an athlete's range of motion. For some bowlers, though, strength training for specific areas of weakness can be helpful. Many people do not have particularly strong forearms and hands, making it difficult to hold on to the ball for the full swing. They often cannot keep the wrist position firm enough to allow for a proper release. Frequently, this weakness forces a participant to use a lightweight ball, limiting the bowler's effectiveness in knocking down pins. Forearm curls and other grip strength exercises would benefit these athletes.

A good general fitness regimen is all a bowler usually needs. A number of professional bowlers run to develop leg strength and endurance. Cycling or swimming gives the same benefits. For the average league bowler who bowls only three games at a time, endurance is not a great concern. Among serious tournament bowlers, who can expect to bowl up to 16 games per day depending on the tournament format, endurance is critical for success.

GETTING INVOLVED

Your local bowling center will have information about leagues, tournaments, and special events in the area. Most leagues and tournaments require membership in one of the sanctioning organizations in order to participate. The WIBC, ABC, and YABA have shared the same headquarter facilities for a number of years. These organizations officially combined to form the United States Bowling Congress (USBC) on January 1, 2005. Local associations will be allowed an extensive transition period for the combination of memberships and functions in order to follow the lead of the national organizations.

American Bowling Congress (ABC):
414-421-6400

College Bowling USA: 800-514-BOWL

USA Bowling: 414-421-9008

Women's International Bowling Congress (WIBC): 414-421-9000

Young American Bowling Alliance (YABA):
414-421-4700

E-mail links to each of these organizations can be found at www.bowl.com. The mailing address for all of these organizations is 5301 S. 76th St., Greendale, WI 53129. Team USA and the U.S. Bowling Coaches Association (USBCA) are extensions of the national organizations and can be reached at the same address.

The following organizations might also be of interest:

Federation Internationale des Quilleurs (FIQ)
Rizal Memorial Sports Complex
Pablo Ocampo Sr. Street
Malate, Manila
Philippines
www.fiq.org

High School Bowling USA,
P.O. Box 5802,
Arlington, TX 76005
800-343-1329
www.highschoolbowlingusa.com

Gripping the Ball for Comfort and Control

Bowling is one of the few sports in which the player puts the hand into the equipment. Successful bowling requires a smooth, controlled release of the ball. Without the control of the ball, which comes from proper selection of equipment, no other skills in the game will develop properly.

A ball that doesn't fit properly creates tension in the hand and arm, negatively affecting the swing and the release. The bowler loses confidence in his ability to complete a shot. He becomes cautious and inconsistent in the footwork. There is a loss of a complete pendulum swing. Variations in footwork and swing lines affect the bowler's ability to achieve a balanced finish position at the foul line. An old adage warns, "You can't coach a bad fit." Likewise, bowlers themselves must realize "You cannot learn your way around a bad fit."

For casual bowlers, it is a great service to be able to walk into almost any bowling center, select a ball, and start bowling. It is doubtful the average tennis club or golf course could provide a wide enough selection of rackets or clubs to satisfy the needs of all the customers using the facility on any given day. The provision of house balls in a variety of weights and grip sizes is a great benefit for introducing millions of participants to the game. Nevertheless, this service has its limitations.

Nothing is more disheartening to a bowler, particularly a serious bowler, than to have a day when the ball just doesn't feel right. Changes in temperature and humidity in particular may cause the hands and fingers to swell or shrink. Many bowlers experience this same response from merely throwing the ball; the wear and tear of throwing the ball can cause considerable changes.

Although various products are available to adjust the feel of the ball, even on a shot-to-shot basis, the first important element for learning correct bowling technique is to get a ball that fits.

ESSENTIALS OF PROPER BALL FIT

Imagine going to a shoe store and not being able to buy a pair of shoes that fit properly. Shoes that are too loose or too tight or that don't provide enough support will soon cause considerable pain and possibly corns, calluses, and blisters.

It is the same with a bowling ball. A ball that fits poorly interferes with the proper mechanics of the swing and release. Inevitably, like shoes that don't fit, a poorly fitting ball will cause pain. A ball that doesn't fit properly may cause blisters and cuts on the fingers as well as pain in the hands, knuckles, wrists, elbows, and shoulders. These conditions will have a debilitating effect.

Because most bowlers begin by using a house ball, we will discuss the factors in choosing a good house ball. However, purchase a professionally drilled ball as soon as you can. In the short run, your own ball will help skill development; in the long run, it will prevent chronic injuries.

Whether purchasing a ball or choosing a house ball off the rack, consider four elements when determining whether a ball is right for you: weight, hole size, span, and pitch (figure 1.1).

Figure 1.1	Ball Fit: Weight, Hole Size, Span, and Pitch

1. Holes fit fingers comfortably
2. Ball slides onto thumb when fingers are inserted
3. Span is not too short or too long
4. Pitch is appropriate for the bowler's grip and needs
5. Ball is the right weight for the bowler's strength

Weight

Proper ball weight depends on the bowler's strength and the fit of the ball. The better the fit, the more easily the ball will stay on the bowler's hand without additional effort on the bowler's part. A ball that fits poorly forces the bowler to use a lighter ball in order to control the ball during the swing.

Refer back to the Sport of Bowling for more information on ball weight (page xviii). An additional test of the bowler's strength is the extension test. This test determines the bowler's strength independent of whether the ball is properly drilled.

Determining Ball Weight. *Extension Test*

Hold a ball in the palm of your hand. Do not insert your fingers into the holes. Extend your arm forward until the ball is straight out from your shoulder. Try to hold that position for four or five seconds. Repeat the test with balls of various weights.

If you cannot fully extend your arm, or if your wrist begins to bend back and your hand no longer supports the ball from underneath, then the ball is too heavy. Use as heavy a ball as you can comfortably control. The better the ball fits, the heavier it can be because your hand won't have to work so hard to hold on to it.

Success Check

- Fully extend the arm from the shoulder.
- Completely support the ball from underneath.
- Hold the ball in the extended position for four or five seconds.

Score Your Success

Give yourself 5 points for finding a ball that is the right weight for you.

Your score ___

Hole Size

The size of the finger hole should closely match the size of the inserted digit. Aim for a smooth, snug fit. The hole should not be so snug that loose skin or the knuckle catches in the hole. A popping or sucking sound may indicate a tight fit, but don't assume that sound means the hole size is too tight. A popping sound may also indicate poor gripping technique. Many bowlers bend the knuckle when gripping the ball. This traps air inside the hole and may cause a popping sound even if the fit is correct. Learn proper gripping technique: Imagine squeezing the thumb and fingers together.

On the other hand, do not allow for too much extra space in the hole. Many bowlers make the mistake of choosing holes that are too loose for fear of the ball sticking on the hand and pulling them down the lane (the Fred Flintstone syndrome). Overly loose holes force a bowler to squeeze excessively just to hold on to the ball. A death grip on the ball causes a great deal of tension from the hand up to the shoulder. The fingers dig into the ball, and the knuckles bend inside the holes. When this happens, the ball sticks on the hand anyway. The bend of the joints inside the hole creates pressure points that cause the fingers or thumb to catch in the hole when the ball is released. If the bowler tries to relax the grip, the excessively large holes will allow no grip on the ball at all. The ball will barely

make it halfway through the downswing before it falls off the hand with an embarrassingly loud thud. Loose finger holes put the bowler in a frustrating drop–squeeze release pattern, destroying all confidence in being able to roll the ball consistently.

The phrase *fits like a glove* is not far off the mark when considering the fit of a ball. Avoid holes that are so loose they allow the knuckles to bend inside the hole. The goal is to maintain control of the ball throughout the swing by gently squeezing the ball. Distribute the pressure of the grip along the entire length of the fingers and thumb. It should feel as though the inside gripping surfaces of the fingers and thumb are being brought closer together (figure 1.2). Gripping the ball will be discussed in more detail later in this step.

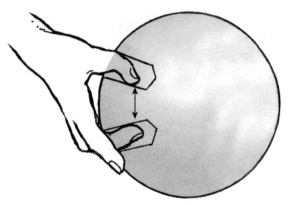

Figure 1.2 Feel as though you are bringing together the surfaces of your fingers and thumb.

Extra space inside the finger hole will lead the bowler to unconsciously bend the knuckle. Bending the knuckle will cause pressure points (figure 1.3). In the short run, these pressure points will cause inconsistent release problems. Over the long run, pressure points will cause pain. Bruises or point sensitivity at the base of the fingers or thumb, tenderness at the ends of the fingers, broken fingernails, and blisters or skin tears at the tops of the knuckles are all possible indicators of holes that are too large.

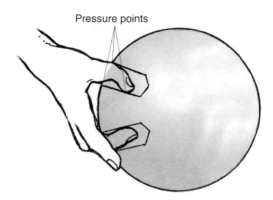

Figure 1.3 Bending the knuckle inside the finger hole will create pressure points.

Misstep

You are able to bend your finger inside the hole, indicating that the finger hole is too large.

Correction

Remember the phrase *fits like a glove*. The holes should be neither too big nor too small. You should be able to hold on to the ball by gently pressing your fingers toward your thumb.

Whether a bowler uses a fingertip grip or a conventional grip, the fingers should fit snugly in the finger holes. The thumb is inserted completely up to its base, and the fingers should be snug to the appropriate knuckles.

Slight variations in the degree of snugness are a matter of personal preference. However, the ability to insert the finger past the appropriate joint is an obvious indication that the holes are too large. The need to cram the fingers into the holes to force them to reach the appropriate joint is an obvious indicator the holes are too small.

Span

The *span* is the distance between the cut of the finger holes and the cut of the thumbhole. After inserting the fingers, the ball should slide smoothly back onto the thumb. The bowler should not need to stretch the hand to get the thumb into the hole. The span should open the hand enough to allow the ball to rest in the palm (figure 1.4a).

A need to reach with the thumb indicates too long a span (figure 1.4b). If the span is too

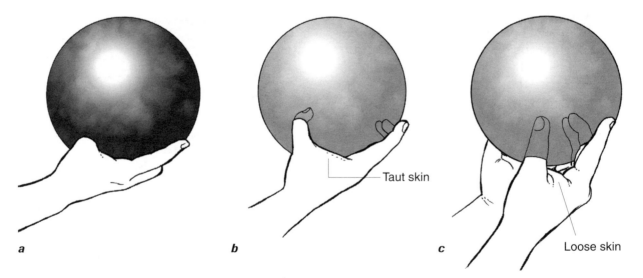

a　　　　　　　　　　b　　　　　　　　　　c

Taut skin

Loose skin

Figure 1.4 *(a)* If the span is the correct distance, the ball will rest comfortably in the palm of the hand. *(b)* If the span is too long, the skin at the base of the thumb will be taut. *(c)* If the span is too short, a gap will appear between the ball and the hand.

long, the bowler may not have the grip strength necessary to hold on to the ball. She may not even be able to completely insert the thumb into the thumbhole. In either case, the bowler will struggle to maintain control of the ball.

Misstep

You experience excessive rubbing or tenderness on the inside of your thumb. Webbing between thumb and index finger is very taut. The ball hangs up on your hand and does not release smoothly.

Correction

If you experience these symptoms, you are using a ball with a span that is too long. Look for a ball that you can hold easily in the palm of your hand. You should not have to reach to get your thumb into the thumbhole.

If the webbing along the base of the thumb is very loose or creased, the span is too short. A short span will cause the fronts of the knuckles to be pushed into the edges of the finger holes. Many bowlers will notice an indentation across the front of the fingers if the span is too short. For some, the pressure against the tendon that extends the finger can be very painful. If the ball appears to be propped up on the ends of the fingers and thumb and does not settle into the palm, the span is definitely too short (figure 1.4c). Try the pencil test (page 6) to determine if the span is too short.

A more precise test of the span compares the position of the knuckles in relation to the finger holes. Insert the thumb entirely into the thumbhole, but do not insert the fingers. Lay the hand flat along the surface of the ball. Let the gripping fingers lie over their respective holes (figure 1.5). Look at the crease of the knuckles in relation to the front edge of the finger holes. For a conventional grip, the edge of the holes should be right at the beginning of the crease for the first knuckle. For a fingertip grip, the edge of the finger holes will be half the distance between the first and second knuckles.

Rarely will you find a fingertip ball on the house ball racks. If you do, the odds are good the ball will not fit properly. If you think your game has progressed enough for you to adopt a fingertip grip, you should already have your own ball. Talk to a trained pro-shop operator when it comes to fitting a ball for a fingertip grip.

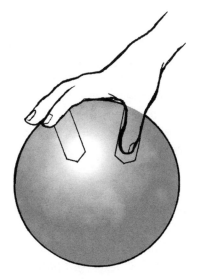

Figure 1.5 To test the span of the ball, lay your hand flat over the ball's surface and look at the creases of the middle finger knuckles in relation to the finger holes.

Misstep

The fronts of your knuckles are bruised or sensitive. The webbing between your thumb and index finger is very loose. Your hand rotates around the ball too early, causing the ball to drop off too soon. The ball does not rest in your palm.

Correction

All of these symptoms indicate that the span is too short. Look for a ball that rests easily in the palm of your hand. Try the pencil test to determine if the span is too short.

Because the first joint does not bend at as sharp an angle as the second joint, there will be some space between the ball and the finger if the ball is drilled for a fingertip grip (see page 12, figure 1.9). Be careful how much the hand is stretched with a fingertip grip. An old ball drilling theory advocated using an extra-long span for the fingertip grip. A bowler who uses a fingertip grip more strongly feels a pull on the fingers when the span is extra long. It was mistakenly thought this pull created more finger lift at the release. In reality, the tension in the hand and forearm caused by the long span restricted the hand's movement around the ball. The looser the hand is, up to a certain degree, the faster the release motion. For many bowlers, the long span not only decreased the amount of hook but also caused injuries.

Some bowlers prefer a somewhat shorter span than what would be judged appropriate for their hand size. A relaxed grip does relieve grip tension. This is helpful for players with hand problems such as arthritis or tendinitis. For these bowlers, an increase in the angle of the pitches in conjunction with a relaxed grip will help them hold on to the ball better.

For those who are not able to rotate the hand around the ball fast enough at the release point to generate the side roll necessary for an effective hook, a relaxed span will help. A word of caution: If the span becomes too short, the release motion frequently will start too early in the downswing. This is called *hitting the ball early*. The overturning of the release causes the ball to drop off the hand too soon. The bowler loses the ability to control the ball throughout the swing, which affects accuracy and speed consistency. The sacrifice of the proper hand position before the ideal release point undermines the bowler's ability to roll an effective hook.

Determining Span. *Pencil Test*

The classic test for a short span is the pencil test. Insert your fingers into the finger holes of the ball. Roll the ball back onto the thumb. Try to slide a pencil between the ball and the palm of the hand. If more than a pencil's width of space remains between the palm and the ball surface, the span is probably too short.

Success Check

- Finger holes should be the right size: not too small, not too large.
- Edge of finger holes aligns correctly with each knuckle of the gripping fingers.
- Fingers and thumb go into the holes up to the correct knuckle.

- Ball should easily roll back onto the thumb.
- Webbing at the base of the thumb should not be too taut or too loose.
- Ball should feel as though it rests snugly and comfortably in the palm of the hand.

Score Your Success

Give yourself 1 point for properly identifying a span that is too short or too long. Give yourself 5 additional points for correcting the problem by finding a ball with the correct span for your hand.

Your score ____

Pitch

Pitch is the angle at which the holes are drilled into the ball (figure 1.6). There are five types of pitches: open, closed, left, right, and neutral. In an open pitch, the fingers and thumb move away from the palm. An open pitch allows the ball to come off the hand sooner. In a closed pitch, the fingers and thumb move toward the palm. A closed pitch allows the bowler to hold on to the ball longer. For left and right pitches, the holes are drilled toward the left or right,

6

respectively. Left and right pitches also influence the release. For instance, in a ball with a right pitch for a right-handed bowler, the thumb will angle toward the palm and the fingers will turn out. This style promotes an earlier rotation at the release. The pitch tilts the ball to the inside of the hand earlier in the swing. The opposite is also true. A left pitch allows the ball to sit in the hand so the bowler can stay behind the ball longer through the release point. Finally, there is a neutral pitch, also referred to as a zero pitch. In a zero pitch, the holes are drilled directly toward the geometric center of the ball.

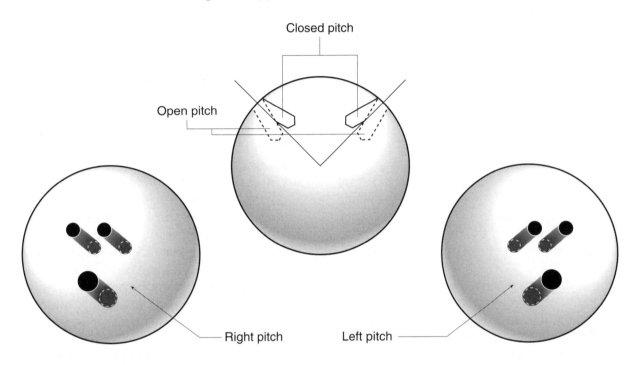

Figure 1.6 Pitches of the finger holes: closed and open, and left and right.

Nearly all house balls are drilled with zero pitch. This is another problem with using a house ball. Not only is it unlikely that the hole sizes and span will be correct, but the pitch angles of a predrilled house ball rarely accommodate the natural strength and flexibility of the bowler using it.

Flexibility of the bowler's hand, particularly the flexibility of the finger joints and the thumb's range of motion, is the most important characteristic to consider when determining the proper pitch angle. The second most important factor is the size of the bowler's hand (i.e., the length of the span). The longer the span, the greater the arc being covered around the circumference of the ball and the less likely the holes are going to point toward the center of the ball.

Use caution when pitching the finger holes. Although slight adjustments may create a different release, it is very easy to strain the joints and tendons of the fingers if the pitch angles are greater than the natural finger positions. Pitches should be altered only after consulting a pro-shop specialist.

Drilling techniques can help a bowler. Proper drilling can facilitate the release motion for a bowler who does not have a particularly strong hand action or help maintain control for a bowler who struggles with the ball during the downswing. For bowlers who hit the ball too hard or who grip the ball too tightly, drill techniques can help them release the ball more smoothly.

Misstep

With your hand inside the finger holes, you cannot feel the pads of your fingers and thumb pressing against the insides of the holes.

Correction

The pitch angle is too sharp (closed). Look for a ball that allows you to feel your fingers inside the holes.

Misstep

The ball feels as if it will fall off your hand early in the swing.

Correction

The pitch is too open. You may also find yourself bending your swing arm to get your hand back under the ball to maintain your hold on it. Look for a ball with a more closed pitch or a neutral pitch.

For example, a bowler might want to create more rotation on the ball and feel a greater lift with the fingers. The ball driller might opt for a slightly open pitch for the thumb. This would cause the ball to come off the thumb sooner, allowing the weight of the ball to transfer onto the fingers earlier in the swing. In addition, the driller might add a closed pitch for the fingers, keeping them in the ball longer through the extension and turn phase of the release.

Consider another example. Say a bowler has difficulty holding on to the ball. The driller might choose a slightly shorter span to allow room for the fingers and thumb to angle inward, creating a closed pitch toward the palm. The wider the grip, the more the fingers and thumb usually angle away from each other. Shortening the grip increases the angle, which in turn helps the hand hold on to the ball with less effort.

Bowlers must go to an experienced, well-trained pro-shop operator. Ask around to learn about the pro shop's reputation. Ask about certifications earned or training courses taken. Given the potential for joint injury, nerve damage, and general aggravation, bowlers cannot underestimate the importance of properly trained pro-shop employees. A good ball driller can help you take your game to new levels, but a bad driller can damage you to the point of ending your bowling career.

CHOOSING A HOUSE BALL

Predrilled house balls give a bowler limited options. As the weight of the balls goes up, typically the size of the finger holes and length of the span increase as well. This will not suit a bowler with short, thick fingers or long, thin ones. It is almost impossible to find a house ball that is the perfect fit. As soon as you can, buy a ball drilled to fit your hand.

Most bowlers use one of two basic grips: the conventional grip or the fingertip grip. Each grip has features that affect the choice of a house ball.

The two grip styles, which will be discussed in more detail in the next section, have characteristics of fit unique to each style.

In a conventional grip, the fingers are inserted up to the second knuckle. House balls are drilled to accommodate a conventional grip. If you use a fingertip grip, it will be difficult to find a house ball that fits your style. If you use a conventional grip, you should have more of a selection of house balls, but be sure to find one that fits your hand.

House Ball Selection. *Does the Ball Fit?*

Choose a house ball and evaluate it based on the following criteria. If the ball does not score at least 6 points, put it back and select a different ball.

- Finger holes offer a smooth, snug fit = 1 point
- Thumbhole offers a smooth, snug fit = 2 points
- Span is the correct length (pencil test, page 6; hand-placement test, page 15; or evaluation of the webbing between the base of the thumb and the index finger, page 4) = 2 points
- Ball is an appropriate weight (extension test, page 5) = 2 points
- You can control the ball (practice-swing test, page xix) = 3 points

Success Check

- Evaluate a variety of balls to find the best one.
- Do not let fashion sway your judgment. Don't be tempted by bright colors or pretty styles.
- Find the ball that is appropriate for you based on how it feels in your hand. Ask yourself, "Am I confident that I can throw this ball consistently?"

Score Your Success

Give yourself 5 points for finding a house ball that scores at least 6 points.

Your score ___

TYPES OF GRIPS

Before making final decisions about a ball, be sure of proper gripping technique. Most bowlers use either the conventional grip or the fingertip grip. Each grip style has certain unique characteristics. As we've discussed, the ball can be drilled to accommodate either style.

For a proper grip (figure 1.7), insert the ring and middle fingers and the thumb of the throwing hand into the ball. The index and pinkie fingers act as outriggers to balance the ball in the palm of the hand. Insert the fingers first, and then roll the ball back onto the thumb. Essentially, you are putting the ball onto the hand in reverse order of the way it will come off the hand at the release. Remember, last in, first out!

When both fingers are in their respective holes, it creates an alignment of the grip. Once both fingers are positioned snugly, the thumb can enter the thumbhole only one way.

Now all that remains is to gently squeeze the fingers toward the thumb. The pressure of the gripping fingers squeezing the ball into the palm of the hand and the thumb is all that is needed to keep the ball in place throughout the swing.

Inserting the thumb first causes certain problems. The thumb and thumbhole are round, so the thumb could be put into the hole from any position. However, not all positions would allow proper placement of the fingers into their respective holes. Also when the thumb is put in first, there is a tendency for it to be set too deep in the hole. Consequently, when the ball is released, the thumb will tend to hang up in the hole. The ball drilling (span, pitches, and so on) is based on the principle of fingers first, thumb last for putting the ball onto the hand. Doing it any other way interferes with proper release mechanics.

Figure 1.7   Proper Grip

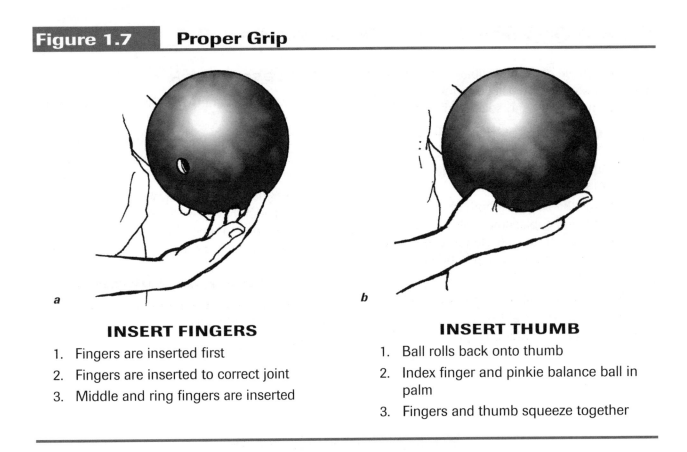

a

b

INSERT FINGERS

1. Fingers are inserted first
2. Fingers are inserted to correct joint
3. Middle and ring fingers are inserted

INSERT THUMB

1. Ball rolls back onto thumb
2. Index finger and pinkie balance ball in palm
3. Fingers and thumb squeeze together

Conventional Grip

The main characteristic of a conventional grip is that the fingers are inserted up to the second joint (figure 1.8). Because more of the fingers are in the ball and because the second joint bends at a stronger angle, the bowler has a better feeling of control with the conventional grip.

Figure 1.8   Conventional Grip

1. Fingers are inserted to second joint
2. Bowler has better feeling of control
3. Fingers and thumb squeeze together
4. Inside the ball, fingers and thumb are flat
5. Bowler needs a ball with a shorter span than if a fingertip grip were used

Although it is called a grip, think about squeezing the ball rather than gripping it. Imagine pressing the long, flat gripping surfaces of the fingers toward the long, flat gripping side of the thumb. Ideally the fingers press harder than the thumb. This is true with any style of grip.

Do not think about gripping the ball the same way you would grip a bar or handle. Keep the surfaces of the fingers and thumb flat inside the ball. This squeezing technique creates a more even distribution of grip pressure. This sense of control will lead to the development of a long, smooth pendulum-type swing. You can focus your attention on accuracy and balance and not have to worry about fighting with the ball during the swing. Remember, hole size should be snug enough to prevent excessive bending of the knuckles inside the holes.

Do not forget about the outriggers, the fingers not inserted in the ball. The pinkie and index fingers press against the surface of the ball. The pressure from these fingers helps lock the wrist in position and supports the ball throughout the swing. The more support the fingers provide, the less pressure is needed from the thumb. Moderating, or even eliminating, thumb pressure reduces the chance of the ball sticking at the release, enabling a quick, smooth release.

When applying grip pressure, imagine holding on to a bird. Close the hand firmly enough to keep the bird from flying away, but don't close it so tightly that you crush the bird's delicate body.

The conventional grip is shorter than the fingertip grip. The finger holes and thumbhole are drilled closer together to allow for a stronger grip. As the hand is opened (stretched out), grip strength decreases. The shortened span of the conventional grip causes the thumb and fingers to release at almost the same time. The longer the fingers are in the ball after the thumb releases, the more time there is for the fingers to drive through and around the ball. The torque applied from a late release of the fingers allows for potentially more revs and side roll, increasing the hook potential of the ball. Obviously, this means that the conventional grip potentially limits the amount of hook a bowler can generate, but it does not entirely eliminate the opportunity to create an effective hook.

Proper release technique creates hook, regardless of the grip used. Maintaining a firm, slightly cupped wrist position; positioning the hand behind the ball during the swing to create drive and maintain accuracy; and applying a turn-and-lift motion of the fingers near the bottom of the swing after the thumb releases the ball will generate a respectable hook, even with a conventional grip.

Semi-Fingertip Grip

You may have heard older bowlers talk of a drilling technique called the semi-fingertip. The semi-fingertip grip is an antiquated drilling technique. As mentioned earlier, fingertip balls used to be drilled with very long spans. The hand was quite tense, and the fingertips felt as though they were locked in place. Because of this drilling, there was a considerable difference in the feel (and the comfort) between a ball drilled for a fingertip grip and a ball drilled for a conventional grip. A bowler who did not want to make such a large jump often used a ball with a semi-fingertip drilling as a way to split the difference between the two extremes. Current drilling techniques, which are based on a better understanding of how the hand most effectively releases the ball, use a shorter span for fingertip drilling.

The current manner of drilling the fingertip grip resembles the old semi-fingertip style. Any discussion of fingertip drilling today essentially includes the concept of what the semi-fingertip used to be.

Fingertip Grip

For a fingertip grip (figure 1.9), the fingers are inserted up to the first knuckle. This lengthens the grip, allowing for a greater time delay between the release of the thumb and the release of the fingers. The extra fraction of a second that the ball remains on the fingers gives the bowler opportunity to create better lift.

11

Figure 1.9 — Fingertip Grip

1. Fingers are inserted to first knuckle
2. Bowler has better chance to generate hook
3. Fingers are squeezed toward the thumb
4. Inside the ball, fingers and thumb are flat
5. Bowler needs a ball with a longer span than if a conventional grip were used

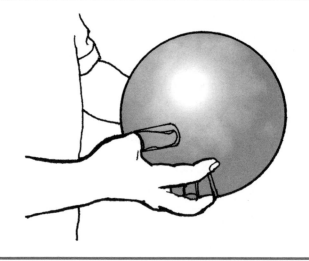

Lift is the resistance of the fingers to gravity. At the bottom of the swing, gravity will try to force the ball off the hand. If the ball is held in the proper grip and in the proper hand position, the fingers will be able to drive through, then around and up, the side of the ball. As the swing carries the hand out and up toward the follow-through, the fingertip grip allows the ball to stay on the fingers longer during the extension and turn phase of the release.

With a fingertip grip, you will experience more noticeable pressing of the fingers toward the thumb. While maintaining this pressure throughout the swing, you will feel as if your fingers are locked in, controlling the ball all the way to the release point. Ideally, this will minimize the urge to press with the thumb, which would cause a feeling of being locked up and would prevent a smooth release.

The fingertip grip does provide a mechanical advantage when creating the side roll needed to make the ball hook. However, the advantage is gained only if the wrist position and the swing movement work toward putting the hand at the correct leveraging point during the release.

A fingertip grip is for more-advanced bowlers. The benefits derived from fingertip drilling are only realized if proper release technique is used. The release is the last element of a long chain of events. The bowler must develop, to an adequate degree, all the rest of her physical game in order for the release to be effective. If other elements of the physical game are lacking, a fingertip grip will do little to increase scoring potential. In fact, it is likely to exaggerate mistakes. The conventional grip is more forgiving, allowing mistakes in swing line, balance position, and wrist position while maintaining some degree of ball control.

Wait until you can play a consistent physical game before moving up to the fingertip grip. If you can affirmatively answer the following questions, you may be ready to advance from a conventional grip to a fingertip grip:

1. Is your body well positioned and well balanced at the line?
2. Do you have reasonably good control of your swing?
3. Is your hand position at the release point consistent and strong enough to create a controllable hook with a conventional grip?

If you answered no to any of these questions, you have other issues to deal with before moving to a fingertip grip.

Because a bowler is likely to use a fingertip grip at some point, some coaches have suggested that the ball be drilled that way to begin with. They contend that a properly drilled fingertip ball is not any more difficult to throw than a ball drilled for a conventional grip. To a certain extent, this is true. If a bowler is developing a reliable set of fundamental skills, then the use of a fingertip grip is a proper step in that development.

It should not, however, be considered a primary step. Of the 50 million people who bowl in the United States every year (about 4 million of them regular participants in leagues and tournaments), a very small percentage seeks out professional coaching. An even smaller percentage has had the benefit of coaching from the very beginning of their involvement in the game. Wouldn't it be great if coaches could begin instructing all bowlers when they're young? Their minds are flexible and expanding, they have no ingrained bad habits, they have no misconceptions or prejudices. Unfortunately, this is not reality.

By the time most bowlers seek advice, bad habits have already been established, and the damage has already been done. The goal of coaches is to help these bowlers straighten out their games, to get them to revisit basic concepts and practice fundamentals. If they have not yet gone to a fingertip drilling, adding it to their games at this point will give them no benefit.

Adopting a fingertip grip from the start fails to take into consideration a few other points. First, it does not account for the bowler's mind-set. A bowler may have seen someone else throw a hook ball and thought it looked cool. In reality, the bowler may lack the interest or dedication to become a more serious player. He may simply lack the understanding to realize a sufficiently effective hook can be generated with a conventional release.

Second, it does not account for differences in physical development among athletes. Although some players seem ready to use a fingertip grip almost immediately after they start bowling, others may not be ready for some time.

When a bowler scores consistently in the 140 to 160 range, she probably has enough control of the other physical skills to consider using a fingertip grip. However, there is nothing wrong with waiting. In fact, some skilled bowlers never use a fingertip grip.

Although it is unlikely that staying with the conventional grip will ruin a bowler's game, no doubt some players have permanently restricted their development by moving to a fingertip grip too soon.

Claw Grip

Some bowlers, often because of weakness or injury, choose to use a *claw grip.* In a claw grip, the middle and index fingers are inserted into the ball rather than the middle and ring fingers. These are not the strongest gripping fingers, and the grip does not center the ball on the hand well. Many inexperienced bowlers who don't know any better try to bowl using this grip. Do not use this grip unless it is absolutely necessary.

Two-Finger (Thumbless) Grip

A current trend in gripping technique is to not insert the thumb at all. In the two-finger (or thumbless) grip, the ring and middle fingers are inserted into the ball just as in a regular grip, but the thumb is not inserted. The ball is cupped in the palm of the hand, and the thumb stays on the outside of the ball.

Many people using house balls experiment with this release. They frequently cannot find a ball with a proper thumb fit, so they don't put the thumb in at all. Specifically, these bowlers are unable to get the thumb out of the ball soon enough to exert the proper torque with the fingers. This may be due to a poorly fitting ball that forces the bowler to squeeze excessively to hold on to it, negating the proper release motion. This technique generates considerable rotation and a strong hook; bowlers frustrated at not being able to achieve the proper release motion for creating a hook often use it.

Commonly, with a house ball, the fingers are inserted up to the second knuckle. Some bowlers use a very lightweight ball with small finger holes. In this case, they insert the fingers only up to the first knuckle. This gives them the benefit of a fingertip release, plus the lightweight ball is very easy to rev up.

Many novice bowlers, impressed by the sharp hook, attempt this technique, regardless of whether they have the skill to achieve it or the properly drilled ball to facilitate it. Many new bowlers who try to hook a house ball employ this technique because most house balls do not fit well enough to promote a good release. Leaving the thumb out of the ball guarantees the fingers will release later than the thumb. This puts the weight of the ball entirely on the fingers at the point of release. Considerable torque can be applied to the ball if the proper hand position and release motion are achieved, though this is a difficult task.

The thumbless technique has considerable shortcomings. For the bowling proprietor, excessive ball damage is an issue. It is very easy to crack the shells of lightweight (8 to 10 pound) balls. Lightweight balls are not designed to be thrown at the velocity many adults utilize. It is difficult, however, to use this technique without dropping down considerably in ball weight.

Second, the bowler is forced to cup the wrist at a sharp angle to hold on to the ball. Often a bend at the elbow is needed to carry the ball through the swing (figure 1.10). This arm position makes it difficult to repeat a shot. The swing rarely achieves the smooth, free-flowing pendulum motion that promotes accuracy and consistency. The bent arm creates a shorter pendulum motion, stealing power from the swing.

Figure 1.10 The thumbless grip forces the bowler to bend the arm, creating a shorter pendulum.

Furthermore, the elbow acts as a lever, pulling the swing away from the body. This action, referred to as *chicken winging,* is commonly seen among those using the thumbless technique. Because the bent arm has a tendency to pull away from the body, the accuracy of the swing line is sacrificed.

Many bowlers who use the thumbless technique suffer shoulder, back, and knee injuries. The swing is very tense and uses many large muscles. In addition, the exaggerated body positions and excessive muscular effort required to throw the ball sacrifice control and accuracy. This style is detrimental to skill development and harmful to the body.

Because many bowlers are not strong enough to maintain the exaggerated wrist cup required to hold on to a heavier ball with the thumbless technique, they must fall back on a lightweight ball, sacrificing pin carry. Many bowlers using this technique are tempted to generate ball speed through excessive body movement, which further sacrifices control and accuracy.

The thumbless grip also lacks versatility. Because of the cupped wrist, a bowler using the two-fingered, thumbless grip will have difficulty not hooking the ball even when a hook is not appropriate, such as when shooting at certain spare combinations or bowling on very dry lanes.

Unfortunately, lane conditions at many bowling centers no longer demand accuracy. The premium is put on trying to string strikes together. Filling frames by spare shooting is becoming a lost art. The bowler merely needs to stand left and throw right and watch the ball roar to the strike pocket. While this may be entertaining for the bowler, it by no means does justice to the athletic demands of the game. It is largely under these playing conditions that even a modicum of success can be seen with the thumbless style.

The use of this style is largely a male phenomenon. Something about the male ego is at work when it comes to throwing a ball with excessive speed and hooking action. Women almost never use this technique, even when just playing around during a fun day on the lanes. Instead, women usually settle for a more reasonable and practical style.

A Notable Exception

Professional bowler Mike Miller was the most prominent bowler using the thumbless technique. Many fans do not realize he was a professional bowler before he adopted this grip. All the important ingredients—physical skill, dedication, mental game—were in place. By everyday standards, he was already an outstanding bowler. He simply lacked the release technique that generated the strike-ball power required to be successful on the demanding lane conditions of the professional tour. After years of little success on the PBA tour, Miller took time off to develop his thumbless style. He quit his career for six months to redesign his game. In the nearly 10 years since the changes, he has had a respectable career (three national titles, including one major), but by no means has he rewritten the record books. He has, however, suffered from a series of chronic injuries.

Realize that just because a particular individual can make an unorthodox style work, it is not a vindication of that style. Often these athletes also have extreme dedication and a unique athletic gift. Furthermore, it definitely does not mean the style is applicable for the vast majority of participants.

Developing Grip. *Evaluating Proper Grip Technique*

You may find it helpful to have a coach or experienced bowler help you evaluate your grip technique. Use the following criteria to determine if your grip technique is sound.

- Middle and ring fingers are inserted before thumb = 1 point
- Middle and ring fingers are inserted to the correct knuckle (second knuckle for a conventional grip, first knuckle for a fingertip grip) = 2 points
- Ball is rolled back onto the thumb after fingers are inserted = 1 point
- Thumb is fully inserted to the base = 3 points
- Thumb and fingers press together = 3 points
- Finger pressure is greater than thumb pressure = 2 points
- Index and pinkie fingers press against ball surface = 3 points

When your grip earns 13 points or more, you are ready to throw the ball.

Success Check

- Have a coach or an experienced bowler evaluate your grip.
- Be sure you are using a ball appropriate for your hand size, style, and strength.

Score Your Success

Give yourself 5 points if your grip passes the scrutiny of an expert.

Your score ___

SUCCESS SUMMARY

Stop using a house ball if possible. Having your own ball instills confidence no matter how seriously you pursue the sport. When buying your own ball, be sure to go to an experienced, well-trained pro-shop operator. Ask other bowlers for advice. Find out about the pro shop's reputation. Look for pro shops that are certified by the International Bowling Pro Shop and Instructors Association (IBPSIA). Ask the operator about other certifications earned or training courses taken.

Review your scores on the evaluations in this step. Record your scores in the spaces that follow and total them.

Determining Ball Weight

Extension Test   ___ out of 5

Determining Span

Pencil Test   ___ out of 6

House Ball Selection

Does the Ball Fit?   ___ out of 5

Developing Grip

Evaluating Proper Grip Technique   ___ out of 5

Total   ___ *out of 21*

If you score at least 16 points, you are ready to move on to the next step. If you score fewer than 16 points, review the sections that are giving you trouble, then repeat the evaluations.

The next step discusses mental preparation. One of the key elements of mental preparation is trust—trust in yourself to learn and trust in your equipment to help you achieve your goals. Confidence in your equipment selection carries over to confidence in your overall game. Just knowing that the ball in your hand fits right and feels right provides a real mental boost.

It will be difficult to focus on other aspects of the game if there are nagging doubts in the back of your mind about the ball you are throwing. Make sure those doubts are put aside. This will eliminate one more concern that could sidetrack you from the objective you really want to achieve. Ball selection is the first step in developing confidence in your game. Once you have the ball-selection process taken care of, you can clear your mind of that detail. Now you are ready to develop aspects of your mental game.

Developing a Bowling Mind-Set

All athletes want to be confident in their ability to perform at the highest level possible. This confidence is solely a product of dedicated preparation. Haphazard and lackadaisical habits will come back to haunt a bowler when the time comes to perform.

Developing the physical skills necessary to perform at a particular level is only part of the picture. Being mentally ready to perform is something else entirely. To many people, mental preparation is what an athlete does just before getting ready to perform. It is true that focusing, making decisions, getting psyched up, and clearing the mind of distracting thoughts are all part of what bowlers call the preshot routine. However, an excellent preshot routine is only the final stage in a series of activities designed to mentally prepare the bowler to bowl. Developing a bowling mind-set involves more than just creating a preshot routine.

With the mind in a relaxed, focused state the athlete can give all his attention to his performance. For a bowler, this mental awareness allows for analysis of his shot without distracting thoughts impeding a quality performance. The bowler must be aware of the feel of a quality performance so he knows what to feel during the next performance. Corrective action cannot be taken without awareness of body movement.

Was the approach smooth and flowing? Did the swing feel relaxed and close to the body? Was the ball comfortably in place on the hand? Was there a sense of control without exertion throughout the swing?

Bowling is a highly repetitive sport. The control aspects are subtle. There is little overt, explosive exertion as one would see in a sprinter coming out of the blocks, a weightlifter jerking the bar over her head, or a tennis player smashing a big serve. What bowling demands is a very fine degree of execution. A subtle variation in the footwork or the swing, just an inch or two, is enough to cause a terrible shot. Minor flaws in balance or body position, just a degree or two off line, and you will be nowhere near your target.

You will commonly hear experienced bowlers say that the game is 90 percent mental. Although I doubt you can put an exact number on the mind's influence over the body, there is no doubt as to its importance. This can be said of elite performers in any activity.

Developing a bowling mind-set must be understood from two perspectives: a short-term perspective and a broad, long-term perspective. The short-term perspective is a narrow, precisely focused here-and-now perspective of what the athlete must do to be ready to perform when the time comes. The broad, long-term perspective requires the bowler to understand and accept how motor skills are developed, to exercise patience and perseverance throughout the learning process, and to set goals. Goal setting has two objectives:

1. To prioritize skill development so the bowler works on the skills that are most in need of correction or that will have the most immediate positive impact when improved.

2. To maintain interest, helping the bowler avoid discouragement and frustration by writing out a set of reasonable, achievable goals that progressively challenge the athlete to achieve a bigger long-term goal.

MOTOR LEARNING

Motor learning refers to how the body learns a movement. First understand that you do not train the body. To accomplish complex athletic movements, linking a series of physical actions together to achieve a desired performance, you must train the mind. The brain sends the signals to the muscles, telling them to contract. Without a signal from the brain, the muscles do nothing. Muscle fibers, in fact, do not retain any information from a previous signal.

Consider how complex this simple game of bowling can be. The swing must engage at just the right time in relation to the steps. The steps and body position align to a visual target. The steps and the swing have to stay on course to a predetermined target throughout the approach. The release must take place at just the right time in the swing for effective roll and accuracy. The bowler must finish in a balanced, controlled position despite the influence of swing force and body momentum. The hand must stay in position behind the ball throughout the swing and then release the ball with just the right amount of movement and force to create the desired roll. All this needs to be done consistently while the bowler evaluates his strategy for targeting, selects the proper ball, and adjusts for lane conditions.

This is a difficult task to perform consistently well, but with the proper learning environment, it can be achieved. This is the challenge of bowling that makes it a worthwhile pursuit.

Bowling requires both gross and fine muscle movement. The brain sends a signal that fires a motor neuron. The motor neuron then enervates the muscle fibers. For gross motor movements, often strong but not particularly precise, many muscle fibers are activated by a single neuron.

For fine motor movements, only a select few muscle fibers are activated by each neuron.

The brain's motor control center determines which motor units are activated. A complex pattern of signals constantly flowing through the body determines which, when, and how many muscles are required for every movement of the body. Proper training will program the brain to send the right set of signals at just the right time so the body will perform the skill in the manner desired.

Some of the larger muscle groups involved in bowling are the muscles of the arms and legs and the stabilizer muscles of the spine. These muscles contribute power to the game, affect the pace of the steps and the drive to the finish, and support the body in a stable position while counterbalancing the force of the swing.

Fine motor movements in bowling include the positioning of the balance arm, the control of the swing, the positioning of the wrist, and the release motion.

Movement alone is not enough; the quality of the movement determines bowling success. Did the body perform the way it was supposed to? Were the goals achieved? A secondary set of nerves called proprioceptors tells the brain whether or not the muscles have moved to the extent required. This is how kinesthetic awareness develops.

Kinesthetic awareness refers to the sense of the body's movement within a given spatial reference. An incredibly complex feedback system involving vision, tactile response, the proprioceptive system, and the cognitive mind creates a qualitative evaluation of the movement. If the performance is not what was desired, alternate patterns of signals must be generated until the desired results are achieved.

This complex program (called an *engram*) is established over many repetitions. If the skill is learned incorrectly, a faulty program is established. Remember this new twist on an old saying: "Practice makes permanent; only perfect practice makes perfect."

Once a motor program is generated, faulty or not, repetition will establish it firmly. Repetition, especially in a structured learning environment, wires the brain to run the program. A few hundred repetitions will develop the motor program. This is equal to bowling a couple of times a week (three or four games per session) for four or five weeks.

A few thousand repetitions makes for a reliable program. This is where trouble can start. What if you are spending all your time focusing on the swing and the release, but your timing and balance are poor? You may find yourself establishing bad habits in one part of your game while working to improve another. This is where goal setting and carefully planned practice sessions will keep skill development on track. Constant evaluation and reevaluation, by you or an experienced observer, will keep the whole package developing in due course.

Perfecting a motor program, in this case flawless bowling technique, requires close to a million repetitions. This is the dedication of the elite athlete (e.g., a bowler who practices more than 100 games per week, every week of the year). This bowler executes more than 100,000 throws of the ball over a year's time.

Earl Anthony (considered by some to be the greatest bowler of all time) once practiced 150 games in two days after a particularly disappointing tournament performance. He had the uncanny ability to re-create a competitive environment in his head. This allowed him to maintain his competitive intensity and focus through seemingly endless hours of practice. After that weekend of practice, he won the very next tournament he entered.

However, even Mr. Anthony was not perfect. In reality, there are no perfect bowlers. You would have to bowl with perfect form 100 games a week for 10 years before perfecting a bowling motor program. Every time you bowled

with even slightly imperfect form, you would establish a faulty program that would need to be unlearned before any progress toward perfection could be made. Should you be discouraged? No, just be realistic. It is all right to be imperfect. Expect to make mistakes, but make sure you are attentive to those mistakes and are willing to work on them.

Eventually, physical performance does become a habit. In other words, the program runs reliably without much guidance from the brain's cognitive center. Ideally, it also will run without any interference from the mind. This is the point at which mental preparation becomes so important. Thinking too much—paralysis by analysis—is a bane to athletic performance at all levels. You want your brain to be able to run the program and alter it as needed without your thinking too much about it. Some athletes refer to this as being in the zone.

It is wondrous to achieve that state of seeming disembodiment, as if the mind and the body are no longer connected, an awareness of the body's movement without the consciousness intruding. No doubts, no second-guessing, just effortless performance. The ability to go on autopilot, as if the athlete is only a casual observer of her own body's actions, is a characteristic of an elite athlete. This is how seemingly effortless displays of athletic prowess are demonstrated despite myriad distractions presented by teammates, opponents, and spectators.

Keep in mind what was stated earlier about muscular function. Because the *motor unit* (a neuron plus its enervated fibers) is small, more neurons must be fired to perform a fine motor action. Fine motor movements are harder to learn than gross motor movements. Simply put, fine motor performances take a more complex set of signals. The brain needs to create a more complex pattern of signals to control all the different motor units in order to achieve the desired results.

For the athlete, this step requires considerable patience. Although some basic elements of the bowling game may come easily (such as the setup), and improvement at the outset may be fairly rapid, eventually the pace of development slows down. As the series of movements becomes more complex (timing of the swing and steps, finish position at the foul line, the release motion for a hook ball) and the increasing performance demands of the game require greater degrees of control and precision, each incremental amount of improvement will take increasingly larger amounts of time.

When first learning a skill, the brain does not have a reference point to determine if the performance is correct or not. The skill must first be learned correctly, hopefully without too many previously established poor habits interfering. Then there needs to be enough practice of the correct form to make it reliable. As more and more different movements must be coordinated to form the complete performance, the number of repetitions needed to develop proper technique increases dramatically.

VISUALIZATION

Visualization is a very valuable tool for the developing athlete. Studies have shown that intense visualization excites the motor center of the brain almost to the same degree as the actual physical performance. The ability to block out distractions and see the performance in the mind's eye allows for nearly countless repetitions. Mental practice can be performed almost anywhere at any time.

The constant comparison of performance to an ideal, along with the opportunity to reinforce preferred behavior, is essential for skill development. The brain can be trained to send the correct signals whether the bowler is at the bowling center or not.

Visualization Drill. *Mental Practice Without a Ball*

Visualization practice can be done at any time. You don't have to be on the lanes, and you don't need a ball. Find a quiet place where you can sit and think. Focus your mind and run through the success checks.

Success Check

- See yourself on the lane.
- No distracting images are around you.
- See yourself perform with flawless execution.

- Repeat the mental performance, emphasizing consistency.
- Believe in your ability to perform as well as you imagine.

Score Your Success

Give yourself 2 points for each element of the checklist you can complete, for a total of 10 points.

Your score ___

GOAL SETTING

A good way to avoid discouragement or distractions is to set goals. By setting goals, you establish a program of skill development. Athletes with a goal structure in mind are more likely to stay on task. They are also more likely to progress faster because they are organizing their time and effort around those elements of the game that are most crucial for their overall development.

It is easy to practice what you do well. It makes you feel good and gives you a sense of satisfaction, but it may not be what you need to improve. The first step in setting goals is to honestly evaluate your skill package. You have to know where you are before you can determine what path will take you where you want to go.

Conscientious practice is essential, and every practice must serve a purpose. Mindlessly throwing ball after ball will do no good. Poor technique will arise without any awareness of what is wrong. Take nothing for granted; be vigilant in the constant assessing and reassessing of technique.

When a flaw in technique is identified, it must be modified or eliminated. Old habits are not broken; they are replaced by new ones. Often a bowler will experience transitional periods in which old habits are no longer reliable but new habits are not yet firmly established. During these periods, scores will suffer. Although this can be disappointing, it is a reasonable expectation. Do not lose confidence. A characteristic of physical skill development is one step back, two steps forward. To avoid some of the disappointment during these difficult times, do not keep score during practice sessions. Devote practice sessions solely to skill development. The score is important only in competition.

Long-Term Goals

Once you've evaluated your skills, the next step is to determine what you want to achieve—your ultimate goal. State the goal in specific terms. In fact, all goals, whether long term or short term, should be stated specifically. Don't be vague or wishy-washy. Make the statement so simple and obvious that you know exactly what you are working toward and exactly when you have gotten there.

Here are some examples of good long-term goals:

- I want to have a 200 average.
- I want to raise my average 10 pins by the end of the season.
- I want to make 90 percent of my single-pin spares.
- I want to win my first tournament this year.

Short-Term Goals

You cannot reach your long-term goal all at once. The long-term goal is the end of a journey. Many little steps need to be taken to reach the end.

Keep your focus on the small day-to-day goals. If your goal selection has been meaningful and practical, each short-term goal will be one step toward the ultimate objective. You are trying to map out a course of progress that may involve the rest of your life, so sit down and have a serious self-chat. Even if you don't have a goal of becoming a professional bowler or rolling a 300 game, any substantial improvement takes commitment. Your goal statement can be either a *process* or a *product* statement. *Process* concerns how something is done, while *product* looks at the outcome.

Focus most of your effort on the process. Identify what you want to feel in all aspects of your physical performance. Focus on just one of those aspects of the process in each individual practice session.

On occasion, seek help from experts to ensure that newly developing skills and the chosen practice regimen are moving your game in the right direction. Reaching a plateau is an indication that something is inhibiting further development. Knowledgeable instructors and coaches can identify flaws as they arise before they become firmly ingrained. The inspiration that comes from good advice or new and creative practice ideas is often all that is needed to break through the frustration or boredom that sometimes arises in practice sessions.

Keep an open mind. Be accommodating to change. By its nature, change is uncomfortable and stressful. If it doesn't feel different, then it is not being done differently, at least not differently enough to effect a significant change in the outcome.

To perform at a higher level, try to determine what is keeping you at your current level. Be honest with yourself. Put away pride and generate an unbiased appraisal of every facet of your game. Sometimes, another person's perception of your skill may be the dose of honesty needed to shake up your game. New ideas or different points of view are useful as catalysts for change. Feedback should not be too brutally honest, however. Humiliation or sarcasm is never helpful, promoting only a lack of self-confidence and a sense of futility.

Do not fall back on what is familiar. Once new motor habits are firmly established and you are comfortable with them, you will wonder why you ever did it any other way. Be confident that the changes you are trying to implement will pay off in the long run. A new game with better skills, better performances, and renewed self-confidence is just around the corner.

THREE ZONES OF THE PRESHOT ROUTINE

You have been practicing hard, you are satisfied with your progress, and now you are confident in your ability to perform. You're ready to bowl, right? Wait just a second. No shot should be made without a little bit of forethought. It is true that competence inspires confidence, but many athletes, even highly skilled ones, do not perform well in competitive situations.

Diligent practice is certainly the first key to becoming a skilled player. When competition starts, though, there is another level to consider. You must be in control of your emotions. Sure you are excited, but are you excited to the point of distraction? Are you focused on your performance? Are you analyzing changes in playing conditions? Can you avoid having your opponent's good breaks, or your bad ones, send you on an emotional roller coaster? Bowling is a game of repetition. It is also an intensely private affair. Nothing your opponent does can prevent you from executing a great shot. Are you ready to make that next great shot? The key is having a preshot routine.

Each section of the bowler's area of focus is a staging zone for the next level of intensity. Find opportunities to relax. Take time to analyze what is going well, what is not going well, and why. Make decisions. Find a place where distractions are set aside and strategy can be developed. Remember this great quote from PBA hall-of-famer Johnny Petraglia. When discussing his outstanding seasons on the PBA tour in the early 1970s, Petraglia said, "In my head I knew I had thrown a strike. I only had to let go of the ball so that everyone else would know it, too."

The area on and immediately near the lanes can be separated into three zones of focus. Each zone has a mind-set and routine particular to it. The bowler uses these zones to recover from the last frame and prepare and implement a strategy for the next one.

Decompression Zone: Relaxation and Contemplation

Zone one is the staging area for your next performance (figure 2.1). Do not let yourself become overly excited or overly upset. Extreme emotions make it difficult to recover before the next shot, so maintain an even keel. An athlete cannot sustain high levels of excitement or intensity indefinitely. The body will begin to tighten up, and the mind will lose its focus, negatively affecting performance. Take advantage of every opportunity to relax, to lower your heart rate, to temporarily remove yourself from the emotions of the situation. Bowling's equivalent to the sidelines of other sports is the settee area.

| Figure 2.1 | Decompression Zone |

1. Relax
2. Sit down
3. Talk with teammates

Grab a seat. Take a deep breath, exhaling slowly. As you breathe out, feel all the tension draining from your body. Talk with teammates. Bowling is a social game, so socialize. This is the opportunity to moderate the emotional ups and downs of the current competitive situation. All athletes feel pressure. Everybody gets excited about the good shots and disheartened by the poor ones. The athletes who can regain control of their emotions and prevent those emotions from influencing physical performance are most likely to perform well in pressure situations. A relaxed conversation or a shared joke with a teammate may be just the thing to relieve tension or dispel anxiety.

Discuss what is happening with the lanes. Don't just sit there and stew about your last shot, angry and confused. Your teammates are bowling on the same lanes; perhaps they have insights and observations that will help you get better scores. Don't think you have to do it all on your own. Ask for their help.

Determine a strategy. In this zone, think about your last shot. Analyze what made the last throw particularly good or particularly bad. You cannot completely ignore what is going on in your game or the competitive environment, but you must adopt a relaxed, rational, contemplative view of your performance. You have little time from one turn to the next, so take advantage of every break in the action. Soon you will need to regain your focus, recognize your mistakes, and implement a plan of action. When it is nearly time for your next turn, get ready to go to zone two, the refocus zone.

Decompression Zone Drill.

Use your time in the decompression zone to regain control of your emotions, gain insights from teammates, and relax in preparation for your next shot. Use the success checks to guide your time in zone one.

Success Check

- Practice relaxation techniques, including breathing control and muscle relaxation.
- Quench negative thoughts. Focus on the positive.
- Analyze your performance on the last shot.
- Discuss strategy with teammates.
- Commit to needed changes.

Using Downtime

Score Your Success

Give yourself 2 points for each element of the checklist you successfully incorporate into your routine in zone one. Give yourself an additional 2 points if you are relaxed and focused when you move into zone two for the next shot.

Your score ___

Refocus Zone: Strategy and Decision

The area just in front of the approach is zone two, the refocus zone (figure 2.2). As the bowler ahead of you starts his next frame, get up from your seat and make your way toward the approach. Frequently bowlers step onto the approach clearly not ready to bowl because they weren't paying attention. The unprepared bowler finds himself hurrying to get ready and make the next shot. Do not fall into this trap. Give yourself time to prepare.

Figure 2.2 | Refocus Zone

1. Make decisions about adjustments
2. Choose a spot and a target
3. Visualize the next shot

Before stepping onto the approach, you must wipe all doubts from your mind. Make decisions based on discussions with your teammates and your own thoughts about your previous performance. Believe in the correctness of those decisions.

Establish an intelligent, well-organized plan of action, devoid of all emotion. Do not think about the score or how badly the team needs you to strike. Thinking about the product takes the focus away from the process. It is better to think about how you should bowl rather than what you want to bowl. If the process is sound and the strategy is well implemented, the results are inevitable.

Visualize the next shot. Imagine you have a video running in your head, allowing you to see yourself making a perfect shot. See the roll of the ball. See the ball's path to the pins. See the pins falling down.

Finalize your strategy. Know what you want to do on the next shot. Know where you will stand on the approach. Know which target you will aim for and what part of the lane to play. Decide what body position, swing, and release you will use to make the next throw effective.

At this point, awareness of your game becomes your total focus. Your teammates fade into the background, as do the other bowlers. You no longer are distracted by sounds—you don't hear the background music, the sounds of the video games, or other people's conversations. You are aware only of yourself, the lane, and your ball. If distractions keep intruding, step away from the lane for a few seconds. Take a deep breath, then return to your ball, ready to bowl.

Understand the mistakes made in the last frame and what you need to do to make a better shot. Now with clarity of thought and great confidence, take your place in zone three, the energy zone.

Refocus Zone Drill. *Preparing for the Next Throw*

In the refocus zone, eliminate any distracting thoughts from your mind, and focus on your game. Use the success checks to guide your preparation in zone two.

Success Check

- Devise a plan of action.
- Visualize the next shot.
- Be confident; believe you will perform well.
- Block out distractions from the environment.

Score Your Success

Give yourself 2 points for each element you successfully incorporate into your preparation in the refocus zone. Give yourself an additional 2 points if you are relaxed and focused as you move into zone three.

Your score ___

Energy Zone: Visualization and Affirmation

As you step onto the approach, you enter the energy zone (figure 2.3). This is the zone of the positive affirmation and the preshot routine. This is the zone in which you feel reenergized, ready to take on the challenge of the next frame. Zone three is the stage from which you will make your next great bowling performance.

Figure 2.3   Energy Zone

1. Go through your preshot routine
2. Say your positive affirmation to yourself

Developing a simple and consistent preshot routine is vital for the mental and physical preparation immediately preceding the next throw of the ball. A good preshot routine prepares the body and clears the mind of distracting thoughts. Have a short mental checklist of items to go over. Ideally, go over your mental checklist in the same order before every throw of the ball. Remember, as each item of the checklist is recalled, physical preparations for throwing the ball are being made. Everybody's routine is different, but figure 2.4 should give you some ideas.

Figure 2.4 | Preshot Routine

a

b

BEFORE STEPPING ONTO THE APPROACH

1. Wipe oil off the ball and from inside the finger holes

2. Dry your hands with the hand dryer, or use a rosin bag or puff ball

3. Check the approach for a comfortable slide

4. Decide where you will start on the lane and what your target will be

5. Look at the lanes to the left and right to see if other bowlers are getting ready

ON THE APPROACH

1. Step onto the approach with the ball in your nonthrowing hand

2. Set your feet on the spot you decided to start from

3. Get in a comfortable stance

4. Check your target on the lane

5. Take a deep breath and put the ball on your throwing hand

6. Set your body and the ball

7. Focus on the target

Misstep

You step onto the approach while another bowler in the lane next to you is getting ready to bowl.

Correction

Always check the lanes to your immediate right and left before stepping onto the approach to see if another bowler is getting ready to bowl. Make lane courtesy a habit.

When you first step onto the approach, the ball should be in your nonthrowing hand. Remember, you are not ready to bowl yet. Set your feet and get into a comfortable stance. After checking your target on the lane, say a positive affirmation to yourself. Visualize your approach and target line; see the ball path from the release, through the target, to the break point, and into the pins. Make sure the ball feels right on your hand, that it fits comfortably and snugly, not too loose and not too tight. Repeat your positive affirmation and breathe again. Set your body and the ball, focus on your target, and go.

When you are on the approach, it is not the time to think about your conversations with your teammates or the people laughing and fooling around behind you. If the distractions are too great, simply step back off the approach. Wait until the hubbub subsides, then restart the pre-shot routine.

When you are on the approach, at no point should you think about your opponent's score or your own. Nothing your opponent can do will prevent your next throw from being anything short of outstanding. Don't worry about your opponent. Bowl against the pins, not the person.

Don't dwell on how badly your team needs the next strike or how high a score you can get. Don't be concerned about the outcome. Concern yourself with the process. Ask yourself what needs to be done. Remember, if the process is correct, the outcome is inevitable.

In the energy zone, you will use a positive affirmation. A positive affirmation is like a mental vacuum cleaner; it cleans up all the unnecessary mental junk and leaves behind only what is essential. An affirmation is a short, simple statement that is easy to repeat over and over. It should be in the form of a positive statement. Focusing on the negative only produces a negative result. Overcorrecting a mistake only produces another kind of mistake. Instead of "Don't pull the ball," tell yourself, *Swing to the target*. Rather than "Don't turn the hand early," think, *Stay behind the ball*. After the throw, assess the result of the affirmation. Did you feel what you wanted to feel? Did your body follow through with the course of action you had in mind? If so, try to feel it again. If not, try to figure out why. Try it again, or rethink your plan of action. Here is a short list of potential affirmations:

- Drop and drive.
- Hips down, head up.
- ICE—I carry everything. (Team USA)
- Swing, swing free, swing to the target. (Earl Anthony's preshot mantra)
- One, two, and through. (Dick Ritger's count for footwork pacing)
- Feel it, don't force it.
- Kick and tuck. (Clear the back leg, and let the swing come down next to the hip.)
- Stay behind the ball.
- Reach out, then up. (Swing along visualized target line to prevent cutting swing short.)
- Swing down and through. (Avoid hitting the release early.)

Energy Zone Drill. *On the Approach*

By the time you reach the energy zone, you should be relaxed, focused, and ready to bowl. Use the success checks to guide your preparation and conduct in zone three.

Success Check

- Check for bowlers to either side before stepping onto the approach.
- Visualize the next shot.
- Take a deep, relaxing breath.
- Go through your preshot routine. Check the slide, your throwing hand, and the ball's surface.
- State your positive affirmation.
- Get in your starting position on the approach: Set your feet (balance), set the ball (comfort), and set the body (positioning).
- Repeat your positive affirmation.
- See the line to the pocket.
- Breathe and bowl.

Score Your Success

Give yourself 2 points for each element of the checklist you successfully incorporate into your routine in the energy zone. Give yourself an additional 5 points if you feel relaxed and focused as you complete the shot.

Your score ___

SUCCESS SUMMARY

Long-term improvement requires the acceptance of the nature of learning. The rate of improvement varies for different skill elements. Motor learning, the development of a motor program, requires considerable repetition. You must learn the correct pattern of movement and practice it in order to avoid establishing a faulty program. You must develop a long-term plan for skill development and improvement.

After establishing a long-term goal, make sure each daily practice session is a step toward that goal. Every practice session must be organized as well. Do not throw the ball for the sake of throwing the ball. Try for a positive development in your game at every outing.

Zone one, the decompression zone, is for relaxation and contemplation. Relax, take a deep breath, have a seat, and take a drink or have a bite to eat. Socialize with teammates, visitors, and spectators. Talk with members of the opposing team. They are your opponents, not your enemies. They may inadvertently give you an insight about the game that you can use to your advantage. Discuss the game with your teammates. Are the lanes changing? Did your teammates notice anything particularly wrong with your last shot? What are their thoughts concerning lane play and ball selection?

Zone two is the refocus zone for strategy and decision making. Analyze the last shot and decide what was correct or incorrect. Choose what needs to be changed, if anything, to make the next shot better. Know what ball you will use, where you will stand, and what target line you will throw the ball along. In your mind's eye, see the next shot. Believe in yourself. Be confident your next shot will be excellent.

Zone three, the energy zone, is for visualization and affirmation. Prepare the ball and your hand for the next shot. Check the lanes for bowlers next to you. Confirm your starting position when you step onto the approach. Visualize your next shot. State your positive affirmation. Identify your target. Set your feet, your body, and the ball. Repeat your affirmation. Breathe, focus, and bowl.

Review your drill scores. Record your scores in the spaces that follow and total them. If you score at least 45 points, you are ready to move on to the next step. If you score fewer than 45 points, review the sections that are giving you trouble, then repeat the drills.

Visualization Drill	
Mental Practice Without a Ball	___ out of 10
Decompression Zone Drill	
Using Downtime	___ out of 12
Refocus Zone Drill	
Preparing for the Next Throw	___ out of 10
Energy Zone Drill	
On the Approach	___ out of 23
Total	___ *out of 55*

You have learned to grip the ball correctly. You have learned the skills to give you the mind of a bowler. The next step is to actually get onto the approach and develop a proper stance. The stance is the launching pad of the approach. Getting into the right position on the approach puts the body in correct alignment to the target line. Step 3 is all about developing the right stance, putting you in position for a straight approach, and accurate swing, and success on the lanes.

Beginning the Approach With a Solid Stance

Think of the stance as the launching pad of the approach. Proper setup position helps create the correct alignment of the body to the target line, a straight approach, and an accurate swing. Ideally, the bowler establishes a line for the body and a line for the swing before initiating any ball or body motion. These lines do not cross during the approach.

The position on the lane is the first element of targeting. The alignment between the starting position and the target on the lane creates the ball's path to the target. It is somewhat a matter of trial and error to figure out where you need to start the approach and what target you will use that creates a path to the strike target. Adjusting one or the other will fine-tune the ball path. Once you are in the pocket, it is a matter of performance to throw it there consistently.

The setup has a critical influence on accuracy. If the body and the ball are not in the correct position relative to each other, it will be difficult to walk or swing straight. The body and the ball will get in each other's way.

Often bowlers use the same terms for more than one element of the game. For the inexperienced bowler, this may lead to some confusion. For instance, the term *approach* has two meanings. One refers to the physical act of walking and swinging the ball until it is released. The other refers to the part of the playing surface the bowler walks on. In other words, you make your approach on the approach.

Starting position is another term that needs clarification. It could mean the positioning of the body parts before putting anything into motion. It could also mean the body's position on the approach, literally where you place your feet before you start walking. In this text, *starting position* refers to the body's placement on the approach. Your starting position is part of your targeting strategy. The *setup position* is about the body itself, its preparation before any actual movement. The terms *stance* or *posture* may also be used.

PROPER POSITION

Before thinking about how to set up, every bowler must decide where to set up. Never step onto the approach until you have decided on an exact starting position. Choose a position in relation to your target or ball path.

To find a proper starting position on the approach, you will need to determine two things about your placement on the approach: the lateral (left-to-right) placement and the distance from the foul line. If you are not sure where to start, just keep it simple.

To determine left-to-right positioning (figure 3.1), first place your slide foot (left foot for a right-handed bowler) on the center dot. Place your other foot next to it. This will put you in a position slightly right of center. If you are left-handed, set up a little left of center.

Next look at the dot on the approach underneath your swing-side shoulder. The swing will pass over this dot if you walk in a straight line down the approach. Directly in front of this dot will be an arrow out on the lane. Focus on this arrow, the one in front of the swing-side shoulder, throughout your approach. (You may find that the setup puts the swing-side shoulder between two dots. This is fine; it means only that your visual focus will be between arrows instead of directly at an arrow.) Watch the ball roll over your visual target, then look up to see where it contacts the pins.

Use the arrows on the lane to your advantage. The arrows are about 15 feet from the foul line. This is much closer than the pins. Teach yourself to focus on a target at or near the arrows. It makes for easier targeting and allows for a more precise determination of errors.

Figure 3.1   Position on Approach

LEFT-TO-RIGHT POSITIONING

1. Place slide foot on center dot, other foot next to slide foot
2. Determine the dot underneath swing-side shoulder
3. Focus on arrow directly in front of dot
4. Visualize ball going over target and contacting pins
5. Target line runs from strike pocket, through target, to throwing shoulder

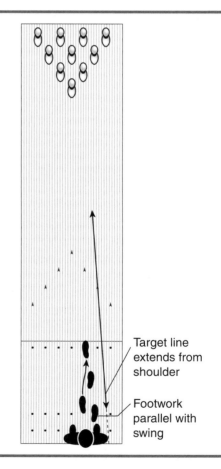

Target line extends from shoulder

Footwork parallel with swing

Now you need to determine your distance from the foul line. The approaches of all lanes are marked by dots (sometimes five, usually seven) that run across the approach. There are two sets of these dots, one 12 feet from the foul line and another 15 feet from the foul line. Remember where your feet are in relation to these dots.

First walk up to the foul line and turn away from the pins (figure 3.2a). Place your heels 4 to 6 inches from the foul line. Using normal steps, pace off the number of steps used in the approach footwork (figure 3.2b). Do not look at your feet. Walk normally, with your focus well past the end of the lane. Take an extra half step to account for the slide. Now turn around and see where you are on the approach (figure 3.2c). Repeat the process three or four times. Use the point from the foul line you reach most often as the starting point for the approach.

Figure 3.2   Determining Distance From Foul Line

FOUL LINE	**STEPS**	**END POSITION**
1. Stand at foul line	1. Walk along the approach	1. Add extra half stride for slide step
2. Back is to pins	2. Use normal steps	2. Turn around to see where you are on the approach
3. Heels are 4 to 6 inches from foul line	3. Pace off number of steps used in the approach	

When positioning yourself on the approach, it is very important to know exactly where you start. Most experienced bowlers use the slide foot as a reference point (i.e., the foot out in front at the end of the approach). Using the same foot at the beginning of the approach as used at the finish will enable you to connect two reference points for determining the direction of the footwork.

Look down at your slide foot when setting up the stance. Some bowlers use the toe; most better bowlers use the inside edge of the bowling shoe (next to the big toe) as the reference point.

Remember the board the reference point is next to, and write it down. Pay attention to the dots and the individual boards between the dots.

Look at what board your slide foot finishes next to, and write this down as well. Keep a log of all your approaches, indicating both the start and finish positions. Note your natural tendencies. Ask yourself these questions:

- Do I finish left or right from where I started?
- Does putting the ball in various positions affect the direction of the steps?

- Does the direction of the steps change when changing the starting position on the approach or the visual target on the lane?

Missing the visual target is usually a result of a physical problem. You simply can't throw the ball to where you are looking. Hitting the target (or at least getting very close to it) but getting bad results is a matter of strategy.

If the ball misses the visual target, check for physical errors. Be sure you walk toward the target. Make sure the slide foot finishes within an inch or two of a straight line from the starting position at the beginning of the approach. In the finish position, the line of the shoulders should face the target. The swing should follow through straight out from the shoulders toward the target.

Misstep

The ball misses the visual target.

Correction

Make sure you are walking toward the target. Check where the slide foot finishes. Check the finish position and the swing.

When the ball rolls over the visual target but misses the strike pocket, creating an unwanted result, you have a problem with your targeting strategy. Move your starting position on the approach in the direction of the error. If the ball was left of the strike pocket, adjust your starting position to the left. If it missed to the right, adjust to the right. Walk back to the same visual target. Changing the starting position while walking toward the same target requires a change of the setup alignment. Change your target. Find a new visual target. If you missed to the right, move the visual target to the left. If you missed to the left, move the target to the right. The new target may not be directly in front of the throwing shoulder. This requires slight changes in body alignment and the direction of the footwork.

Misstep

The ball rolls over the visual target but misses the strike pocket.

Correction

Move your starting position on the approach in the direction of the error. Change the target.

Trace a mental line from the strike pocket, through the target, and back to the beginning of the approach (figure 3.1, page 30). The direction of this imaginary ball path determines where the starting position should be.

After deciding on a target line, trace it back to your throwing shoulder. The ball swings from the shoulder. For the swing to follow the target line, aim must come from the shoulders, not the eyes. Imagine the head positioned over the throwing shoulder, looking down the arm. This puts the sight line along the arm toward the target. The bowler knows two things at this point: the direction of the swing and the direction of the footwork.

Position Drill 1. *Stringing Them Along*

Many bowlers have a difficult time visualizing the target line. They think they are aligned with the proper target, but they are not. Sometimes a physical prop is needed. This visual practice drill requires the help of a partner.

Set up in your preferred starting position. Tape one end of a piece of string to the lane on top of your intended target. Draw the string back to your throwing shoulder. Practice your setup five times while holding the string in place. After each setup, close your eyes and try to imagine the line to the target.

Once you have a feel for the drill, lay the string loosely on the ground. Set up in your starting position. Have your partner bring the string back into position on your shoulder. Did your setup using a visualized target match the real line determined by the string? Practice this five times. Score 1 point each time your mental line matches the real line.

Score Your Success

Mental line matches real line = 1 point

Your score ___

Position Drill 2. *Parallel Tracks*

Once you think you have determined the proper setup for your intended target, go ahead and bowl. Retape the string a couple of inches away from the intended target. Pull the string tightly along the floor. It should lie just outside of the throwing-side foot. You should be able to walk alongside the string without walking on it or away from it. If you throw toward the original target, the ball path should be parallel to the placement of the string. Practice five times, checking to see if both the approach and the ball path are parallel to the line of the string. Score 1 point each time your

footwork does not deviate from the string. Score 1 point each time the ball path is parallel to the string and rolls over the target.

Score Your Success

Footwork doesn't deviate from path shown by the string = 1 point

Ball path is parallel to the string's path and rolls over the target = 1 point

Your score ___

PROPER STANCE

After determining the proper position on the approach, your next order of business is to get in the proper stance (figure 3.3). Set up in a balanced yet active position. The body must be ready to make an aggressive and forceful yet accurate and controlled movement to the foul line. The proper stance is key for this to occur.

When first learning the elements of the stance, practice without a ball. Use shadow bowling (practicing without a ball in hand) every time you first attempt any particular position or movement. Shadow bowling allows you to concentrate on the elements of concern without

worrying about holding on to the ball or rolling it down the lane. Whether it is a particular position or a series of motions, shadow bowling lets you develop a feel for that element before concerning yourself with ball control.

From a standing position, a few small adjustments are necessary to determine the initial setup. The primary focus is on the throwing side of the body; determine, first, where the swing is in relation to the body. This is very important. At no point during the approach do you want the swing and the body to get in each other's way.

Assume an anatomical position: face forward, elbows to the sides, palms turned forward. In this position, it is obvious that the elbows are closer to the body than the hands are. Maintaining this "elbow in, hand out" relationship between the swing and the body throughout the approach is a characteristic of an excellent swing. Now bend the arm, bringing the hand straight up to a position in which the throwing hand is in front of the shoulder.

Do not move the ball to the body. Instead, move the body to the ball. Imagine an arrow sticking out of your shoulder, pointing toward the target. This arrow will point right over the top of the ball if it is properly positioned.

Figure 3.3   Establishing a Good Stance

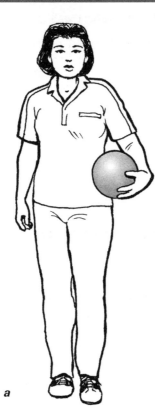

a   b   c

FACE FORWARD

1. Focus eyes on target in front of throwing shoulder
2. Align hips and shoulders toward visual target
3. Both hips and shoulders may have a slightly preset angle

BEND THROWING ARM

1. Place elbow of throwing arm next to hip
2. Palm is turned forward; hand is directly behind ball
3. Elbow is closer to the body than the hand is
4. Bend elbow, bringing ball straight up to a comfortable height
5. Ball is directly in front of shoulder or center of upper arm

LIFT NONTHROWING ARM

1. Bring nonthrowing hand across front of body
2. Place nonthrowing hand under ball or slightly off center
3. Allow nonthrowing hand to take some of the ball's weight
4. Keep elbow of nonthrowing arm comfortably close to the body; avoid contorted positioning
5. Adjust ball height to comfortable position while keeping it in front of shoulder or center of upper arm

Misstep

After bringing the throwing hand to a position in front of the shoulder, you move the ball toward the chest, bringing it closer to the body's center of gravity.

Correction

Although this movement feels natural, unfortunately it is very detrimental to accuracy. Placing the ball in front of the body forces the bowler to throw the ball around the body as the swing is put in motion. In many instances, the bowler will walk around the ball as well, affecting both the footwork and the swing.

Bring the nonthrowing hand across to a supporting position under the ball. Turn the shoulders toward the throwing hand, a movement referred to as *opening the shoulders* (figure 3.3c). This action not only turns the shoulders to face the target but also accommodates the line of the swing. For most bowlers, the backswing pulls the shoulders to an open position eventually; a slight presetting of the shoulder angle moderates the twisting of the shoulders during the approach. This helps keep the upper body on line to the target.

Now that the position between the ball and the body is established, let's consider the rest of the stance, beginning with the lower body.

Balance in the stance is the primary concern. Everything should be centered as closely over the feet as possible in an active, ready-to-move position.

Feet are slightly apart in a front-to-back staggered position. A 1- to 3-inch separation is usually enough for a comfortable, balanced stance. For most bowlers, this is slightly less than shoulder-width apart.

The foot on the nonthrowing side is 3 to 5 inches ahead of the foot on the throwing side. In bowling, because the movement is front to back, the stagger is front to back. Compare that with a sport such as tennis that requires crosscourt movement. A crosscourt movement goes side to side, so the feet are spread side to side.

Flex the knees slightly—it is difficult to generate power with stiff knees. Slightly flexing the knees in the initial stance also prepares the bowler for the considerable knee bend at the end of the approach.

Hips are in a slightly open position. To preset the hips, place the foot on the nonthrowing side ahead of the foot on the throwing side (figure 3.4). Ideally, you want to create as small an obstacle as possible for the swing to work around. Think of bowling inside a box. If the hips and shoulders are square, the box is wide. Presetting the angle compacts the box.

Figure 3.4   Lower Body Position

1. Feet are a few inches apart
2. Feet are staggered, with foot opposite the ball 2 to 5 inches ahead
3. Both knees are slightly flexed
4. Hip angle is preset slightly to an open position

The preset of the lower body matches the preset of the upper body. The spine is tilted forward slightly, about 10 to 15 degrees, depending on the bend in the knees. The back is kept straight. A curved spine promotes a poor postural position that affects balance throughout the approach to the line.

With the knees flexed, the upper body must tilt forward to maintain proper balance. Consider what happens when you sit in a chair. As the knees flex, the upper body moves further and further back behind the feet. Eventually the center of gravity is no longer over the feet, and the rump plops down onto the chair. The approach is not the place to sit down, so avoid leaning backward. Leaning back is a passive, slow way to initiate the approach. Create a forward, active, ready-to-move aspect to the body tilt. The ball moves forward at the initiation of the swing; the body must be prepared to move forward with it.

Place the elbow at the side of the body, above the hip (figure 3.5). Accuracy starts at the elbow. The body should not get in the way of the swing; keep your elbow at your side. Do not hold the ball near the middle of the chest or place the elbow near the abdomen. These positions do not promote a straight swing. When in the ideal position, you should be able to trace an imaginary straight line from the shoulder through the ball to the target. This establishes the potential swing line. This line should not cross in front of or behind the body at any point.

Figure 3.5 Upper Body Positioning

1. Spine tilts forward slightly (10 to 15 degrees)

2. Shoulder angle is preset to an open position

3. Preset angle of shoulder is similar to that of the hips; lower body faces the same direction as the upper body

4. Place ball and swing arm in proper position after complete stance position is established

Keep both hands under the ball. The non-throwing hand must share some of the weight. Hold the ball at a height that suits your game—a little higher if you use slower footwork, lower if you use faster footwork. Holding the ball lower allows it to drop into the downswing sooner, a necessary move for the ball to catch up with fast footwork. Holding the ball higher helps emphasize the pushaway. This delays the ball's descent into the backswing so the swing does not get ahead of slow footwork.

Experiment! When you find a position that works well with your footwork, the ball will release from the hand cleanly. Good timing makes for a good release.

A good setup is vital for establishing alignment, balance, ball positioning, and other factors. In fact, recalling the elements of a proper setup (feet, knees, hips; spine, shoulders, swing arm) in a short, easy-to-recall checklist is an important part of an effective preshot routine.

Another function of the stance is to prepare the body at the beginning of the approach for the position it will assume at the end of the approach. In the finish position, the bowler balances on one foot with the front knee bent and the leg on the throwing side behind and out of the way (figure 3.6). Essentially, the hip and shoulder are in an open position, the knees are bent, and the spine is tilted forward. This is similar to the characteristics of a good setup in the stance, just to a greater degree than at the start.

A good finish position is the foundation for the rest of the bowling performance. Taking considerable care to ensure everything is in its proper place in the beginning will help you get in proper position at the end. A properly aligned, well-balanced starting position is the first step toward an accurate and powerful movement to the foul line.

Figure 3.6 Balanced end position.

Stance Drill 1. *Look in the Mirror, Front View*

Practicing in front of a mirror is a great way to evaluate your game and develop a feel for proper positioning and movement—without ever stepping foot in a bowling center. You can practice the stance setup almost anytime. All you need is a large mirror, preferably full length, or a window you can easily see your reflection in. Use a piece of tape to mark a straight vertical line going up from the floor. This straight line will be your reference point for proper alignment.

First look at your stance from the front. Stand straight and align your body with the mirror so that the tape line runs up the throwing side of your body past the center of your shoulder. Set your body in the proper stance position without moving the shoulder away from the reference line. Remind yourself of the three items for the lower body (feet, knees, hips) and the three items for the upper body (spine, shoulders, swing arm).

When placing the ball in position, keep it centered on the reference line. Keeping the ball on the line in front of the shoulder will help you learn what a well-positioned ball feels like.

If space allows, practice the entire approach, from setup to finish, in front of the mirror. When you practice your pushaway and swing, keep the shoulder and arm centered on the vertical reference line throughout your approach.

To Increase Difficulty

- Try to establish the position without looking at the mirror as a reference.
- Practice 10 setups from the front view without looking at the mirror. After each setup, look at the mirror to see if each element of the proper setup is correctly positioned.

Success Check

Look for these five items of a proper setup:
- Stagger of the feet
- Spacing between the feet
- Position of nonthrowing hand under ball
- Placement of elbow next to hip
- Alignment of ball in front of shoulder

Score Your Success

Give yourself 1 point for every item correctly positioned without first looking in the mirror. Use the mirror only to confirm positioning.

Your score ___

37

Stance Drill 2. *Look in the Mirror, Side View*

Now evaluate your stance from the side. Stand with your throwing side turned to the mirror. Position yourself so that your toes just touch the vertical reference line. Flex your knees just until they appear to touch the reference line. Tilt your upper body forward, keeping the spine straight, until the shoulder touches the line. This is your vertical balance line, the line that runs from the shoulders through the knees down to the toes. Place your elbow above your hip. It will be directly under the shoulder. The upper arm will be parallel to the reference line on the mirror. Position the ball at the preferred height without moving the upper arm.

To Increase Difficulty

- Try to establish the position without looking at the mirror as a reference.
- Practice 10 setups from the side view without looking at the mirror. After each setup, look at the mirror to see if each element of the proper setup is correctly positioned.

Success Check

Look for these six items of a proper setup:
- Stagger of the feet
- Bend of the knees
- Preset of the hips (ball-side hip will appear behind other hip)
- Tilt of the spine
- Preset of the shoulders (ball-side shoulder will appear ahead of throwing shoulder)
- Placement of the elbow (line from shoulder to elbow points down to the floor)

Score Your Success

Give yourself 1 point for every item correctly positioned without first looking in the mirror. Use the mirror only to confirm positioning.

Your score ___

Stance Drill 3. *Evaluating the Starting Position*

Step onto the approach and assume the starting position. Have a qualified instructor or experienced bowler analyze your stance. Earn points based on the following checklist:

- Upper body (hip to head) tilted slightly forward (___ out of 2)
- Knees slightly flexed (___ out of 2)
- Feet staggered 3 to 5 inches (___ out of 2)
- Throwing side of the body preset to an open position (___ out of 3)
- Elbow of throwing arm above hip (___ out of 3)
- Nonthrowing hand helps support ball (___ out of 1)
- Ball directly lined up in front of shoulder (___ out of 3)

It is sometimes difficult for new bowlers to analyze themselves without a bit of help. A mirror may not always be available. Sometimes you may need to rely on the observation skills of a knowledgeable individual. The scoring system for this drill can also be used when you simply need to evaluate yourself.

Success Check

- Tilt the upper body about 10 to 15 degrees from the hip.
- For a right-handed bowler, the right foot is back. For a left-handed bowler, the left foot is back.

Score Your Success

If you score 13 to 16 points, give yourself 5 points for the drill. If you score 10 to 12 points, give yourself 3 points for the drill. If you score 7 to 9 points, give yourself 1 point for the drill. If you score fewer than 7 points, give yourself 0 points for the drill.

Your score ___

SUCCESS SUMMARY

A proper setup is the foundation for the rest of the approach. Before you can even think about putting things in motion, a number of elements must be in place:

- The body has to be in the correct location on the lane, relative to the desired target line.
- The body has to be positioned in a manner that best allows the footwork to proceed straight toward the target and the swing to move unimpeded.
- The bowler must be ready to initiate a series of powerful movements with great control and precision.

A proper setup position gives the bowler the opportunity to do just that. Carelessness in preparation leads to inconsistency. There is a purpose for every element of the stance. The positioning of the feet and overall posture of the body help promote balance while generating a powerful movement. The alignment of the shoulders and hips, as well as the positioning of the ball, influences the accuracy of the swing.

Generating force, being in control, maintaining accuracy of footwork and swing, all can be best realized with diligent preparation in the setup. A bowler should feel in control with every throw of the ball. When you step onto the lane, ready to knock down the pins, you should have a sense of being comfortable, relaxed, balanced, and ready to move.

Review your drill scores. Record your scores in the spaces that follow and total them. If you score at least 25 points, you are ready to move on to the next step. If you score fewer than 25 points, review the sections that are giving you trouble, then repeat the drills.

Position Drills

1. Stringing Them Along   ___ out of 5

2. Parallel Tracks   ___ out of 10

Stance Drills

1. Look in the Mirror, Front View   ___ out of 5

2. Look in the Mirror, Side View   ___ out of 6

3. Evaluating the Starting Position   ___ out of 5

Total   ___ *out of 31*

The next step discusses the topic of footwork. It seems natural that once a proper position is established, we will want to get things moving. The progress from the beginning of the approach to the finish position now becomes the prime concern. Footwork, though, is not a matter of merely strolling down the lane and letting go of the ball at some point.

In the setup, alignment and balance are established. The goal of all bowlers is to maintain this positioning and body control while generating some power. The direction, position, and pace of steps are key to allowing this to happen. All the good work done in creating a proper stance and position of the lane will go to waste if it is followed by lackadaisical effort once things get started. With the target line, you have identified your destination. The setup position prepares you, but the footwork is what actually gets you there.

Moving Your Feet With Timing and Efficiency

Many bowlers do not give footwork much thought. If asked about their approach, the usual reply is something like "I don't know. I just start walking." This is an unfortunate oversight.

Every action serves a purpose. There are no wasted movements. Every step of the approach helps the bowler reach a destination. Footwork serves as the launching pad for generating a powerful series of movements. Footwork establishes the synchronization between body momentum and swing momentum. Until the elements of footwork and the swing become perfectly blended, nothing else—not the release, not balance, not accuracy—will be reliable.

The previous step established a starting position and the setup. Now it is time to get things moving. There are only two major movements in bowling: the arm swing and the footwork. Arm swing will be discussed in a later step. In this step, the progress of the entire body to the foul line is our concern.

The pace of the footwork is an important part of overall ball velocity, and the direction of the footwork is a vital component of accuracy. The best arm swing in the world won't do you any good if you can't walk straight. Either you will miss your target, or you will hit the target from the wrong angle because the approach ended in the wrong spot.

FOOTWORK CHARACTERISTICS

The six characteristics of footwork are direction, speed, number of steps, stride length (spacing between steps), rhythm (tempo or beat of the steps), and contact angle.

Direction

Without fail, the bowler should walk in a straight line. By that, I mean a straight line toward the target, not necessarily a straight line down the approach (figure 4.1). Imagine two parallel lines, one for the footwork and the other for the swing. These lines will be side by side throughout the approach.

The one exception is the slide step. Execute a complete weight transition from the power step onto the slide foot. The body does not chase the foot. Therefore, the slide step must work its way

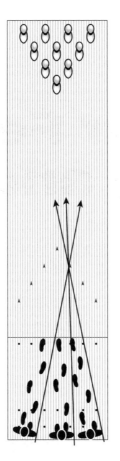

Figure 4.1 Three different straight approaches. All align to the same target even though they are not straight down the lane.

direction intended. The preferred finish point will depend on which target you are aiming for and how far the swing is from your slide foot. The distance from the slide foot to the swing line is called the *lay-down point*.

The lay-down point is the point at which the ball is released relative to the bowler's ankle (figure 4.3). Knowing your lay-down point will help you learn where the slide should be in relation to the target you are using to line up the swing.

For instance, you would like to roll the ball straight down the 12th board. Unless you know your lay-down point, you will not know where to finish the approach in order to put the swing over the 12th board. Let's say the lay-down point is 6 boards to the right of the slide foot. Be sure to have your slide foot finish next to the 18th board; if your slide is here, the swing will be over the 12th board.

To make subsequent adjustments, first determine where the release should take place. Once you identify the release point, merely add the number of boards of the lay-down point to the board number of the release point. This determines which board the approach finishes next to. Let's say you adjust your target and want to release over the 15th board, which is in front of the third arrow. Assuming the same 6-board lay-down point, expect to find the adjusted slide position on the 21st board.

under the body in order to maintain balance (figure 4.2). The body weight is centered over the base of support; the slide foot is that base.

Part of knowing the direction is recognizing where the approach should end. Check the finish point regularly to ensure you are walking in the

Figure 4.2 Weight is centered over the base of support, the slide foot.

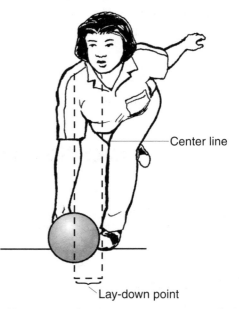

Center line

Lay-down point

Figure 4.3 Knowing your lay-down point—the point at which you release the ball—will help you adjust your slide step.

You cannot watch yourself swing the ball. After all, the visual focus is out toward a target. You can estimate the position of the swing, but pay close attention to where the approach fin- ishes, and know your lay-down point. A simple practice drill for determining the lay-down point will help.

Direction Drill. *Determining the Lay-Down Point*

Assume a finish position. The slide foot is under the body. The leg on the throwing side is behind the front leg. The back is straight, and the body is balanced over the slide foot. Slowly bend the knee of the slide leg until the knee of the back leg touches the ground. Keep the back leg behind the body, out of the way. Let the throwing arm hang down loosely. Note what board the middle finger of the throwing hand points toward. Count the number of boards from the inside of the slide foot to the board under the hand. This number is your lay-down point.

Success Check

- Have a partner help you.
- Get in a good finish position.

Score Your Success

Determine your lay-down point = 5 points
Your score ___

Speed

Strive for smooth, continuous acceleration to the line. For the beginning bowler, the pace of the swing dictates the speed of the footwork. As a player gains experience, the ability to adjust ball speed becomes an important tool for adjusting to changing lane conditions. Slowing the ball down to generate some traction when there is heavy oil and speeding it up to create some skid as the lanes dry out are important adjustment skills. Foot speed has an important influence on overall ball velocity.

Ultimately, how fast a bowler walks depends on her ability to control the stop at the slide. Do not run up so fast you lose control at the finish. Conversely, do not make the approach a slow, plodding march to the line. Think of the footwork as a fast dance, not a sprint—quick and smooth, powerful and precise.

When determining ideal foot speed, pay attention to the pace of the swing. Count out the speed of the swing, then try to match the speed of the steps to that of the swing.

Don't be overly cautious. The swing has a surprising amount of speed. Practice increasingly faster footwork. Eventually you will get to the point of panic, where you feel out of control, as if you cannot stop in time to keep from falling over the foul line. That is when you know you have reached your own limit. Back off slightly from there, and you will be fine.

Emphasize a good knee bend and a smooth slide. The knee is the shock absorber for the approach, absorbing some of its force. The long, soft slide is the braking action; bring the body to a smooth stop.

Number of Steps

Now things get interesting. The number of steps a bowler chooses to use will influence some of the other characteristics of the footwork. As will be discussed in step 5, there are four parts to the swing: pushaway, backswing, downswing, and follow-through. To provide enough time for the swing to complete its full motion, it makes sense to have at least four steps in the approach.

Some bowlers prefer to move the leg opposite to the throwing hand on the first step. In this case, when starting and finishing on the same foot, the approach should have five steps. There is a pretty even split between the number of bowlers using four steps versus those using five.

Other numbers of steps (three steps, six steps, and so on) are rare, probably less than 1 percent of all experienced bowlers. A three-step approach is a possibility, but three steps does not allow for a complete swing movement. Some bowlers who try to use a three-step approach start the swing early. The swing is already falling into the backswing as the first step is taken. Although not unheard of, this is awkward for most bowlers.

Stride Length

For the characteristic of stride length, the emphasis is on a power step. The power step sets up the body for the final drive into the slide. There is a strong push-off from the power step.

The power step is the next-to-last step. It is relatively short. Keeping the power step short keeps the drive foot (the right foot for a right-handed bowler) under the body. This puts the body weight slightly forward, over the ball of the drive foot. From this position, with the knee well flexed, the bowler can make a strong push-off, or drive, into the slide step.

The power step is the last opportunity to add body momentum to the overall velocity of the ball. It has to be taken at just the right time. If the power step is taken too early, the body launches forward while the swing is still going back. This forces the swing forward prematurely, ruining the natural pace of the swing. If the power step is taken too late, it does not contribute to ball speed.

When does the power step push off? Although timing will be more fully discussed in another step, we cannot talk about footwork without mentioning a little about timing. If the pace of the steps properly matches the pace of the swing, the ball will reach the top of the backswing at the end of the next-to-last step. At this point, the ball is ready to swing forward, and the power step should drive forward with it.

The acceleration of the body should lead the swing. It will feel as if the swing is following along. Just as the foot enters the slide, the ball approaches the bottom of the swing, gaining speed from gravity the whole way.

Not all instructors teach a power step, nor do all bowlers implement it in their games. The power step is not easy to implement if a bowler has poor timing. It is a somewhat more-advanced skill. Although it can be useful for beginning bowlers, other elements of the game must be in place before emphasizing the development of a power step. Beginning bowlers should focus on a shorter next-to-last step as a positioning tool. Be concerned first about keeping the hips on line to the target and the body balanced over the foot before the slide, then worry about how much force to put into the power step.

Some bowlers prefer a relatively even spacing. These bowlers will have a relaxed, somewhat modest pace. In general, they do not have a strong acceleration to the foul line, and their footwork is paced like the "tick, tick, tick" of a stopwatch or metronome. This is not necessarily a bad practice. It has its merits. The beginning bowler finds it easy to learn, and it does promote consistent speed. Some bowlers don't like the feel of the acceleration that comes from a power step. They prefer a relaxed, consistent rhythm from start to finish.

One important aspect of a shorter next-to-last step is the positioning of the body relative to the swing. The short power step works with the mechanics of the swing. When the ball reaches the top of the backswing, the leg on the throwing side is forward. You cannot produce a backswing of any significant height with a long stride into the next-to-last step. The body is too stretched out. Almost all experienced bowlers shorten the next-to-last step, especially players with a high backswing, even if they are not aware of it.

The shortened step allows for a forward positioning of the body—the foot is under the body instead of ahead of it—which counterbalances the pull of the backswing. By shortening the step, the swing can go higher without creating excessive tension on the throwing side of the body. It puts the body in a stronger position, ready to move forward as the downswing comes forward.

Today's game is about power and generating speed and hook. Increasing the ball's speed generates more pin action. Hooking the ball increases the ball's entry angle, creating a larger strike pocket. Bowling balls are designed to hook much more than they used to, and lane conditions change much more quickly than in the past. With strong hooking equipment and rapidly changing lane conditions (lanes become increasingly dryer as the oil is removed during play), generating ball speed is an important factor for potential success. Increase in ball speed is achieved by two means: a higher backswing and a faster acceleration of the steps of the approach. The short power step helps with both of these requirements.

The power step does not always need a lot of power put into it, however. Sometimes the short step is used only for positioning—getting ready for the finish—without trying to generate any extra drive. Bowlers should practice varying the force used in the drive of the power step, sometimes driving hard, other times being much softer.

You may not always need the extra power, but it's nice to know it is there. This is called versatility. If you learn to hook the ball, you can always learn not to hook it. If you learn to play all parts of the lane, you can play any part of the lane. If you can learn to throw harder, you can always learn to tone it down. The goal is to have a large set of tools at your disposal.

In a previous step, we talked about the setup. In the setup, the throwing side of the body is preset to an open position to accommodate the swing and to get the body ready for its position at the end of the approach. Wouldn't it be nice if the hips and the shoulders, essentially the entire upper body, could keep their preset angle without any movement during the approach? We could eliminate the extra body movement, the twisting and turning, that has a very negative effect on the swing and overall balance. The nature of the steps can allow this to happen

The alternating length of the steps in a "short, long, short, long" walking pattern actually helps maintain correct positioning throughout the approach. If the first step is short, the hips will stay in the open position. That is, the hip on the swing side will not get ahead of the hip on the throwing side.

The longer second step allows for two things. First, it keeps the hips open, which helps prevent the body from getting in the way of the swing. Second, the longer step takes a slightly longer amount of time. This allows the swing to pass by the throwing-side hip and clear the throwing-side leg before that leg starts moving forward into the power step.

The next short step, the power step, also has two functions. Again, it keeps the hips open, preventing the lower torso from turning away from the position established in the stance. It also provides the firm base from which the power step can drive the body forward into the slide. The next-to-last step should not be so long as to move the hips out of position. This is absolutely the wrong time to get the throwing-side hip ahead of the other hip. If this happens, the bowler will need to perform a more dramatic hip and leg kick to provide clearance for the swing. Either the leg will not clear in time and will get in the way of the downswing, or the exaggerated kicking movement will throw the body out of kilter.

The last long step, the slide, is the control step. It provides the long, smooth braking action to the approach, as well as the balance point for the body. At the finish, the opposite foot is forward, and the back leg is kicked behind. The body is now in position to allow the swing to sweep forward past the hip, with the swing passing under the shoulder in line with the target.

To promote a short power step and a long slide step, the bowler with a four-step approach should implement a short, long, short, long walking pattern (figure 4.4a). For a five-step approach, the pattern is short, short, long, short, long (figure 4.4b).

The five-step approach begins with a small step with the opposite foot. This step helps in the weight transitions. The body and ball should move forward together. Everything moves together. If the opposite foot moves first, the first step is small to make the weight transition controllable and easy to repeat. The second small step, with the foot on the throwing side, is just like the first step of the four-step approach.

In either case, the next-to-last step—the power step—is short. The short step keeps the foot under the body so the bowler can drive forward more easily. If the step is too long, the body weight will be behind the foot, making the weight transfer forward more difficult.

The short step is not a stutter step. It is merely a little shorter than a normal walking step. The long steps are close to a person's normal stride length, with the addition of the slide to the last step.

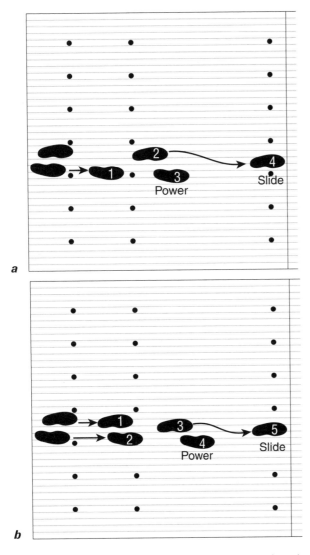

Figure 4.4 Stride length for *(a)* four-step approach and *(b)* five-step approach.

Rhythm

Rhythm is sometimes referred to as cadence. The bowler literally counts out the beat of the steps, similar to counting out the beat in music. The swing has a "one, two, one, two" or "out, down, back, down" beat to it. The downbeat is felt from the weight of the ball (the ball feels heaviest at the bottom of the swing). However, never pause during the swing. The swing is a single fluid movement. This should also be true of the footwork.

Feel the pattern of the footwork from the spacing of the steps. Do not add obvious pauses in the footwork in an effort to emphasize tempo. Such pauses interrupt the smooth flow of the footwork. Strive for a smooth, constant acceleration. Although there may be an inherent meter, or timing pattern, to the pace of the steps, do not try to force the rhythm by pausing between beats.

Contact Angle

The degree of the bowler's heel-to-toe gait influences the smoothness of the footwork. The normal walking heel strike needs to be slightly modified while bowling. If the heel plants too firmly, the footwork will not be as smooth as it should be. This frequently happens when the bowler's stride is too long and the knees lock out when the leg is at full extension. If the heel hits hard, there is a recoil effect. Essentially, the leg pushes back. This stop-and-go pattern is very disruptive to the flow of the footwork and the swing.

Conversely, if the toes strike first, the bowler will tend to lean into the shot. Once the body leans too far forward, the footwork has to be hurried in order to catch up, and the bowler reaches the line too quickly. This running to the line is similar to a sprinter running a dash. A bowler who is in sprint mode will not have a controlled, well-balanced stop at the foul line. The feet should make full contact with the floor, at least temporarily, to promote balance and speed control.

Good footwork incorporates a shufflelike step. It is not a true shuffle step—the foot lifts completely off the ground, and the heel does strike the floor a little bit sooner than the rest of the foot. Imagine a rolling step. The weight rolls onto the heel at contact, then rolls off the toes at release. Attempt a very smooth distribution of weight along the length of the foot during the stride.

Many excellent bowlers have used shuffle steps in their approaches, though, with great success. With a true shuffle step, the foot is kept flat. The steps glide along the approach, a familiar feeling for those who have ever ice skated or inline skated. The stride is usually shorter; the feet are under the body. The shorter shuffle steps can help with balance. The bowler may be able to generate faster foot speed while still feeling in control.

The closer the footwork approaches a heel-to-toe gait, however, the more it will feel like normal walking steps. This may be more comfortable for a beginning bowler to learn. The stride may be a little longer; it will frequently be more methodical. In a walking gait, there is an obvious heel strike, foot plant, and toe release.

Additionally with a heel-to-toe walking gait, the bowler is more likely to feel the heel strike, making it easier to count out the rhythm. Each step becomes a beat in the cadence of the approach. This helps a bowler learn timing. He can better feel for each different position of the swing that coincides with each particular step of the approach. Also, this is a good way to slow down a bowler who has a tendency to rush the line. Making the bowler think about or feel each step will tend to slow his progress to the line.

Once again, the slide step is the exception to the rule. The slide step is the one step of the approach in which the toe hits first. If the toe contacts first, the foot will glide in for a smooth landing. Then as the heel contacts the approach, the bowler will enjoy a smooth, gradual stop. This long, smooth braking action helps the bowler control the body during the release phase of the swing. An abrupt stop, usually caused by planting the heel on the approach first, has two immediate negative effects.

First, trying to stop the momentum of the approach too quickly sacrifices balance at the line. The foot will plant, but the body will keep going. A long slide absorbs some of the energy of the approach and allows most of that energy to transfer into the swing. Bowlers who have a tendency to stand up at the line or step away from the shot often do so because they plant the heel first on the slide step.

Second, an abrupt stop disrupts the fluid mechanics of the swing. The swing will jerk forward, just as the body jerks forward. Not only will the swing move offline, but also the release will be less consistent. Stopping the approach triggers the brain to release the ball. If the stop is abrupt, the release will not happen at the correct part of the swing. This affects ball control in the swing as well as the leveraging effect of the release motion.

One way to ensure a toe-first slide is to not lift the slide foot completely off the ground when taking the last step (figure 4.5a). As the toe releases, glide it along the floor, then point it into the slide (figure 4.5b). A consistent approach will ensure a consistent swing and release. Conversely, bad feet equal a bad release.

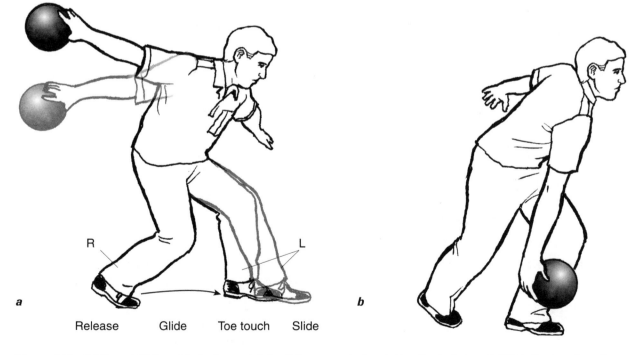

| Release | Glide | Toe touch | Slide |

Figure 4.5 *(a)* Do not lift the slide foot completely off the ground when taking the last step. *(b)* Glide the toe along the approach, pointing it into the slide.

FOUR-STEP APPROACH

On the first step of the four-step approach, the leg on the throwing side moves first (figure 4.6a). The first step is short and smooth, and the stride should be easy to repeat. The whole body moves forward with the first step. Once the foot is firmly planted, the body is centered over the foot.

If you want a faster approach, use a shuffle step. Quickly transfer your body weight to the ball of the foot. If you want a slower approach, let the heel strike first, and transfer your body weight to the ball of the foot more slowly.

The knee is flexed slightly on the first step. The knees stay slightly flexed throughout the approach. Do not stride out so far as to force the knee to lock out.

The second step of the four-step approach is slightly longer than the first (figure 4.6b). The second step is more like a normal walking step.

Again, do not let the stride get too far ahead of the body. Smoothly transfer your body weight from one foot to the other. Maintain a slight flexion at the knees.

The third step is short (figure 4.6c). The foot stays under the body. Again, be sure this step does not get too far ahead of the body. Transfer your body weight onto the ball of your foot. You should feel your body centered over the ball of the foot. The knee is flexed to about 45 degrees. As your body weight passes over the ball of your foot, push off directly forward.

On the fourth step, the toe of the slide foot glides along the approach (figure 4.6d). The slide step begins with toe contact. As the body weight transfers forward, the heel makes contact. Turn the heel inward to guide the slide under the center of your body.

Figure 4.6 | **Four-Step Approach**

a   *b*

FIRST STEP	**SECOND STEP**
1. Leg on throwing side moves first	1. Step is slightly longer than first step
2. Step is short and smooth	2. More like normal walking step
3. Stride is easy to repeat	3. Do not let stride get too far ahead of the body
4. Entire body moves forward with the step	4. Maintain smooth weight transfer from one foot to the other
5. Body is centered over foot once foot is firmly planted	5. Maintain slight knee flexion
6. Knee is slightly flexed	

For some people, the four-step approach feels a little mechanical. As soon as the foot goes forward, the swing starts forward. The start can be uncomfortably abrupt for some bowlers. A weight transition can be built into the four-step approach. This weight transition, which promotes a smooth, balanced start to the approach, is covered in the practice drills.

FIVE-STEP APPROACH

The five-step approach (figure 4.7) really isn't very different from the four-step approach. Bowlers who choose the five-step approach prefer to move the foot opposite the throwing side first. Many inexperienced bowlers are not aware of which foot they move first; they simply start walking. The first step of the approach is largely unconscious, and it makes no sense to go against natural inclination. If a bowler tends to move the opposite foot first, the approach will start and finish on the same foot. This merely requires an odd number of steps—five steps instead of four.

When the throwing-side leg moves, in this case on the second step, the arm swing begins as well. Essentially, the five-step approach is exactly like the four-step approach except it has an extra initial step. This initial step gets the body moving just before the ball starts moving into the swing.

This is perhaps the only real advantage of a five-step approach. The initial step gets the body moving. The transfer of the body weight forward leads into the weight transfer of the ball that comes during the pushaway. This gets everything—the ball, the feet, and the body—moving forward smoothly and consistently.

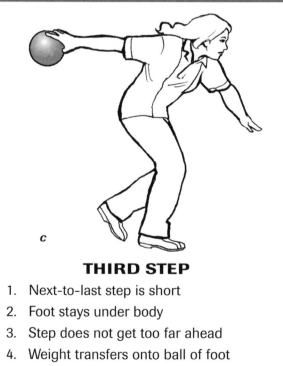

c

THIRD STEP

1. Next-to-last step is short
2. Foot stays under body
3. Step does not get too far ahead
4. Weight transfers onto ball of foot
5. Body is centered over ball of foot
6. Knee is flexed to about 45 degrees
7. As body weight passes over ball of foot, push off directly forward

d

FOURTH STEP

1. Toe of slide foot glides along approach
2. Slide step begins with toe contact
3. As body weight transfers forward, heel makes contact
4. Turning heel inward guides slide under center of body

Figure 4.7 **Five-Step Approach**

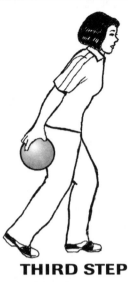

FIRST STEP

1. Step with foot opposite throwing arm

SECOND STEP

1. Leg on throwing side moves
2. Step is short and smooth
3. Stride is easy to repeat
4. Entire body moves forward with the step
5. Body is centered over foot once foot is firmly planted
6. Knee is slightly flexed

THIRD STEP

1. Step is slightly longer than first step
2. More like normal walking step
3. Do not let stride get too far ahead of the body
4. Maintain smooth weight transfer from one foot to the other
5. Maintain slight knee flexion

FOURTH STEP

1. Next-to-last step is short
2. Foot stays under body
3. Step does not get too far ahead
4. Weight transfers onto ball of foot
5. Body is centered over ball of foot
6. Knee is flexed to about 45 degrees
7. As body weight passes over ball of foot, push off directly forward

FIFTH STEP

1. Toe of slide foot glides along approach
2. Slide step begins with toe contact
3. As body weight transfers forward, heel makes contact
4. Turning heel inward guides slide under center of body

Weight Transition Drill 1. *Four-Step Approach*

This very simple drill ensures the body moves forward when the ball moves forward in the pushaway. It incorporates a small, almost imperceptible back-and-forth hip slide. This gradual shifting of the weight from back to front helps the bowler get the body moving forward as the ball is ready to move forward into the pushaway.

Many bowlers have a tendency to move the ball without the body or vice versa. This error (among other things) may lead to bad timing, a topic that will be discussed in detail in a later step. In addition, this lack of coordinated movement also disturbs the body's balance over the feet. A simple shifting of body position as the swing starts will help maintain a well-balanced start.

Assume the starting setup position. Feet are slightly staggered, and knees are slightly flexed. Shift your weight onto your back heel by sliding the hips back. Shift your weight forward to the ball of your front foot by sliding your hips forward. Practice 8 to 10 times, feeling for the shift from back to front.

Once you are comfortable with the weight shift, add the first step of the approach. As the balance point moves past the front toe and you feel the urge to take a step, move the throwing-side leg and the ball forward. You will feel as though the first step has caught or taken the weight of the body and the ball as they move forward.

Success Check

- Transfer weight smoothly from back heel to front toe.
- Move upper and lower body together.
- Transfer weight smoothly past front toe on the first step.
- When first step is firmly planted, body weight is balanced over foot.

Score Your Success

Weight transition from back heel to front toe is smooth = 1 point

Upper and lower body move together = 1 point

Weight transition past front toe on the first step is smooth = 1 point

When first step is firmly planted, body weight is balanced over foot = 2 points

Your score ___

Weight Transition Drill 2. *Five-Step Approach*

One of the benefits of the five-step approach is a built-in automatic weight transition in the form of the first step. Instead of merely shifting onto the front foot, the bowler actually steps with that foot. With the body weight gently moving forward with the first small step, there is a seamless continuation of the weight shift onto the second step. The weight transition includes the movement of the ball.

Assume a setup position with the feet slightly staggered. Slide the hips back until the weight is over the heel of the back foot. Smoothly slide your hips forward until the weight goes past the toe of the back foot. Slide the foot opposite the throwing arm forward. The body weight transfers forward to the opposite foot as the step is taken. Practice the weight transition with the first step 8 to 10 times before incorporating the second step and pushaway.

As the body weight moves past the opposite foot, take a small step with the throwing-side foot. The ball moves forward into the pushaway just as the throwing-side foot moves for the second step. When the second step is firmly planted, the body weight will be centered over the throwing-side foot.

Success Check

- Transfer weight smoothly from back heel to first step with foot opposite throwing arm.
- Move upper and lower body together.
- After first step, body weight is balanced over foot opposite throwing side.
- As second step begins, move body weight and ball forward.

51

FOOTWORK TROUBLESHOOTING

Fixing footwork problems is not always easy. For many people, the way they walk is as unique as their signatures or fingerprints. The unbalancing effect of the swing also influences footwork. Sometimes ball position or swing line may be as much a cause of approach problems as the way a bowler walks. Nevertheless, with patience and diligent practice, a bowler can learn smoother, more accurate footwork.

Crossover steps must be corrected. Other than the slide step, the feet should move side by side. Imagine straddling a line that goes down the length of the approach. The feet should remain on either side of this line. When the approach is complete, the slide foot will end up right on the line.

As a reminder to keep the feet together and moving directly forward, brush the heels of your shoes together as the feet pass each other (figure 4.8). This will keep the feet together and moving in a straight line.

Figure 4.8 Heels brush against each other as the feet pass.

Tempo variations can create problems with the approach. Walk with as consistent a pace as possible, and correct any obvious changes in the pace of the footwork. A step that is excessively longer or shorter than any other step often indicates a tempo problem.

Choppy steps or extra-long strides change the pace of the footwork, causing abrupt speed changes, pauses, or accelerations that disturb the smooth progress of the steps. Even when the steps are all close to the same length, some bowlers struggle to keep an even tempo in the footwork. Many bowlers tend to pause in the steps and then rapidly rush forward to the finish. It's as if they feel the urge to load up the muscles and then spring into action.

The approach should accelerate smoothly to the release point. Note any obvious hesitations or accelerations. Remember, the pendulum of the swing is a smooth, fluid action. Keep the progress of the steps smooth and fluid as well. Count the rhythm if you have to. Match your steps to the pace of the count. At first, this will feel mechanical and restrictive, but eventually the tempo of the steps will even out.

Once the tempo evens out, work on speeding up the later steps. Practice matching the steps to a faster beat, especially a beat that is quicker at the end of the approach than at the beginning. Speed up the footwork as you get closer to the foul line. This will allow for natural acceleration as the approach progresses.

The difference in the stride length in the "short, long, short, long" pattern is not as dramatic as you might think. However, those who are struggling to even out the tempo of their steps need to work on keeping all their steps about the same length. There might be a tendency for the steps at the end of the approach, especially the slide, to be a little longer because of acceleration. If this occurs, stay with it as long as the lengthening is not overly dramatic.

Beware of marching to the approach. Emphasize quick shufflelike steps. Walk as quickly as possible while maintaining balance over each step.

Watch for steps that are excessively short or long. Practice keeping the body centered over the feet with each step of the approach.

FOOTWORK PRACTICE

Accuracy is the foremost concern of all bowlers. Essentially, bowling is a targeting game. The ability to walk in a straight line to a predetermined target is the first requirement of accuracy.

For all the following drills, first practice without a ball. The practice drills are appropriate whether using a four-step or a five-step approach. Gain confidence in the pattern or direction of the step before moving on.

Eventually, practice with the ball cradled in both hands to get yourself used to the weight. Do not try to swing and throw the ball until your body movement is controllable. Finally, practice the footwork drills using a full swing and release. This is the last test to determine whether the correct movements have been truly adopted into your game.

Now is a good time to enlist the help of an experienced coach or trustworthy fellow bowler. People rarely watch themselves walk. Walking comes so naturally, whether swinging a bowling ball or not, it is difficult for a bowler to determine whether effective changes are occurring. An extra pair of eyes is frequently beneficial.

Footwork Drill 1. *Line on the Approach*

Using tape or string, mark a line on the approach from a point starting between your feet and ending at the foul line. If you use tape, be sure it is not sticky-side down. Tape leaves a residue on the approach that is hazardous to bowlers and difficult to remove. Two long pieces of medical tape stuck to each other will have sufficient weight to stay in place on the approach without sticking to anything else.

The line should end about 4 feet from the approach to allow for the kick of the back leg. Project an imaginary line from the end of the tape to the foul line. Put a small piece of tape or other marker at this point on the foul line. This is where the slide foot should end up.

Set up with the feet straddling the line. Practice walking along this guideline 8 to 10 times before trying to incorporate a swing. The steps of the footwork will be along the line (figure 4.9). Touching the line with part of the foot is acceptable, but make sure no step crosses completely over to the opposite side of the line. The slide step crosses over to a point directly on the center of the line. Tell yourself, "Heel in," as a way of directing the slide foot under the body.

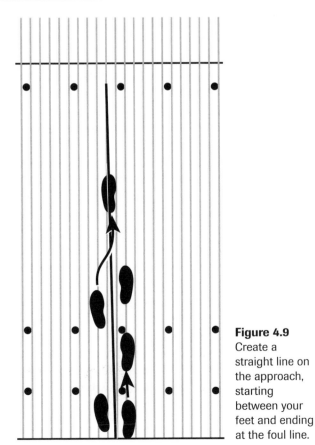

Figure 4.9
Create a straight line on the approach, starting between your feet and ending at the foul line.

To Decrease Difficulty

- Walk more slowly, feeling for the placement of each step.
- Watch your step. Look down at the line while walking until you are confident in the footwork.

To Increase Difficulty

- Walk at different angles on the lane by pointing the line in different directions. This is an important skill for rolling at cross-lane spares or when playing atypical lines to the strike pocket.

Success Check

- Each step is along the line.
- Body is balanced over feet with every step, with no excessive side-to-side sway.
- Slide step ends in front of predetermined finishing point.

Score Your Success

Each step is along the line = 1 point

Body is positioned over the line with each step = 1 point

Slide foot ends under center of body = 2 points

Slide foot ends up in front of slide-point marker = 2 points

Your score ___

Footwork Drill 2. *Bowling Within the Box*

Without trying to swing a ball, the previous drill may be easy. Once the swing is included with footwork practice, a tendency to walk off line may become apparent. The inability to walk straight is referred to as *drift*.

The most common tendency is to walk away from the swing; right-handed bowlers frequently drift left and vice versa. Many bowlers have the unconscious tendency to walk away from the ball, whether or not the swing path is getting in the way. These bowlers must learn what a straighter approach feels like.

Outline your path on the approach with towels or sheets of paper. In most cases, the towels need only be placed on the side you drift toward. Lay the towels so their edges make a straight line that points in the desired direction. Practice the approach 10 to 15 times without a ball.

Once you have confidence in the footwork, attempt the drill while swinging the ball. When you are comfortable with the placement of the guides, incorporate a normal swing with the footwork.

Finally, remove the towels to test for elimination of the drift. If the drift returns when the guides are removed, repeat the practice with the guides in place.

To Decrease Difficulty

- Place the towels slightly offset from a truly straight line. This will allow for some drift. The allowance for drift should be decreased as time goes on.

To Increase Difficulty

- Place the towels next to the spot where each step should fall so you can practice the length of your steps as well as their direction.
- Place the last towel (for the slide step) slightly inward. This will remind you to direct the slide foot under your body rather than try to get the body over the slide foot.
- Imagine you are on a balance beam about 10 inches wide. Place guides (towels, papers, pieces of tape) on each side of the approach. The guides outline a path about 12 to 14 inches wide, depending on your size. A larger bowler's natural stance is wider than average.

Success Check

- The setup directs the body toward the desired target.
- Steps are along the towels.
- No step crosses over, landing between or on any towel.
- The slide step moves in and is centered under the body.

Footwork Drill 3. *Step Placement*

This drill can be practiced with or without a partner. Without a partner, you will need to place a marker such as a piece of tape, a small rubber pad, or a towel on the lane next to where each step is supposed to land.

Slowly walk through each step of the approach. Pause slightly after each step. Make sure your body is centered over your foot after each step. Emphasize the short–long alternating pattern. On the next-to-last step, feel the drive leg load up (take the body's weight) before pushing off into the slide. Point the toe a little, keeping the foot mostly flat, to develop a better slide. Practice turning the heel in. Practice 8 to 10 times while watching the feet land on each marker.

To Increase Difficulty

- Practice 8 to 10 times with your eyes focused ahead. Look down only after each step to see if the feet landed next to the appropriate marker.
- Have a partner watch your approach. Walk through the approach at normal speed. Your partner will say "Yes!" each time a step lands next to the proper mark and "No!" each time a step misses. Stop the footwork on the first no. Start over. Repeat footwork until every step is a yes.

- Slowly increase the pace of the footwork.
- As you get more comfortable with the acceleration, start incorporating the swing into your footwork practice.

Success Check

- Steps are smooth and natural.
- Steps follow short–long pattern if preferred.
- The next-to-last step is short.
- The slide step goes toward the visual target.

Footwork Drill 4. *Evaluating Footwork*

Step onto the approach and go through your footwork. Have a qualified instructor or experienced bowler analyze your footwork on the approach. Earn points based on the following criteria:

- Each step moves toward the target (___ out of 3)
- Footwork has a smooth rhythm (___ out of 2)
- Knees are slightly flexed and never lock out during stride (___ out of 1)
- Steps use a soft heel-to-toe gait, almost like shuffle steps (___ out of 2)
- Next-to-last step is short (___ out of 2)
- Strong push-off into the slide is evident (___ out of 1)
- Toe touches the lane first on the slide step (___ out of 2)
- Slide step crosses over and finishes under the midline of the body (___ out of 3)

Success Check

- Steps are smooth and rhythmic.
- Body feels well balanced and firmly set over the foot after each step.
- Leg push from power step is strong.
- Slide step moves under body to a center position.
- When footwork finishes, you are balanced over the slide foot.

Score Your Success

If you score 14 to 16 points, give yourself 5 points for the drill. If you score 11 to 13 points, give yourself 3 points for the drill. If you score 7 to 10 points, give yourself 1 point for the drill. If you score fewer than 7 points, give yourself 0 points for the drill.

Your score ___

Footwork Drill 5. *Stride Length*

Many beginning bowlers greatly alter the way they walk as soon as they have a ball in their hands. The footwork is much closer to a normal walking pattern than many people think. Sometimes exaggerating a movement will help you feel the difference between variations.

Practice this drill while cradling the ball in both hands in front. While practicing the steps, strive to achieve a strong finishing drive into a well-balanced finish position.

Practice 10 approaches using extra-long strides. Practice 10 approaches using very short, choppy steps. Practice 10 approaches using normal walking steps. Rate each type of approach on a scale from 1 to 5. Enter your scores in table 4.1.

Add up all the points from the categories for each type of approach. Which stride length received the highest score? Ask yourself these questions:

- With which stride length did I feel most comfortable and in control?
- Which stride length gave me a sense of smooth, rhythmic motion?
- Which stride length gave me the greatest sense of momentum and power?

Table 4.1 Stride Length Scores

	Extra-long strides	Short, choppy strides	Normal strides
Easy to repeat	1 2 3 4 5	1 2 3 4 5	1 2 3 4 5
Smooth and rhythmic	1 2 3 4 5	1 2 3 4 5	1 2 3 4 5
Feeling of balance and control with every step	1 2 3 4 5	1 2 3 4 5	1 2 3 4 5
Able to gradually accelerate to a strong finish	1 2 3 4 5	1 2 3 4 5	1 2 3 4 5
Able to finish in balanced position consistently	1 2 3 4 5	1 2 3 4 5	1 2 3 4 5
Totals			

Success Check

- Continue to practice the footwork using the stride that best satisfies the questions.

Give yourself 10 points for finding the stride that best suits you.

Your score ___

SUCCESS SUMMARY

The feet stay under the body for balance while driving the body forward for power. This is not as easy as it sounds. Sure we all know how to walk, but can we learn how to walk with power? Keep a consistent rhythm with the footwork. Make sure every step is toward the target. Think of the footwork as a smooth transfer of energy that brings the body along with the swing.

Review your drill scores. Record your scores in the spaces that follow and total them. If you score at least 40 points, you are ready to move on to the next step. If you score fewer than 40 points, review the sections that are giving you trouble, then repeat the drills.

Direction Drill

    1. Determining the Lay-Down Point   ___ out of 5

Weight Transition Drills

    1. Four-Step Approach   ___ out of 5

    2. Five-Step Approach   ___ out of 5

Footwork Drills

    1. Line on the Approach   ___ out of 6

    2. Bowling Within the Box   ___ out of 6

    3. Step Placement   ___ out of 5

    4. Evaluating Footwork   ___ out of 5

    5. Stride Length   ___ out of 10

Total   ___ *out of 47*

The proper placement and pace of the steps allow a bowler to generate power without sacrificing consistency and control. A smooth, balanced approach is an important element of the game, but at some point, the bowler needs to throw the ball. The goal of all bowlers is to have a flawless blending between the pace of the steps and the rhythm of the swing. The next step in skill development is to develop the swing.

Swinging for Power and Accuracy

The swing is the most important physical skill in bowling. Work hard to build your game around your swing. Swing control—directing the swing line—is the essential element of accuracy. The pace of the swing, its rhythm and speed, establishes the pace of the footwork to which it is matched. The velocity the ball achieves as it falls through the arc of the swing is the largest component of the ball's final velocity. Yes, a bowler can walk more quickly or add more drive during the power step to increase speed. Nevertheless, there is a limit to what a bowler can do before losing control in positioning or before overall balance begins to have a negative impact.

The speed at which the ball leaves your hand is, in large part, a product of the swing. Furthermore, a truly free swing, one that is neither constrained nor manipulated by muscular effort, is inherently consistent.

Consistency, rhythm, accuracy, and power are all initiated from, and largely influenced by, the type of swing the bowler develops. Proper swing development cannot be overemphasized. A proper swing influences balance, control, and the mechanics of the release, so time spent perfecting the swing is time well spent.

What is it about the swing that influences the nature of the game of bowling? How can you use that knowledge to your benefit, helping you develop both consistency and versatility?

After all, a swing is not necessary to put a ball in motion down the lane. As children sometimes do, you could simply cradle the ball in both hands, hold it in front of your abdomen, run up to the foul line, and push the ball with the palms of your hands to send it toward the pins.

In the long run, this run-and-push technique has its limits. With this method, there is no development of a release technique. The bowler cannot learn to manipulate ball roll and create angle into the pins (hook) with this method. More important, ball speed is severely limited. A bowler can run down the approach only so fast, trying to impart ball speed through body momentum, before losing control.

To generate adequate speed and free the hand for the release, at some point the ball must be moved to the side of the body. Proper positioning allows for the development of a pendulum swing. Moving the ball from in front of the body clears the way for a long, unimpeded swing, a movement that generates considerable speed in a short amount of time.

Although the swing is one continuous motion, the ball passes through recognizable points in the arc during the swing. The arc of the swing starts with its initial movement and finishes with the follow-through after the release. Throughout the swing, the bowler should strive for as free and effortless a motion as possible.

PENDULUM MOTION OF THE SWING

The most obvious physical trait of the swing is its pendulum motion. The gravity-driven pendulum nature of the swing is a physical constant. A pendulum has a couple of important qualities. First, once put in motion, a pendulum will follow the same swing path without error. Unless some force acts on it, the path of the swing is inherently reliable and accurate. Second, the time a swing takes to complete its full motion is consistent. If no muscular effort accelerates it or slows it down, the swing will travel back and forth along its swing path at the same rate every time.

A true pendulum, solely driven by gravity, is inherently consistent. You can reliably determine the direction, speed, and amount of time a pendulum swing takes. If the position of the swing and its initial movement are carefully determined, any one characteristic of the pendulum swing may be adjusted, as needed, without any of the other characteristics being disturbed.

However, keep in mind that the arm is not a true pendulum. A true pendulum has only one anchor point around which the swing rotates. The ball-and-socket structure of the shoulder is considerably more complex. The arm has a large range of motion in a number of different directions, or planes, of movement. It takes a complex series of muscular engagements and, more important, disengagements to simulate a pendulum motion. To see a great swing is to observe a beautiful lesson in the graceful, fluid generation of power, something not easy to achieve. With practice, though, you can replicate the characteristics of a pendulum motion to the benefit of your game.

The first consideration is the timing of the swing, also referred to as the tempo or rhythm. A principle of physics states that the length of a pendulum determines the period of oscillation. In other words, the amount of time it takes to complete a swing depends solely on the length of the pendulum being swung. To a bowler, this means the length of the arm determines how long the swing takes. Height of the swing does not matter.

This may seem strange to the casual observer. It seems logical that the higher the starting point of the swing, the longer it should take to complete its full path. This assumption is wrong. Although it is true that a higher starting position will cause the ball to fall along a longer swing path, it is also true that a higher starting position allows for a greater acceleration due to gravity. The net result is that the ball travels the path in the same amount of time as if it had started from a lower position (figure 5.1).

This understanding leads us to two very important bowling skill elements. First, timing is based solely on the length of the bowling arm. It does not matter where the swing starts. The bowler needs to match the footwork to her own unique swing rhythm. Second, ball speed can be manipulated solely as a function of the swing starting height. Unlike the use of muscular effort, which tends to be variable among all but the most highly skilled performers, reliable changes in ball speed can be achieved through the careful selection of ball height.

An important skill for all bowlers is to discover the pace of their own swings in order to find the footwork pace that is an appropriate match. The synchronization of the steps with the swing is commonly referred to as *timing*. Although timing is not the specific topic of this step, developing a feel for the rhythm of your own swing is an important first step toward developing this important skill.

Time of swing

$$B_1 \rightarrow B_2 = A_1 - A_2$$

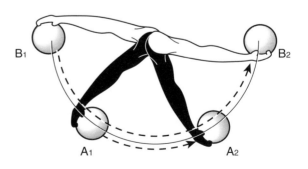

Figure 5.1 Long swings do not take more time to finish the motion than short swings.

Ideally, the body momentum generated by walking speed complements the swing momentum. Recognizing the relationship between the length of a bowler's arm and his stride is an important element for determining proper timing. For instance, a taller bowler who has a longer swing arm will need a decidedly slower footwork pace than a shorter bowler who has a relatively short, quick swing rhythm.

Considering the importance of consistency and accuracy in bowling and the inherent accuracy and consistency of a pendulum swing, it seems to be in a bowler's best interest to implement a pendulum-type swing as part of her skill set. To maintain the pendulum properties beneficial for skill development, the swing should be as free as possible. Restrictions or additions by muscular force should be avoided. Do not match the swing to the steps; match the steps to the swing.

If a bowler walks at a certain pace and then tries to fit the swing to that pace, there is a good chance the swing will not be free. Muscular effort will be needed to slow down or speed up the swing to fit the pace. The swing will no longer be a true pendulum, and the bowler runs the risk of losing the advantageous properties of a pendulum. However, it is easy to walk a little slower or faster, as necessary, to fit the pace of the swing.

Remember, an important principle is that the height of the swing determines the ball's final velocity. Speed control is largely a matter of choosing the correct height from which to initiate the motion. The higher the swing, the more gravity contributes to the ball's final velocity (figure 5.2). Because the swing takes just as long to complete its path from a lower starting position as it does from a higher one, you can manipulate ball speed fairly accurately without disturbing the synchronization of the steps and the swing.

The average bowler throws the ball 14 to 18 miles per hour (about 20 to 26 feet per second). A long, free pendulum swing can do most of the work toward achieving this velocity

As mentioned earlier, a common misconception is that a shorter swing takes less time. Based on this misconception, bowlers with quick approaches, or fast feet, might be taught

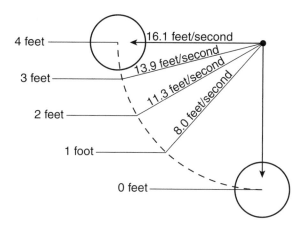

Figure 5.2 Potential speed from various swing heights.

to start the ball in a lower position. However, based on what is known about pendulum motion, this is neither necessary nor desirable. In reality, a lower starting position reduces the potential velocity attained at the bottom of the swing compared with the velocity that could be generated using a higher starting position. The answer to fast feet is not necessarily a lower starting position. Adjusting the swing to fit the tempo of the steps is solely a matter of when the swing is initiated, not how high the ball is when the swing starts (figure 5.3).

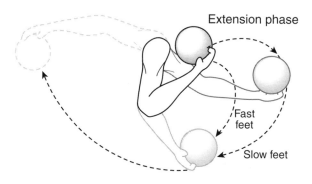

Figure 5.3 Starting position affects the time of the swing. For a bowler with slow feet, more extension time delays the ball's drop into the swing. For a bowler with fast feet, the quick extension drops the ball into the swing sooner.

PARTS OF THE SWING

When executing a full swing, emphasize its arcing, or circular, nature. Avoid erratic or forceful movements. It may seem strange to think of a continuous motion as having parts. Instead of thinking of them as parts, think of them as identifiable positions the swing passes through. The swing has four positions: the pushaway, the backswing, the downswing, and the follow-through.

The pushaway (figure 5.4a) is the initial movement of the ball from its starting position to the point at which it begins to fall into the arc of the swing. The pushaway is something of an outward movement away from the shoulder as the ball drops down into the arc of the backswing. During the pushaway, the swing arm has not yet reached full extension. The ball is not yet in a free fall.

The backswing (figure 5.4b) covers the movement of the ball after the pushaway to its highest point behind the bowler (the top of the backswing). As the ball clears the hip, it should continue to a point about as high as the initial starting position. If the starting height and back-

---

| Figure 5.4 | Full Swing |

a

PUSHAWAY

1. Pushaway is straight out from the shoulder toward the intended target

2. Pushaway is in a smooth arcing motion

3. Initial movement is out and down into the arc

b

BACKSWING

1. Arm extends fully as it approaches the bottom of the backswing

2. The ball is not pulled back; it will fall through the backswing on its own

3. At the top of the backswing, the ball is at about the same height as it was in the starting position

---

swing height are not similar, there is muscular interference. At the top of the backswing, the ball should be in line with the shoulder. Positions either away from the body or behind the body indicate that lateral movement has taken the ball off its ideal swing line.

At the top of the backswing, the ball should be at about the same height as it was in the starting position. Sometimes flexibility problems will result in the height of the backswing being lower than it should be. Adjust your style to accommodate a more restricted range of motion.

Misstep

You are forced to loop the swing around your hip during the backswing.

Correction

This error has two possible causes. Either the ball is positioned inside during the setup or it is positioned outside during the setup. If the ball is positioned inside, it must be pushed outward in order to swing around the body. From there it will continue to loop around the body to a position behind the back. This half-circle motion wreaks havoc on accuracy. The smaller the loop, the greater the accuracy of the swing. Be sure to start with the ball directly in front of your throwing shoulder. If the ball is positioned outside in the setup, the swing angle brings the ball behind the back. For a right-handed bowler, the backswing will be from right to left.

c

d

DOWNSWING

1. Downswing is a long, smooth arc
2. The swing is not pulled forward; it will fall through the downswing on its own
3. Little or no bending of elbow evident before release point

FOLLOW-THROUGH

1. Throwing hand extends out and up past shoulder
2. The swing line follows the ball to the target
3. The momentum of the swing will cause it to finish above shoulder height

A lower backswing position also may be caused by too much tension. Learn to let the swing flow. If a free swing seems impossible without feeling as if you will lose control of the ball, the ball may not fit properly. If your ball does not fit correctly, your swing may be restricted as you fight to hold on to the ball.

If the ball is higher than expected, you may be accelerating the downswing. Be sure to avoid a pulling motion. You may also have changed your body position. Leaning forward or turning the shoulders can put extra impetus into the swing. This changes the swing rhythm as well, sacrificing accuracy and balance.

Misstep

You lose balance during the swing.

Correction

Keep the swing close to the body. The force of the swing will pull the body out of position. Assuming a proper swing, you can do a few other things to stay balanced over the slide foot. Kick the throwing-side leg farther around. This leg counterbalances the force of the swing. Do not kick the leg so far around, however, that excessive tension is felt in the hip or knee. Bend the knees more and lower the center of gravity for better stability. Make sure the nonthrowing arm extends fully from the shoulder. The weight of this arm also helps counter the force of the swing.

The downswing (figure 5.4c) is the forward movement of the swing from the highest point of the backswing until the ball is released. The ball comes off the hand at or near the bottom of the downswing. Ideally, the ball should feel as if it is falling. (Another interesting physics tidbit: A ball falling from a certain height will attain the same speed whether it is falling in a straight line or falling along the arc of a pendulum.) The sense of the ball's being in a free fall is valuable to the notion of a muscle-free swing.

Assuming a proper grip and ball fit, the momentum of the swing will keep the ball pressed onto the hand. Remember, the pressure of the fingers on the surface of the ball will keep the wrist in a firm, straight position. The ball should not come off the hand until the bottom of the swing.

Misstep

You relax your hand or break back the wrist, causing you to drop the ball too early during the downswing.

Correction

Maintain proper wrist position and correct finger pressure to keep the ball in place. The fingers feel as if they press the ball into the palm.

Misstep

The thumb turns toward the floor during the downswing. The ball either drops off early or the bowler is forced to squeeze in order to hold on to it.

Correction

Do not rotate the forearm inward during the downswing. Save all rotation for the bottom of the downswing. Do not push the thumb forward during the swing. The thumb essentially does no work during the downswing.

The follow-through (figure 5.4d) is the upward movement of the arm after the ball is released. The swing will feel as if it is driving forward through the back of the ball before it moves upward. After the ball comes off the hand, it is like releasing a spring. The swing will kick out and up. The follow-through continues to a point above shoulder height. The arm should be allowed to bend at the elbow. A stiff, straight arm extension all the way through the follow-through indicates excessive tension in the swing. The swing should have a quick, free, almost whiplike motion after the release.

Many bowlers have difficulties reconciling changing ball position as a way to vary ball speed with the pace of the footwork. It is the nature of the pushaway that determines when the ball begins to fall into the swing. For instance, many bowlers use a lower starting position because of fast feet. They assume the shorter swing takes less time. What is really happening is that the swing is already significantly extended during the pushaway. The ball does not have far to fall in the backswing to reach the pendulum part of the motion. The lower position allows the ball to be placed into the swing sooner, keeping the swing on pace with the steps, even though the short swing takes just as much time as a swing with a higher position.

However, ball height does not have to be adjusted to accommodate variations in foot speed. A bowler can simply adjust the direction of the pushaway, either pushing the ball more outward to delay its descent or downward to quicken it. This will coordinate the swing with the footwork without affecting ball velocity. An extended outward pushaway delays the point at which the ball falls into the swing, a suitable option for those choosing a slower approach (figure 5.5a). A quick descent into the swing, essentially a *drop-away* motion rather than a push, accommodates faster foot speed (figure 5.5b). A blend of a drop-away motion and a pushaway, which one could call a *swing-away* motion, creates a smooth, arcing initial move-ment (figure 5.5c). This is the preferred option for many bowlers. This type of initial movement utilizes both the outward and downward ele-ments simultaneously.

Although this appears to violate the "don't fit the swing to the steps" principle, there are times when the bowler must use foot speed to alter ball velocity. For instance, a bowler who is trying to generate more ball speed but is unable to swing the ball any higher may need to increase the speed of the footwork to increase ball velocity.

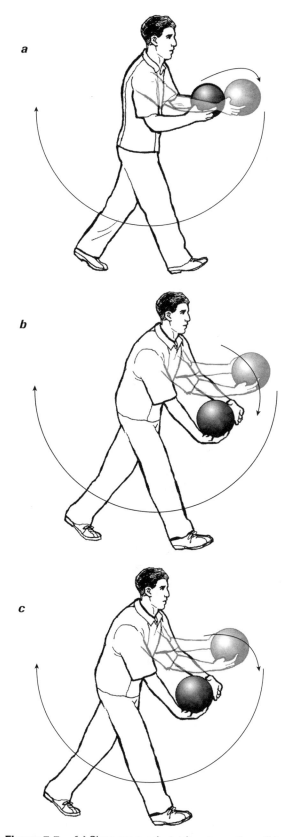

Figure 5.5 *(a)* Slow approach, pushaway motion. *(b)* Fast approach, drop-away motion. *(c)* Medium approach, swing-away motion.

The height of the backswing is largely limited by the bowler's flexibility. Exceeding the normal range may cause the bowler to twist the upper body away. The bowler must find an option for increasing ball speed without sacrificing proper alignment to the target or causing considerable discomfort.

Two important factors determine the accuracy of the swing: the ball's starting position relative to the shoulder and the direction of the pushaway (left or right) relative to the shoulder. If the ball is aligned directly in front of the shoulder in the starting position and the pushaway is straight out from the shoulder, the swing path will be straight, moving back and forth, passing along the side of the hip (figure 5.6a). The ball should be directly under the shoulder at the bottom of the swing. If the ball position or initial movement is not in line with the shoulder, the swing will not be accurate.

If the starting position or pushaway is in front of the body, the backswing will move away from the body. The ball will still fall along a swing line,

but that swing line will no longer align with the target. The downswing will typically follow the same path as the backswing—the swing will end up in front of the bowler. The ball will be pulled across the lane rather than swung out toward the target.

Sometimes, when the positioning is on the inside, the tendency is for the pushaway to move. Frequently, this causes the backswing to wrap around the back, and the swing will not be able to go straight down toward the target. The downswing must come back around the hips, which causes the follow-through to go away from the body (figure 5.6b).

Outside positioning is a problem seen in many bowlers (figure 5.6c). Some bowlers support the weight of the ball by sticking the elbow into the hip or stomach, which angles the arm away from the target line. Other bowlers simply push the ball away from the body as a matter of habit. Perhaps it is an unconscious avoidance of the ball. In reality, there is plenty of space between the ball and the body.

Figure 5.6 *(a)* Straight swing. *(b)* Wraparound swing. *(c)* Outside swing.

In other cases the bowler overrotates the hand to an open (palm up) position. The swing follows the thumb. Even after being made aware of the problem or seeing it on videotape, a bowler may have difficulty resisting the urge to move the ball away from the body.

The ideal pushaway moves in the direction of the target. Assuming the starting position in the stance places the swing out of the way of the body, the bowler should be able to swing the ball back and forth without it getting out of line with the target.

Learn to push the ball straight out from the shoulder. The swing should stay along the target line throughout the entire swing. The follow-through will finish in a position in line with the shoulder. You will feel as if you are reaching out and trying to touch the target on the lane.

During the swing, be sure to maintain upper body tilt. Establish the tilt of the spine from hips to head at the beginning, and do not change it during the approach. If the head leans too far forward, the swing gets artificially high. The arc of the swing drives the ball down into the lane, frequently causing an early release into the lane rather than sending the ball out along the lane. In addition, leaning out past the slide foot will cause a loss of balance, adversely affecting body control and swing accuracy. Remember, toe down and head up.

Misstep

You look at a target straight ahead and try to swing to that target.

Correction

Your eyes are in the middle of your head. If you swing toward a target directly in front of you, you will establish a swing that crosses in front of the body. Make sure you are looking at the target that is in front of the swing shoulder.

Do not allow the shoulders to pull back. Maintain the tilt and the knee bend. Almost every bowler, even highly skilled bowlers, have been admonished at some time for not staying down at the line. Remember, establish upper body position in the stance, and do not change it from start to finish.

Shoulder movement, whether twisting left or right or moving up or down, causes inconsistency in the release. Because the swing arm is attached to the upper body, variations in the movement of the upper body will cause changes in the swing as well as in the hand position on the ball.

Upward movement of the body just as the ball is swinging downward, whether caused by straightening the slide leg or pulling back the upper body, is one of the most common errors in bowling. This pulling not only affects the release but also takes the swing away from the target line.

Remember to drop and drive. Bend the knees to lower the hips on the next-to-last step, then use the power step to drive the hips forward as the swing brings the ball forward toward the release point.

PRACTICE DRILLS FOR DEVELOPING THE SWING

Each successive drill in this step either changes body position or adds a movement. The goal is to add levels of complexity without a subsequent loss of balance or swing integrity. The practice drills described in this section will promote awareness of the rhythm of the swing, the direction of the swing, and body position relative to the swing.

To understand the rhythm of the swing, you must learn how a pendulum swing feels.

Thanks, Dick Ritger

Some of the drills described in this text have their basis in the training regimen created by Dick Ritger. Mr. Ritger was an outstanding professional bowler who took his physical education experience and applied it to bowling training. Although he may not have been the first person to bring somebody up to the foul line to isolate the swing or learn proper balance, he was one of the first to develop a complete training system for the sport of bowling. Mr. Ritger has taught his system all over the world since the mid-1970s.

The game has evolved considerably since that time. The emphasis on increasing ball speed and revolutions has altered the need for generating power from what was expected of bowlers during that earlier era. Although I do not promote all elements of Mr. Ritger's training, his concepts and drills for establishing basic skills such as hand position, balance, and swing are fundamental to bowler training. As one internationally acclaimed instructor noted, "I don't know where I would be without one- and two-step practice drills."

A muscled swing, one that tries to either control the ball's movement on the backswing or direct it during the downswing, must be avoided. Although sometimes a gentle, continuous press or push against the back of the ball during the downswing has a useful accelerative effect, this technique should be used with caution—and not until a truly pure swing has been developed.

To understand the direction of the swing, you must be comfortable with a swing line right next to your body. Avoid the urge to direct the swing to a target. Learning to trust the swing is a complex interaction between what is felt and what is seen. The goal is to learn how to look at where you want to swing instead of swing to where you are looking.

Understanding body position relative to the swing requires first realizing that the width of the ball is greater than the width of the arm. Adjustments in positioning are essential to maintain swing accuracy. The swing weight (the ball weight accelerated by the force of gravity during the swing) has considerable force. This swing weight is entirely on one side of the body. Correct body position will counteract the swing weight, allowing you to keep your balance. A later step discusses more fully the particulars of balance, but its development starts with the swing.

While performing these drills, remember you are not trying to throw harder, you are trying to throw smoother. Any increase in ball speed is a natural consequence of body momentum working with swing momentum.

At this point, you should be comfortable with using the arrows out on the lane. Only 15 feet from the foul line, the arrows are easy to see and provide a precise target on the lane. It is easy to determine whether you have rolled the ball where you intended it to go. Before starting any of the practice drills involving targeting, make sure you can identify what target you are focusing on.

Learn to focus on a specific area on the lane; initially, this area can be a few inches across. The first concern is not aiming the ball but rather relaxing and letting the swing take the ball down the lane. With practice and improved concentration, you will learn to identify the specific board over which the ball rolled.

A bowling lane typically has 39 boards. Seven evenly spaced arrows mark the lanes on both the right and left sides. They appear on the 5th board (first arrow), 10th board (second arrow), 15th board (third arrow), and 20th board (fourth arrow). The 20th board is the center of the lane. A left-handed bowler counts boards from the left gutter. A right-handed bowler counts from the right gutter.

Swing Drill 1. *Kneeling Swing Isolation*

Your goal is to use only the swing to send the ball down the lane. Avoid moving the shoulders side to side. Keep the upper body slightly tilted forward; do not lean or pull back.

Kneel in front of the foul line, with the throwing-side knee on the ground (figure 5.7). Center the foot opposite your throwing hand (what would be the slide foot) under your body. Keep your nonthrowing hand on the knee of the front leg to prevent the nonthrowing arm from flailing around and turning the shoulders from the target line. The back knee should be behind the front foot to clear room for the swing line. If you feel unbalanced, bring the back foot further around to make a tripod out of the front foot, back foot, and knee.

Do not be too concerned with your position on the lane. Simply put the front foot on the center dot and swing toward the target (an arrow out on the lane) directly in front of the throwing shoulder.

Grip the ball and raise the throwing shoulder, bringing the ball off the ground. Angle the shoulder in an open position (facing slightly right for a right-handed bowler) to help direct the swing toward the target. Slowly swing the ball back and forth, letting the swing get longer each time. You will feel a slight pulling motion on the way back but a completely relaxed swing on the way forward. Do not take more than three swings or you could lose your grip on the ball. Do not stop the swing at any time. Say to yourself, "Back, relax. Back, relax. Back, release."

Look down your arm while swinging to be sure the swing is straight. Imagine a line drawn from the shoulder to the target; the swing will follow directly down that line. The inside edge of the elbow will brush the hip on the way by. The elbow crease on the front of the arm, the point just below the biceps, will point at the target during the swing. Release the ball at the bottom of the swing. The momentum of the swing should carry the ball past the foul line. Do not swing to where the eyes are; look to where you want the swing to go.

The follow-through extends directly out from the shoulder. The hand will come next to the ear after the throwing arm bends. When the arm is bent, the elbow will point toward the target. Watch the ball roll over the intended target.

Practice at least 15 throws, preferably with a partner. Stay in the drill position on the lane, and let your practice partner bring the ball to you. Rotate positions after every few throws. Some players may be uncomfortable staying down in this drill position for an extended amount of time. Increase comfort by placing padding of some sort under the knee.

Success Check

- Keep the throwing shoulder up.
- Do not swing the ball more than three times.
- Swing the ball in a straight line.

Score Your Success

If you hit the target 11 to 15 times, give yourself 5 points. If you hit the target 6 to 10 times, give yourself 3 points. If you hit the target 0 to 5 times, give yourself 1 point.

Your score ____

Figure 5.7 Kneeling swing-isolation drill.

Swing Drill 2. *Backswing Alignment*

To many bowlers, the proper position of the back-swing feels strange. They may be so used to the ball swinging behind their backs that the proper swing feels as if it is going away from the body. This drill teaches the sensation of the correct backswing. Remember that the swing reaches out from the shoulder.

This drill requires a practice partner to stand directly behind you. From this position, your partner can tell you how accurate your swing is.

Have your partner hold his hand directly behind your swing-side shoulder. As you near the top of the backswing, you should feel the ball touch your partner's hand (figure 5.8). If the swing is considerably off line, your partner should stop the ball at the top of the backswing, reposition it in line with your shoulder, and let it swing forward from the correct position. This will help you feel the difference between a good swing and a misaligned swing.

Figure 5.8 Swing-alignment practice with a partner.

Success Check

- Swing reaches out from the shoulder.
- Backswing stays in line with the shoulder.

Score Your Success

Five consecutive swings touch your partner's hand = 5 points

Your score ___

Swing Drill 3. *Swing-Line Practice*

This drill requires a practice partner to stand next to you, on your throwing side. This position allows your partner to guide the swing.

Have your partner grasp your arm in a position that does not interfere with the release. Your partner grips your forearm just above the wrist, with the thumb positioned under your hand (figure 5.9). This position helps you maintain a loose swing that stays in a straight line. Swing the ball two or three times before releasing it. Execute five throws, then switch roles with your partner. For each throw, have your partner grade your execution based on the following criteria:

- Smooth swing; partner feels no resistance = 3 points
- Straight swing; partner does not feel the swing pull away = 3 points
- Wrist maintains position; partner does not feel the back of the hand press against the supporting thumb = 2 points

Figure 5.9 Partner's grip on the forearm during the swing-line practice drill.

Success Check

- Execute a smooth, loose swing.

Score Your Success

If you score 35 to 40 points over five swings, give yourself 10 points for the drill. If you score 30 to 34 points over five swings, give yourself 5 points for the drill.

Your score ___

Swing Drill 4. *Shoulder Level*

From a position at the side, a practice partner can help you maintain shoulder level. There should not be an excessive shoulder drop or side-to-side movement with the swing.

Have your practice partner place a hand on your throwing shoulder. You want to keep your shoulder in contact with your partner's hand throughout the swing. Swing two or three times before releasing the ball. Execute five throws, then switch roles with your partner.

If practicing without a partner, place a soft object such as a folded towel, beanbag, or rosin bag on your throwing shoulder. Do not allow the object to slip off during the practice swings. If the shoulder drops, the object will slide off. Excessive shoulder drop will cause the ball to hit the floor

before it is released. Swing two or three times before releasing the ball.

Success Check

* Maintain shoulder level throughout the swing.

Score Your Success

If you execute five consecutive throws without your shoulder dropping away from your partner's hand, give yourself 5 points for the drill. If you execute five consecutive throws without the object slipping off your throwing shoulder, give yourself 5 points for the drill.

Your score ___

Swing Drill 5. *No-Step Balance Drill*

Essentially, the no-step balance drill is the kneeling swing-isolation drill from a normal finish position. The important thing to be aware of is the pull of the swing. Because the body is in a higher position and the center of gravity is higher, it is easier to lose balance. Pay careful attention to positioning to prevent any loss of balance.

Stand in front of the foul line with the throwing-side leg back. Flex the knee of the slide leg approximately 45 degrees. The knee will be over the slide foot. Tilt the upper body forward just enough to position it over the knee of the slide leg. Extend the nonthrowing arm from the shoulder, holding the hand about waist high. With the upper body in an open position facing a target in front of the throwing-side shoulder, the nonthrowing arm will be slightly ahead of the body. Position the throwing-side leg behind the slide leg. The rear leg will be mostly extended, and the toes on the nonthrowing side will touch the floor (figure 5.10).

Once you are in this position, the drill is the same as the kneeling drill. Assume a well-balanced finish position. After establishing the proper grip, let the ball hang freely from the side. After two or three swings, release the ball toward the target. If the drill is performed properly, the

Figure 5.10 No-step balance drill.

ball will swing out onto the lanes in much the same manner as if you had gone through a full approach. The only significant difference will be somewhat less ball speed due to the absence of footwork momentum. Practice at least 15 times. Grade yourself or have a practice partner grade you based on the following criteria:

- Balance is maintained during swings = 3 points
- Swing is straight and in line with target = 3 points
- Follow-through extends from shoulder toward intended target = 2 points
- Ball is released smoothly; momentum sends ball out past foul line = 2 points

Success Check

- Maintain balance during the swings and the release.

- The swing is free and uninterrupted.
- The ball swings out toward the target.

If you score 140 to 150 points, give yourself 10 points for the drill. If you score 130 to 139 points, give yourself 5 points for the drill. If you score 120 to 129 points, give yourself 1 point for the drill.

Your score ___

Swing Drill 6.   One-Step Timing Drill

For the one-step timing drill, imagine being on the next-to-last step of a full approach, the power step, with an obvious push-off into the slide. This practice drill incorporates a complete weight transfer from the power step into the slide step.

Put all of your weight on the nonsliding foot. The only part of the slide foot that should touch the ground is the toe. Flex the knee. If you sense a loss of balance, bend the knee more. Extend the nonthrowing arm from the shoulder, just as it is at the finish.

As in the other drills, let the ball swing three times. Count the rhythm: "Back, relax. Back, relax. Back, step, swing." Be sure the swing is straight and the body is not pulling out of position. When the ball reaches the top of the backswing and you feel the stretching sensation, begin the push-off. The push from the back leg will be strong enough to drive the body weight over the slide foot. With the weight centered over the slide foot, the back leg will then be free to kick out of the way before the swing comes down. The push-off will slightly precede the downswing, allowing the slide to finish just before the ball gets to the release point at the bottom of the swing. This is bowling's equivalent of stepping into the shot.

As the swing goes toward the target, the body should be in a well-balanced position, centered over the slide foot with the head up. Imagine bowling against a glass wall. You want to slide up to the wall, allowing the toe, knee, and chest to touch the wall without any of them breaking through or pulling away from it. Practice this drill at least 15 times. Grade yourself or have a practice partner grade you based on the following criteria:

- Step does not start until ball is near top of the backswing = 1 point
- You finish in a balanced position = 1 point
- Ball rolls over intended target = 1 point
- Throw is perfect—on time, in balance, and accurate = 3 points

Success Check

- Maintain upper body tilt.
- Do not allow the shoulders to pull back.
- Do not start the slide step until the ball reaches the top of the backswing.
- The slide step crosses over to a position under the center of the body.

If you score 80 to 90 points, give yourself 10 points for the drill. If you score 70 to 79 points, give yourself 5 points for the drill. If you score 60 to 69 points, give yourself 1 point for the drill.

Your score ___

Swing Drill 7. *Towel Variations*

Certain tools are useful for developing a proper swing. One of the most useful is also one of the simplest. A small towel can serve a variety of purposes in addition to placing it on the shoulder to correct a shoulder-drop problem (as previously mentioned).

Use a towel during the kneeling drill (figure 5.7, page 69). To correct the problem of dropping the ball too early in the downswing, put the towel next to your slide foot. The swing should carry the ball over the towel. As you move on to other drills, such as the balance drill (page 71) and one-step timing drill (page 72), move the towel farther ahead of the foot. The higher release point and greater ball speed will cause the ball to swing farther out onto the lane.

Use the towel-tuck practice method with any of the drills or as part of a full approach. To correct a swing that moves away from the hip, tuck the towel under the armpit (figure 5.11). If the swing moves away from the body, the towel will drop to the ground before the ball is released. Gently pressing the towel to your body will give you a sense of what a straight swing—one that stays close to the hip on the way back as well as on the way through—feels like.

Don't forget about footwork when practicing the swing. Eventually you will need to get all of these parts working together, so remember what was practiced in the previous step. Try blending some of the practice elements for footwork with the elements of the swing. As a reminder of proper foot placement, put an additional towel just outside where the slide foot should end up. This will get you to step toward the target while practicing the swing.

Many bowlers sacrifice accuracy by stepping away from the swing. It is difficult to control the ball if you are stepping one way and swinging another. Stepping toward the target promotes body movement in accord with the direction of the swing.

Success Check

- The swing is always a smooth, pendulum motion.

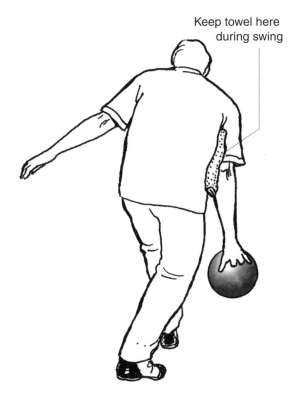

Keep towel here during swing

Figure 5.11 Practice keeping the swing straight by holding a towel under your arm.

- The body is well balanced in the finish position.
- A smooth release rolls the ball down the lane.
- The momentum of the swing carries the ball past the towel.

Score Your Success

Swing the ball over the towel while performing the kneeling swing-isolation drill = 1 point

Swing the ball over the towel while performing the no-step balance drill = 1 point

Swing the ball over the towel while performing the one-step timing drill = 1 point

With the towel tucked under the throwing arm, swing without dropping the towel = 2 points

Your score ____

73

Swing Drill 8. *Kneel and Roll With a Partner*

Perform the kneeling swing-isolation drill, except roll the ball to a partner instead of at the pins. Your partner kneels 10 to 12 feet away and places her hand directly in front of your throwing shoulder, as if it were a target. When rolling to your partner, do not throw the ball too hard. A good swing will roll the ball directly to your partner's hands. If your partner has to move her hands to stop the ball, your swing was off. Your partner can provide suggestions about your swing, body position, and release before rolling the ball back to you for another attempt.

The simplicity of this drill allows for many repetitions. If you are both working on your swings and releases, you can trade off. The bowler who is not throwing merely sets his ball to the side until it is his turn. Each bowler should easily complete two or three sets of throws, with 10 throws per set, in a short amount of time. Try starting a day of bowling by practicing this drill for 10 to 15 minutes.

Execute 10 consecutive throws, earning up to 4 points per throw.

Success Check

- Assume a well-balanced kneeling position.
- The swing is a smooth, relaxed pendulum.
- The ball releases cleanly from the hand.
- The ball rolls smoothly down to your partner—no bounces or drops.
- The ball goes directly toward your partner's hands.

Score Your Success

Roll is smooth; no drops or bounces = 1 point

Roll is on target; ball goes to partner without partner having to move his or her hands = 1 point

Roll is perfect, both smooth and accurate = 2 points

Your score ___

Swing Drill 9. *Playing Catch*

Playing catch promotes a strong follow-through and also helps correct a tendency to release the ball early. This drill is similar to the one-step timing drill (page 72). You will throw the ball in the air to a partner standing 10 to 12 feet away.

Again, your partner should position his hands directly in front of your throwing shoulder. Much like pitching a horseshoe, take a step forward as the swing comes down. Imagine the catcher's hands are a target on the lane; both the step and the swing go toward the receiver's hands. Take a couple of practice swings before throwing the ball to your partner. The emphasis is on creating a smooth, relaxed swing while releasing the ball at a point that allows it to go in a forward direction.

It is important to make sure the area is clear and there is no chance of anybody wandering in the ball's flight path. Practice on a carpeted area. This prevents damage to either the floor or the ball should the throw land short.

Do not throw until your partner is ready. The catcher in this drill should have both hands out, ready to receive the ball. As the ball approaches, the catcher should receive the ball with both hands and allow the momentum of the ball to come forward. He should catch the ball with the hands and bring it toward the body instead of catching it on the chest or the abdomen.

The catcher should have a fair amount of experience in the game. He needs to understand the momentum generated by the ball and have the confidence to control that momentum.

As you swing the ball back and forth, your partner should remind you not to throw hard but rather to let the swing propel the ball. The flight of the ball should be a soft arc, not a hard, straight line.

For most players, it takes only three or four throws to develop the sense of a later release and a strong follow-through. Once they realize how easy it is to throw the ball to a person 10 to

12 feet away, they will have little trouble being confident in their ability to release the ball a foot or so over the foul line.

Note: You may be reluctant to do this drill (perhaps even shocked it was suggested), but you should have no problems with the drill if you observe some basic rules of safety:

- Be sure to have plenty of clearance on both sides and that there is no chance of any pedestrians getting in the way.

- The catcher should be prepared for errant throws. An early release will send the ball down toward the catcher's feet or result in the throw falling short. A late release, caused by squeezing the ball too tightly, will send the ball at or over the catcher's head.

- Start slowly and cautiously. As both of you become more comfortable with the technique, this drill will prove useful for practicing balance, swing line, and release.

- Find a partner who is evenly matched. Do not expect a petite lady to catch a heavy ball.

Execute five consecutive throws, earning up to 4 points per throw, then switch roles with your partner.

To Decrease Difficulty

- Stand closer together (but no closer than about 8 feet).

- Have the thrower in a kneeling position, practicing just the release.

Success Check

The swing is a long, smooth pendulum motion.

- The ball comes off the hand cleanly.

- The step and swing go directly toward the catcher's hands.

- The ball reaches the catcher's hands on the fly.

Score Your Success

Ball makes it to the catcher in the air = 1 point

Catcher does not have to move hands to catch the ball = 1 point

Throw is perfect = 2 points

Your score ____

Swing Drill 10. *Swing Motion With a Partner*

It is easy to practice the initial swing motion with a partner. Have your partner place her hands directly in front of you. When you push the ball away, your partner will catch the ball, but do not relax your grip on the ball. This practice will help you feel a relaxed swing. Your hand should be firm, but your shoulder should be loose. You can practice this initial movement time after time, with or without a step. Dry your hands occasionally to ensure a good grip on the ball. Practice the pushaway 10 times to get a sense of the ball falling into the swing, earning up to 3 points per swing.

Once you feel comfortable with the drill, ask your partner to move her hands unexpectedly. If the swing is genuinely free, the ball will pass right through the position where your partner's hands were on its way into the backswing.

After developing a full approach, you can use the partner method to test your pushaway. Your partner stands to the side, holding out a hand as a target. As the pushaway extends the ball toward the hand, your partner pulls the hand away to allow you to complete the full approach. If you hesitate when dropping the ball in a smooth arc, have your partner put one hand lightly on top of the ball during your setup. As you start the approach, your partner's gentle push against the ball will remind you of the proper time and direction for the pushaway.

Success Check

- Move the ball directly toward your partner's hand.

- Your arm is relaxed; the weight of the ball is entirely in your partner's hand.

- Your grip is still firm, and the ball stays in your hand.

Score Your Success

Per set of 10 throws.

Partner catches the ball without having to move hands = 1 point

Swing passes freely through the right spot after partner moves hands = 2 points

Your score ___

SUCCESS SUMMARY

The swing is a fluid, powerful generation of force. It should never feel rushed or erratic. Your goal is to keep the footwork and the swing working together side by side as you move down the approach. Try to make the motion as smooth and effortless as possible. Gravity (pendulum) and momentum (footwork) are doing all of the work. Do not muscle the shot. Just let it swing, and enjoy the ride!

Review your drill scores. Record your scores in the spaces that follow and total them. If you score at least 125 points, you are ready to move on to the next step. If you score fewer than 125 points, review the sections that are giving you trouble, then repeat the drills.

Swing Drills

1.	Kneeling Swing Isolation	___ out of 5
2.	Backswing Alignment	___ out of 5
3.	Swing-Line Practice	___ out of 10
4.	Shoulder Level	___ out of 5
5.	No-Step Balance Drill	___ out of 10
6.	One-Step Timing Drill	___ out of 10
7.	Towel Variations	___ out of 5
8.	Kneel and Roll With a Partner	___ out of 40
9.	Playing Catch	___ out of 20
10.	Swing Motion With a Partner	___ out of 30
Total		___ *out of 140*

The swing takes you to the finish. The finish position is the culmination of all the forces at work in the approach, swing, and footwork. Everything comes together at the finish. In the next step, you will learn to finish in balance, achieving that bowling-trophy position that every bowler aspires to.

Finishing the Approach in Balance

The finish position is the point of stability, the culmination of all the forces. The force of the swing and the momentum gained through the footwork come together at the finish. The finish position determines body alignment to the target and is also the anchor point of the swing. It is critical for swing control that the body reach a controlled finish.

Keep in mind that your ability to hit a solid finish depends on the alignment of movement during the approach, not just at the end. If the body and the swing get too far out of line from each other, you will have difficulty recovering to a balanced finish position. The steps preceding

this one emphasize footwork and swing. With these force elements of the game under your control, it will be easier to achieve a balanced, aligned finish.

On the approach, keep an image in mind, a reference point against which you can compare positioning. This reference image is called a *visual template*. A template is simply a standard form of an image used to re-create that image (e.g., plastic templates for making circles, triangles, engineering symbols, or flowchart symbols). When the template is placed on paper, the correct form can be traced and perfectly re-created.

VISUALIZING AND BUILDING THE FINISH POSITION

Use a visual template to determine how closely the actual finish matches the ideal finish position. The goal is to visualize a mental picture of the position. In your mind's eye, see yourself repeat the image, throw after throw.

The first step in the visualization process is to conjure the image of a clock face. Picture yourself within the clock. Your head points up to 12:00,

and your feet stand on 6:00. For a right-handed bowler, the follow-through extends to 1:00 while the back leg kicks around to 7:00. We have now established our image lines. The basic image of the visual template consists of only two lines: a static balance line and a force–counterforce line (figure 6.1).

77

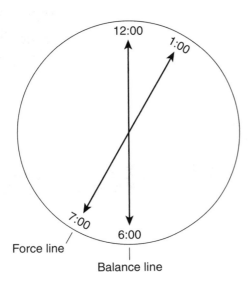

Figure 6.1 The visual template has a static balance line and a force–counterforce line.

Draw a line straight down from the head to the slide foot. This 12:00 to 6:00 line is the static balance line. For the bowler to hold position at the finish, all weights and forces must be equal on both sides of this line. The body needs to be centered over the slide foot. When the center of gravity is positioned over the base of support, static balance is achieved. The forces cannot be so imbalanced as to pull the body away from the base of support.

The force of the swing (i.e., momentum of the ball weight as it swings) is considerable. There must be a comparable counterforce (the kicking behind of the back leg). The line drawn from 1:00 to 7:00 is the force–counterforce line. This

image is the same whether viewed from the side or from the back (figure 6.2). The perfect finish position can be built by using this template.

Keep a few things in mind. First, the static balance line is set in the stance and does not change from start to finish. Second, the force of the swing on one side of the balance line requires the action of an opposing counterforce on the other side of the balance line.

The static balance line is maintained through every step of the approach. At the beginning of the approach, center the body over the feet, and keep it centered over the feet on every step. The position of the upper body is established in the stance. Try not to change any of these stance elements—the tilt of the spine, the open position of the hips and shoulders, and the close proximity of the swing line to the body—during the approach. Eliminating as much extraneous movement as possible—no twisting or turning, no leaning or pulling—is important for overall balance of the body. The more controlled the movement during the approach, the more likely a well-balanced finish will be achieved at the end of the approach.

The main difference between the starting and finishing positions is the knee bend. Bending the knee at the finish lowers the swing toward the lane. The knee is the body's shock absorber. It must be ready to receive the body weight plus the force of the downswing as you enter the slide. If the front knee is locked straight, there will be nothing to absorb the momentum of the

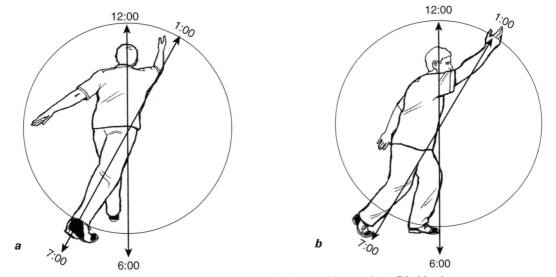

Figure 6.2 Use the visual template to build the perfect finish position: (a) rear view; (b) side view.

approach, and you will need to redirect your energy in a different direction to keep from falling over the foul line. Some bowlers redirect the force vertically (referred to as standing up at the line) or laterally (spinning away from the swing) or by taking an extra step (stepping out of the shot).

Be sure to sufficiently bend your front knee as you follow through. Planting the back toe on the ground promotes a better knee bend and ensures the leg is counterbalancing the swing. Do not drop the shoulders.

Imagine two parallel lines, one for the footwork and another for the swing (figure 6.3). Both lines are oriented toward the target. The ball is put in motion, and the bowler need only walk next to the swing. The less a bowler deviates from a straight line to the target, either with the swing or the footwork, the better. This requires the bowler to pay attention to the footwork leading up to the finish. The swing has a considerable unbalancing effect as it is. Any additional movement away from the swing causes even more problems.

Unfortunately, many bowlers tend to walk away from the swing. This is particularly noticeable during two different phases: when the ball is dropping down toward the bowler after the pushaway and as the ball is coming forward in the downswing. If the steps are moving the body away from the swing, it becomes difficult to recover to a balanced and accurate position by the time the approach finishes. The most basic tenets of the game—walk straight, swing straight, and stay on line to your target—are violated.

If a bowler walks away from the swing as the ball is dropping down toward her after the pushaway, she will experience accuracy problems.

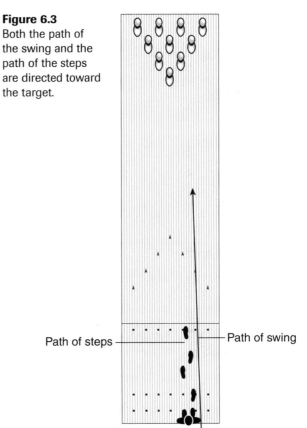

Figure 6.3
Both the path of the swing and the path of the steps are directed toward the target.

Path of steps ———   ——— Path of swing

Once the feet start in a certain direction, they tend to keep moving in that direction unless the bowler makes a conscious effort to reorient the footwork back toward the target. This footwork drift also affects the swing. The arm attaches to the body; if the body is not moving in a straight line, neither can the swing.

As the ball is coming forward in the downswing, many bowlers, of all skill levels, step away because of an unconscious tendency to avoid being hit by the ball (figure 6.4). This sidestepping as the bowler enters the slide dramatically affects the balance position. Make a conscious effort to center the slide foot under the body.

Misstep

You lock your front knee.

Correction

Bend your front knee as you follow through on the swing. It may help if you keep your back toe on the ground. This promotes a better knee bend so the leg counterbalances the swing.

If the slide step is going one direction and the pull of the swing is going another, the bowler will lose balance at the release (figure 6.5).

The release takes place at the bottom of the swing, when the momentum of the ball is greatest. At this point, the swing will exert the most

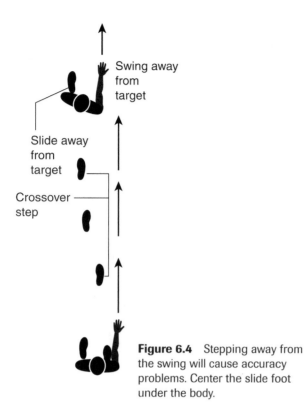

Figure 6.4 Stepping away from the swing will cause accuracy problems. Center the slide foot under the body.

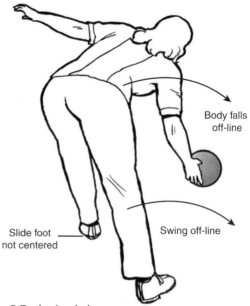

Figure 6.5 Losing balance.

dramatic unbalancing effect. Proper positioning will allow for the countering of the swing weight. The placement of the slide foot is a key element of proper position.

Remember these two bowling phrases:

1. Head up, hips down.
2. Drop and drive.

One of the best ways to promote a balanced finish is to learn a slight crossover step. The goal is to work the slide foot under the center of the body. It is the only crossover step of the approach; all other steps are side by side.

To promote this movement, turn the heel slightly inward as the foot enters the slide. With the slide leg moving in front of the push-off leg, the push-off leg will not have as far to go to counterbalance the swing. A weight or force of some kind must be on the opposite side of the balance line from the swing. The sweep of the back leg provides the needed counterforce, and the extension of the nonthrowing arm acts as an additional balancing aid. Now we have a good picture of the finish position (figure 6.6).

Figure 6.6 **Finish Position**

1. Slight forward tilt of upper body is evident
2. Knee is flexed to about 45 degrees
3. Body is centered over slide foot
4. Nonthrowing hand extends from the shoulder straight out to the side
5. Follow-through extends out from throwing shoulder in the direction of the target
6. Line of the shoulders and line of the swing make a 90-degree angle
7. Back leg is positioned around opposite of throwing side

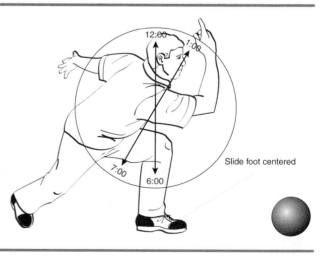

In this position, referred to as *bowling against the glass wall,* you want the knee, the chest, and the toe to touch the wall but not be so far out in front as to break through. Using the clock image helps you imagine the finish position. Remember, for a right-handed bowler, the throwing hand should follow through at 1:00, and the balance leg is at 7:00. For a left-handed bowler, the throwing hand should follow through at 11:00, and the balance leg is at 5:00. Fit your form within the template as perfectly as possible. The swing leg and throwing arm are on the opposite sides

of the dial; the rest of the body is centered over the slide foot.

The nonthrowing arm is the rudder that steers the upper body; the back leg steers the lower body. Avoid oversteering. The arm should extend out from the shoulder, the hand somewhat below shoulder level but above waist height. The placement of the arm to the front or back modifies the shoulder's alignment to the target. The arm will be slightly back (closed) if the target is inside the shoulder line and slightly forward (open) if the target is outside the line (figure 6.7).

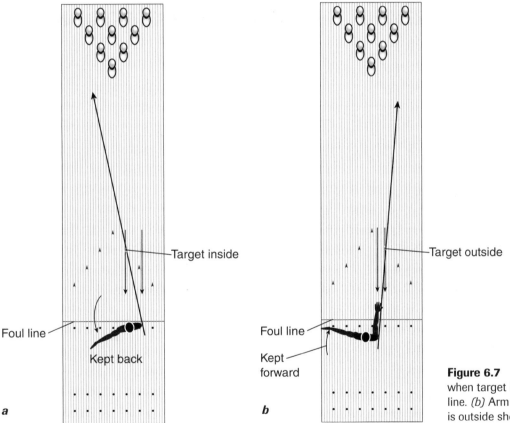

a

b

Figure 6.7 *(a)* Arm is closed when target is inside shoulder line. *(b)* Arm is open if target is outside shoulder line.

When swinging the back leg out of the way, do not pivot on the front hip. Freely swing the back leg. The rotation should occur only at the non-weight-bearing hip joint (figure 6.8). If the front hip pivots, the line of the hip will turn away from the target. Additionally, with the heel turning in at the slide, any outward rotation of the hip will put tremendous strain on the knee. Knee problems have ended many bowling careers.

Figure 6.8 Rotation occurs at the non-weight-bearing hip joint only.

Many bowlers have difficulty with balance. Learn to establish balance in a stationary position before trying to achieve it after an active approach.

Misstep

You can't keep your balance when in the finish position.

Correction

Be sure to keep your feet under your body. Use the crossover step to bring your slide foot under your body. Have a coach or trained bowler look at your entire approach from behind and from the side. Is there any point at which the steps veer away from a centered position? Does the body lean forward or pull back from a position over the slide foot? A balance issue early in the approach can become a problem at the finish.

PRACTICING THE FINISH POSITION

Practice each of the finish-position drills in gradual steps or levels. Execute 10 to 15 repetitions at each level of challenge for every practice drill.

- Level 1: Practice the drill without a ball.
- Level 2: Practice the drill while holding the ball at chest level. This adds the weight of the ball.
- Level 3: Practice the drill with the ball held to the side, hanging from the swing arm. This adds the unbalancing effect of the ball at the side of the body.

- Level 4: Incorporate a full swing, including the release of the ball toward the pins, as the last stage of the practice regimen for a particular drill.

Not all challenge levels apply to all the drills. However, be sure to follow a sequence of increasing weight and unbalancing effect as the skill progresses.

Finish-Position Drill 1. *Balance Practice*

From a stationary position and without a ball (level 1), put all your weight on the slide foot. Lift the other foot and move the leg behind the slide foot. Position your body according to the visual template. Bend the front knee just until the back toe touches the floor, approximately 45 degrees (figure 6.9). Close your eyes and hold the position for 15 to 20 seconds. Try to get a sense of what this position feels like without any distractions or visual reinforcement.

Notice the tilt of the spine. What does the flex of the knee feel like? What is the most comfortable placement for the back leg? Your goal is to fully investigate what a solid balanced position feels like. Once you are fully aware of the finish position, remember the sensation. This is the position you want to be in after every throw. If you do not feel you have achieved the ideal finish at the end of a throw, something likely went wrong.

Figure 6.9
Finish-position balance practice.

To Decrease Difficulty

- Keep your eyes open as you hold the finish position.

To Increase Difficulty

- Practice the drill at level 2 (hold ball at chest level).
- Practice the drill at level 3 (hold ball to side).

Success Check

- Front knee is bent.
- Balance foot is touching floor behind slide foot.
- Body is centered over slide foot.

Finish-Position Drill 2. *One-Step Practice*

Drill 2 emphasizes the weight transfer from the drive leg to the slide foot. Execute the drill at level 1 first, then proceed to levels 2 and 3. From a stationary position, balance all your weight on the throwing-side leg. Pick up the slide foot. Only the toe will touch the ground. Flex the push-off leg about 45 degrees. Let the body weight shift forward. As the weight shifts past the push-off foot, push off from the toe. As the push-off drives the body forward, center the opposite foot under the body. Facilitate the centering movement by slightly turning the heel of the slide foot inward. Finish in visual template position.

To Increase Difficulty

- Close your eyes as you go through the sequence. The goal is to sense the weight transfer as the body moves from a balanced position over the drive foot to a balanced position over the slide foot.

Success Check

- You perform a smooth toe-first slide. (1 point)
- Slide foot moves to centering position under body. (3 points)
- Upper body angle does not change. No leaning over! (2 points)
- Back leg kicks to a counterbalancing position. (3 points)
- Nonthrowing arm extends out from shoulder. (1 point)

Finish-Position Drill 3. *Full Approach*

Once you can complete the one-step practice drill with your eyes closed, you are ready to try a full approach. Be confident your footwork will bring you to a finished position before adding a ball to the exercise (levels 2 and 4).

When ready to use a ball, either holding it next to you or going through the full swing motion, make sure the finish position is attained consistently before attempting another level.

To Increase Difficulty

- With a ball, go through the full approach, and close your eyes just before starting the last step. Keep your eyes closed as you finish.

- Close your eyes on the last step while using a full swing and approach. Release the ball as you normally would. This exercise will teach you not to aim (i.e., to try not to force the ball toward a particular visual target).

- Practicing with your eyes closed on the last step teaches you to trust the swing. You will not feel the urge to aim the throw if you have nothing to look at. Trying to force the ball to a particular visual target by aiming it frequently causes the body to turn out of position and pull the swing off line.

Success Check

- You perform a smooth toe-first slide. (1 point)
- Slide foot moves to centering position under body. (3 points)
- Upper body angle does not change. No leaning over! (2 points)
- Back leg kicks to a counterbalancing position. (3 points)
- Nonthrowing arm extends out from shoulder. (1 point)

Score Your Success

Grade yourself based on the point values noted in the success check. You can earn up to 10 points for each attempt at each level. Execute the drill once each at levels 1, 2, and 3. Earn 2 bonus points if your swing extends from your shoulder toward the target on level 4.

Your score ___

Finish-Position Drill 4. *Evaluating the Finish Position*

Step onto the approach and assume a balanced finish position. Have a qualified instructor or experienced bowler analyze your finish position. Earn points based on the following criteria:

- Upper body is moderately tilted forward (___ out of 3)
- Back is straight; shoulders are not hunched (___ out of 2)
- Front knee is bent at about 45 degrees (___ out of 2)
- Upper body is positioned over front knee (bowling against the glass wall) (___ out of 3)
- Back leg is in position to counterbalance swing (right-handed bowler: throwing arm is at 1:00, back leg is at 7:00; left-handed bowler: throwing arm is at 11:00, back leg is at 5:00) (___ out of 2)
- Nonthrowing hand extends out from shoulder (___ out of 2)
- Position can be held after the release (___ out of 3)

To Increase Difficulty

- Go through a full approach, including the swing and the release of the ball. Hold your position at the line after the release. Have a skilled observer or instructor perform the same evaluation after you have completed a full approach. Does the evaluation of the finish position change as the movement elements of the footwork and the swing are added?

Success Check

- Upper body is positioned over the slide foot.
- Back leg and nonthrowing arm counteract the force of downswing.
- Movement of back leg and nonthrowing arm do not turn body out of position.
- Body position is held after throw is complete.
- A sense of control is felt at the finish.

Score Your Success

If you score 15 to 17 points, give yourself 10 points for the drill. If you score 11 to 14 points, give yourself 7 points for the drill. If you score 6 to 10 points, give yourself 4 points for the drill. If you score fewer than 6 points, give yourself 0 points for the drill.

Your score ___

SUCCESS SUMMARY

Examine your finish position often to be sure it matches the visual template in your mind's eye. The visual template is your reference point for the finish. After you have the visual template, it becomes a matter of sticking the landing.

Review your drill scores. Record your scores in the spaces that follow and total them. If you score at least 70 points, you are ready to move on to the next step. If you score fewer than 70 points, review the sections that are giving you trouble, then repeat the drills.

Finish-Position Drills

1. Balance Practice	___ out of 9
2. One-Step Practice	___ out of 30
3. Full Approach	___ out of 32
4. Evaluating the Finish Position	___ out of 10
Total	___ *out of 81*

The discussion of the basic bowling skills footwork, swing, and balance concludes with this step. Now it is time to put them together. The goal of the bowler is to coordinate the moving parts of the body. To be precise, bowling requires blending the rhythm of the swing with the pace of the steps to achieve a powerful, yet graceful, athletic movement.

The skill element of *timing* refers to the seamless blending of movements to create this smooth, powerful progression to the line. Excellent timing not only allows for the near effortless generation of power but also permits accuracy and balance. With good timing, the bowler will arrive at the line at just the precise moment in exactly the right position to send the ball to the intended target. The next step in bowling skill development involves the concept of timing.

Coordinating the Steps and the Swing

The coordination of the footwork with the swing provides for the effortless generation of power. The momentum of the swing combined with the momentum of the body allows a bowler to send the ball down the lane with decent speed. In addition, this coordination puts the body in the right place in the correct alignment so the bowler can throw the ball where it is intended to go. The coordination of the swing and feet, referred to as *timing,* influences a bowler's ability to throw the ball how he wants as well as where he wants.

Many bowlers, however, have a misconception of how power is generated. Many take what they are familiar with in other sports and try to apply the same movement to bowling. Picture what happens when you throw a ball. The leg drive leads into the hip turn, which leads into the shoulder turn. The upper body's rotation transfers to the arm, the upper arm in particular. The angular momentum of the upper arm then accelerates the lower arm. The whole movement terminates with the wrist snap at the release.

Essentially, levers are at work. A wrench is a lever that turns a bolt. If the bolt won't turn, you grab a bigger wrench—the longer the lever, the farther away from the point of rotation the force is applied, and the greater the force. Our bodies are a system of levers. Because our levers are too short, individually, to apply much force, we need to put them together to form bigger levers. A system of connected levers is called a *kinetic chain.* A kinetic chain is efficient only if the movement of each link is properly coordinated, or timed.

Our goal is the conservation of momentum. A basic tenet of the conservation principle is high mass at low velocity transfers into low mass at high velocity. For the athlete, the high mass of the body moving around a rotation point transfers its angular momentum into the low mass of the arms, which are farther away from the body.

How does the conservation of momentum apply to bowling? In bowling, there are only two links in the chain—the body and the swing. Many bowlers try to generate speed using too many links. They attempt to perform as if bowling were a high-velocity game, trying to get the hips and the shoulders into the shot as if they were throwing a baseball. There are two problems with this approach.

First, bowling balls are typically among the heaviest projectiles in the sporting world (in men's shot put, the shot weighs 16 pounds). Baseballs weigh 5 ounces, softballs about 9 ounces, and footballs between 14 and 15 ounces, or almost a pound. These objects are easy to throw fast and far. There is no way a person could control the momentum created by throwing a 14- to 16-pound ball 40 or 50 miles per hour. That force would literally pull the athlete all over the place. It is doubtful that the body could handle the stress of that much force; things would strain or break.

Second, the accuracy demands of bowling require the bowler to focus not just on how the ball is thrown but where. The home plate in baseball is 14 inches wide. If any part of the ball passes over the plate, it could be a strike. The strike pocket in bowling is only 2 to 3 inches wide. And it's not as if any part of the ball can touch that area; the center of the ball must be driven through that 2- to 3-inch window when it makes contact with the pins, or a strike will

be unlikely. The strike pocket is 60 feet from the foul line. This is equivalent to a golfer hitting a 60–70-foot putt or driving a 250-yard tee shot down a fairway 10 yards wide. How about a pitcher throwing strikes over a plate 3 inches wide?

A bowler does need to generate some force. After all, there are 10 pins down the lane that weigh 3 1/2 pounds apiece. You have 35 pounds of wood to knock around. However, the power must be delivered with great precision. All of the movements that create the force must be very finely controlled. Synchronizing the footwork with the swing allows for this force generation while addressing the needs of movement precision. Timing lies at the heart of bowling success.

TIMING

As the braking action of the slide slows the approach, the body momentum generated by foot speed transfers into the free-moving swing just as the swing accelerates toward the release point. If the timing is off, the result is a loss of momentum.

With late timing, the footwork finishes before the downswing approaches maximum acceleration (figure 7.1). The body momentum is wasted before it can transfer into the swing.

Figure 7.1 Late timing causes the slide to finish before the hand is ready to release the ball.

Frequently, bowlers who have late timing pull the ball through the last portion of the swing, trying to make it catch up to the footwork. Rotation of the shoulders enables this pulling motion. If this happens, the shoulders will be in an open position when the slide foot hits the foul line, and they will no longer keep their alignment to the target. A bowler cannot allow the shoulders to pull out of alignment. If you are not facing the target, you probably won't hit it. Unless the shoulders are forced to rotate back, the swing will go away from the body. In addition, forcing the shoulders to rotate back on line toward the target does not promote consistency.

With very late timing, the ball frequently falls off the hand early in the downswing. With ideal timing, the ball will near the bottom of the swing as the approach finishes. This allows the momentum of the swing to carry the ball out onto the lane, smoothly rolling off the hand. In cases of late timing, the momentum of the body stops. Once the momentum of the approach stops, there may not be enough momentum in the swing to keep the hand pressing against the ball, and the ball drops off the hand.

Other signs of late timing include the following:

- Pulling up at the line and using the legs to finish the shot.

- Muscling the swing (trying to pull the swing through the release point). The forceful tension in the upper arm pulls the swing away from the target line.
- Using a shortened backswing. The later the swing starts in relation to the feet, the less time there is to complete a full, natural pendulum swing. Tension in the backswing and a forced forward swing frequently cause problems in both accuracy and release consistency.

With early timing, the ball reaches the release point before the footwork finishes (figure 7.2). The last bit of momentum from the footwork cannot transfer into the swing because the swing finishes before the steps do. The swing arrives at the release point before the slide foot moves under the body. If the body is not in a stable, balanced position before the release, the release will be ineffective. Frequently, bowlers with early timing drop the ball. Early bowlers also struggle with balance. They occasionally need to take an extra step after the release. Early timing also affects accuracy. When the ball arrives at the release point early, it pulls the shoulder forward and down, causing the swing to come across the body.

With perfect timing, the slide foot enters the slide just ahead of the swing. As the body slows down from the braking action of the slide, the momentum transfers into the swing, essentially accelerating the swing through the release. Just before the swing passes through

Figure 7.2 In early timing, the ball is ahead of the body and ready to be released before the slide is finished.

the release phase, the momentum of the body should finish.

Imagine running while trying to throw a ball forward at the same time. Throwing with both power and accuracy while on the run is very difficult; simply ask a baseball infielder or a football quarterback. Instead, plant the foot, then drive with the legs and the hips as you throw the ball. Though not as dramatic as a football or baseball example, there is still a subtle plant-and-throw sensation to the bowling movement. For some of the true power players of the game, the action is decidedly plant and fire.

PACING

For perfect step–swing synchronization, consider the pace and size of the steps in the footwork pattern. Swing practice drills will help you develop a sense of the swing's rhythm and pace, but close attention to the footwork is needed to improve step–swing synchronization. The near effortless generation of ball speed comes about by combining body momentum with swing momentum.

First, in all footwork patterns, the foot opposite the throwing hand (left foot for a right-handed bowler) must take the last, or slide, step. This is essential for balance. Finishing on the wrong foot causes the bowler's weight to shift to the throwing-side leg just as the swing force pulls along

the throwing side of the body. Without adequate counterbalance for the weight of the swing, the bowler will have little control at the finish.

Second, there must be enough steps to allow the swing to complete its full four-part motion (pushaway, backswing, downswing, and follow-through). If the number of steps is even, then the approach starts with the foot on the same side as the throwing arm. If an odd number of steps is used, then the foot on the nonthrowing side starts the approach.

Third, the approach usually has at least four steps. Some prefer to take five. Fewer than four rushes the swing, forcing it to play catch-up with

Doing Well on the Wrong Foot

In 1958, a bowler who finished on the wrong foot won the first PBA event. "Wrong Foot" Lou Campi developed his finish position from playing bocce ball, a game similar to lawn bowling played for centuries in Italy. The wrong-footed finish is common among bocce players, and Lou Campi adapted this technique to his bowling game. Keep in mind that a bocce ball is light compared with a bowling ball. In addition, bocce players usually take only one step. In other words, they do not have significant ball weight or body momentum to deal with. I can't think of anyone else, before or after Mr. Campi, who won any event of any status, amateur or professional, using the wrong-footed style.

the footwork. This usually results in late timing; the footwork finishes at the foul line before the swing reaches the ideal release point.

More than five steps makes timing difficult as well; it becomes harder to integrate the swing rhythm to the pattern of the steps. It is rare to find professional players or even very successful amateurs who regularly use other than four or five steps in the approach. They may modify the approach under certain extreme playing condi-

tions, but a vast majority of these players use either a four- or five-step approach.

Finally, with every step of the approach, the body is centered over the feet. At no point is a step excessively in front of the body, nor is the body leaning out in front of the foot. The position and balance line established in the stance do not change during the progression of the approach. Balance while in motion is a key characteristic of skilled performance.

FOUR-STEP APPROACH

Most bowlers new to the game start with the four-step approach (figure 7.3). Because the arm swing has four parts, the four-step approach is the most basic step pattern for synchronizing the steps with the swing. For each step of the approach, the details of the body position and swing position are described.

When initiating the approach, do not suddenly lurch forward at the outset of the prestep motion (figure 7.3a). Instead, try to achieve a smooth weight transition. Set your feet in a staggered starting position. Slightly rock back onto the heel of the back foot. Move the whole body back. Do not change the overall setup position. Gently shift your weight forward onto the ball of the front foot. Rock back onto the heel again. As the weight transfers forward the second time, let the body move out past the ball of the foot. You should feel the need to take a step. Push the ball away and take a step.

The first step of the four-step approach is a short, smooth step that initiates the pattern and the rhythm (figure 7.3b). Remember, the four-step approach has a rhythm of short, long, short,

long. The step pattern matches the rhythm, or beat, of the swing—out, down, back, down. Each long step matches a downbeat in the swing. If done properly, the first step promotes a relaxed weight transfer of the body synchronized with the weight transfer of the ball.

The initial step is soft and smooth. Glide the foot along the lane, keeping the knee slightly flexed. Start the pushaway at the same time as the step. The extension of the arm is only slightly longer than the step; the arm is not fully extended yet. The pushaway of the ball transfers the center of mass of the body–ball system slightly forward. For balance, the foot needs to be under the center of mass, not under the ball. Because the body is constantly moving, the center of mass should pass through the base of support. The heel should strike just ahead of the center of mass. This will put the ball about 2 to 4 inches ahead of the first step after the pushaway (figure 7.4). As the body moves forward, it will pass over the base of support established by the foot. As the center of mass passes beyond the foot, it is time for another step.

Figure 7.3 **Swing and Footwork, Four-Step Approach**

PRESTEP MOTION

1. Slightly stagger feet
2. Rock back on heel of back foot, and shift weight forward onto ball of front foot
3. Again, rock back on heel of back foot and shift weight forward, moving body past ball of front foot
4. As body weight transfers forward past the foot, you will feel the need to take a step

FIRST STEP

1. Step forward
2. Push ball away, out and down in a smooth arcing motion
3. Slightly flex knee
4. Heel strikes just ahead of center of body
5. Pushaway places the ball a few inches past the length of the first step

SECOND STEP

1. Move leg on nonthrowing side forward
2. Use normal walking stride in a heel-to-toe pattern
3. Fully extend arm during backswing
4. Ball is at bottom of backswing
5. Keep head still
6. Upper body tilt does not change

THIRD STEP

1. Flex front knee
2. Take a short step
3. Hips drop down
4. Transfer weight onto ball of foot
5. Ball swings back to top of backswing
6. Stay in balance over foot

FOURTH STEP

1. Push off from power step
2. Toe of slide foot contacts floor
3. Transfer weight onto slide foot
4. Slide foot is under centerline
5. Sweep back leg away to make room for the swing
6. Ball falls through downswing
7. Finish in visual template position

Figure 7.4 The heel strikes just ahead of the center of mass.

The second step is long and balanced (figure 7.3c). By *long* I mean the second step should be as long as a normal walking step. Do not over-step. As the leg on the nonthrowing side moves forward, you should have enough time for the swing to pass the throwing-side leg.

Use a normal stride length and a slightly stronger heel-to-toe walking pattern than was used on the first step. The swing comes back, and the arm fully extends. Keep your head still. Do not let your upper body pull forward and down, following the swing as it goes forward and down.

With the leg on the nonthrowing side forward and the leg on the throwing side back, the hips are in an open position. This presents a smaller target to swing around. A bowler who has late timing, in which the swing starts after the initiation of the steps, will notice the throwing-side leg is into the third step before the swing has passed it. This bowler has two choices: to cross the third step in front of the body to move it around the swing or to change the swing line to avoid the throwing-side leg. Often a bowler with late timing makes these adjustments without even being aware of it. However, just because it feels natural does not mean it is correct.

Learn to evaluate your timing, and make sure you are not starting late. These errors can negatively affect your game. If you cross the third step in front of your body, you will not be walking straight toward the target. If you need to move your swing around your leg, you will have difficulty with accuracy. Recognize these problems and correct them immediately, no matter how uncomfortable or weird the new technique may feel initially.

The first and third steps are arguably the most important in the approach. The first step initiates a smooth, consistent start. The third step sets up a strong finish. Step three is a short power step (figure 7.3d). A short third step accommodates for the stretch from the backswing. With proper four-step timing, the swing reaches the top of the backswing on the third step. If the third step is too long, the bowler will feel stretched out. The leg on the throwing side will be too far forward just as the swing is at maximum extension on the way back.

Take a short third step. Flex the front knee. Your goal is to drive forward with the leg just as the swing moves forward. The throwing-side leg must be in a strong position. Imagine being a sprinter and pushing off the starting blocks on the track. The optimal strength angle for the knee joint is about 45 degrees (figure 7.5). For the leg to perform a strong drive into the slide, the knee bend should be close to this angle. Feel your hips drop down as the body sets up for a drop and drive into the last step. Transfer your weight onto the ball of your foot, and feel the ball of the foot and toes dig in. The swing moves to the top of the backswing. Avoid turning the shoulder excessively. Maintain the balance line over your foot. At this point, many bowlers feel the urge to put something extra into the shot. Resist that urge. Do not ruin all the careful preparation and smooth movement by leaning forward, pulling back, or forcing the swing forward.

On step 4, you hit the landing (figure 7.3e). The quality of the last step is the result of the quality of the previous steps. The slide foot must work its way under the body. The body maintains its balance line over the slide foot. The back leg sweeps behind the body, out of the way of the downswing, which starts forward just as the

Figure 7.5 For a strong drive into the slide, on the third step have the front knee at a 45-degree angle.

last step begins. The last step touches the floor slightly ahead of the swing. The slide should finish just before the swing gets to the release point. The body will be stable and balanced a brief moment before the release happens.

For the final step, push off from the power step. Keep the hips down as the body drives forward. Because of the knee bend going into the third step, you will not experience an exaggerated drop into the last step. The toe of the slide foot contacts the floor first. As the body weight transfers to the slide foot, the heel begins a braking action, slowing the body's momentum. Turn the heel of the slide foot in slightly to direct the slide foot under the centerline of the body. Sweep the back leg away to clear room for the swing. Let the ball fall through the downswing next to the throwing-side leg. Finish with your body in visual template position (see step 6 for more about the visual template).

Remember the most important characteristics of the four-step approach:

- Maintain the short, long, short, long walking pattern. This pattern accommodates for the mechanics of the swing, opening the hips and getting them out of the way as the swing passes the side of the body.

- The rhythm of the step—a strong one, two, one, two beat—matches the rhythm inherent in the swing's pendulum motion. In general, use a heel-to-toe walking gait.

- Be careful, though. Do not march up to the line. Keep the knees flexed and the feet fairly flat. Think of the approach as a dance. It is neither a lazy shuffle nor a rigid march. The steps are quick, soft, and smooth.

FIVE-STEP APPROACH

The most common variation of the approach is the use of five steps instead of four. Whenever a bowler starts and finishes the approach with the same foot, they will use an odd number of steps. Some bowlers are more comfortable moving the foot opposite the throwing hand first. A bowler must find out what comes naturally before determining the number of steps or any other adjustments. If you prefer to move the opposite foot first, go with the five-step approach.

There is little difference between the four- and five-step approaches. The five-step approach simply has an extra cheater step that initiates body movement before the start of the swing. The second step is with the leg on the throwing side, and the pushaway begins with the second step. This leaves the last four steps in the approach to match the four parts of the swing.

The five-step approach (figure 7.6) requires some changes in the nature of the footwork. This approach frequently has slower, somewhat more controlled, initial steps. For the cadence, count "one . . . two, one, two, three" or "step . . . push, three, four, five." The spacing of the feet still must match the rhythm and mechanics of the swing. The first step is short. The remaining steps are like the four-step approach. This yields a walking pattern of short, short, long, short, long.

Some bowlers find starting the swing and the steps together, as in the four-step approach, somewhat jolting. Because of the extra cheater step, the five-step approach has a built-in weight transfer. The movement of the body flows into the movement of the swing.

For a bowler of shorter stature, the extra step allows for more momentum. On the other

Figure 7.6   Swing and Footwork, Five-Step Approach

a   *b*   *c*

PRESTEP MOTION TO FIRST STEP

1. Slightly stagger feet, with foot opposite throwing hand in front
2. Rock back on back heel, and shift weight forward onto ball of front foot
3. Again, rock back on back heel and shift weight forward
4. Move front foot forward with a short step
5. Transfer weight; movement of body with first step flows into movement of swing on second step

SECOND STEP

1. Step forward
2. Push ball away, out and down in a smooth arcing motion
3. Slightly flex knee
4. Heel strikes just ahead of center of body
5. Pushaway places the ball a few inches past the length of the second step

THIRD STEP

1. Move leg on non-throwing side forward
2. Use normal walking stride in a heel-to-toe pattern
3. Fully extend arm during backswing
4. Ball is at bottom of backswing
5. Keep head still
6. Upper body tilt does not change

d   *e*

FOURTH STEP

1. Flex front knee
2. Take a short step
3. Hips drop down
4. Transfer weight onto ball of foot
5. Ball swings back to top of backswing
6. Stay in balance over foot

FIFTH STEP

1. Push off from power step
2. Toe of slide foot contacts floor
3. Transfer weight onto slide foot
4. Slide foot is under centerline
5. Sweep back leg away to make room for the swing
6. Ball falls through downswing
7. Finish in visual template position

hand, one sees tall bowlers trying to cover the entire length of the approach (as much as 17 feet) in only four steps. The momentum created by these long steps makes approach control difficult. Additionally, with the feet always out in front of the body, these bowlers have difficulty maintaining balance. An extra step forces them into a shorter, more controlled footwork pattern.

When initiating the approach, the prestep motion leads into the first step. The body does not suddenly lurch forward. Keep it very smooth and soft. Set your feet in a staggered starting position. Slightly rock back onto the heel of the back foot, moving the whole body back and forth. Rock back onto the heel again. Without changing the body position established in the setup, gently shift your weight forward as the first step moves forward.

TROUBLESHOOTING STEP AND SWING TIMING

The initial movement causes the most trouble in coordinating the steps and the swing. Many players simply will not move the ball when they take the first step. About 70 to 80 percent of all untutored bowlers have late timing. It is somewhat rare to find an athlete who falls into a natural timing rhythm without any instruction. Why is this? Perhaps some bowlers need the trigger of a starter step before unloading the swing. Others may be uncomfortable with the sudden weight shift that occurs when the first step and pushaway move together.

If you have difficulty with the initial movement, try using the five-step approach. The body is in motion on the first step, and the swing follows on the second step. Starting the pushaway on the second step of a four-step approach is trouble, but that is the proper sequence for a five-step approach.

If you prefer to stay with the four-step approach, try moving the ball first. Anticipate the hesitation by initiating the swing just before the first step. This may feel uncomfortable at first, but practicing the pushaway drills described later in this step will help.

Be sure your first step is not too long. If the initial step is too long, the leg will be way out in front, and the body and the ball will hang back. Remember, for a proper four-step approach, the ball and the step move at the same time, in the same direction, and for the same distance.

Avoid making an upward movement during the pushaway. Pushing the swing up and out takes more time than the proper out and down movement. Women and younger players often

tend to push the swing up and out. Those of smaller stature try to generate more ball speed with a bigger swing. You can add power a couple of ways: Start the ball in a higher position and use a drop-away swing. Or walk faster, using the extra momentum and a strong leg drive at the end to create extra speed.

Keep in mind, an up-and-out movement can be useful if performed correctly. Initially, this type of swing is not a true pendulum. If you want to create a bigger swing using the up-and-out initial movement, you will need to start the swing early. It requires extra time to push the ball up before it falls into the pendulum stage of the swing. This technique is espoused by one of the premier instructors on the professional tour.

When attempting to create more power with this type of swing, the swing has to move first. To accommodate for the extra time needed for the upward motion, start the pushaway before you start the first step of the four-step approach. Take the first step as the ball falls into the swing and reaches a point forward and down from the initial starting position. The upward push starts on the first step of a five-step approach. In either case, the ball will start to drop down into the pendulum portion of the swing just as the throwing-side foot moves.

If early timing is the problem, try to extend the pushaway. The up-and-out technique may help those who drop the swing down too soon. Slow feet and a fast drop away of the swing contribute to early timing. For these bowlers, there is no noticeable pushaway. A short swing generates less speed. These players need to work on a smoother (perhaps slower) and more complete swing rhythm.

Exaggerating an opposite movement helps some athletes fix a problem. In the case of early timing, imagine pushing the ball over a bar. This creates a better extension into the pushaway, allowing time for the steps. Try pushing out stronger toward the target. Take a longer initial step. Be sure the ball is carried forward with that step before allowing the ball to move down into the backswing.

Timing Drill 1. *One-Step Swing Away*

This drill will help you develop a sense of the swing's movement in time with the first step. While practicing the timing of the movement, try to create a smooth arc of the swing as well.

Stand in the setup position. Push the ball into the swing. Let the ball arc out and down. Just as the swing starts, take a short, smooth step with the swing-side leg. Let the ball swing completely back and forth. As the ball swings back to the starting position, catch it and take a step back into the setup position.

If you use a five-step approach, start with the opposite foot out in front, as if you had already taken the first step. Or take two steps, pushing the ball on the second step.

Practice this drill 10 times, earning up to 5 points each time, before adding another step.

Success Check

- Ball arcs out and down.
- Your step is short and smooth.

Score Your Success

Ball and foot move together = 2 points

Swing starts with an out-and-down motion = 2 points

The complete swing, without hesitation, brings the ball back to the start = 1 point

Your score ____

Timing Drill 2. *Discover the Rhythm*

This exercise allows you to feel the "one, two" and "out, down" synchronization of the steps and swing. It is similar to the preceding drill, except you will take the first two steps of a four-step approach. If performed properly, the ball will have reached the bottom of the backswing just as the second step lands.

In proper setup position, begin the swing with a smooth, arcing out-and-down movement. Start the first step when the swing begins. Continue to the second step as the swing comes down. Stop after two steps. Let the swing go completely back and forth to return to the starting position. As the swing returns toward the body, take two steps back, returning to the setup position.

As in the previous drill, for those who use a five-step approach, the opposite foot will move forward first. Then the throwing-side leg and swing move together.

Practice this drill 10 times, earning up to 5 points each time, before enlisting the help of a partner or attempting a full approach on your own.

Success Check

- Ball moves in a smooth arc, out and down.

Score Your Success

Throwing-side leg moves out when swing starts = 2 points

Ball reaches bottom of swing when opposite leg moves = 1 point

Swing is a smooth, full pendulum arc = 1 point

Upper body position does not change as the swing moves back and forth = 1 point

Your score ____

Timing Drill 3. *Partner Drill for Initial Movement*

A bowler may think he is performing a skill correctly, but the help of another participant can ensure correct form. This drill is similar to swing drill 10 described in step 5 (page 75). However, now the partner looks for the body to be in motion with the swing. The bowler should be moving toward the partner at exactly the same time the ball is placed into the partner's hand.

The catcher stands 1 1/2 to 2 feet in front of the bowler, with her hands out directly in front of the bowler's shoulder at about waist level. As the pushaway moves out and down, the catcher reminds the bowler to step. If properly performed, the ball and the bowler will move toward the catcher. The ball should land in the catcher's hands, with the bowler's arm completely relaxed. The bowler does not let go of the ball, but there is no tension in the arm. The catcher takes all of the ball's weight. The catcher helps return the ball to the starting position as the bowler takes a step back.

Perform 10 repetitions, earning up to 5 points each time, then switch roles.

Success Check

- Watch for good timing.
- Swing stays in line.

Score Your Success

Ball and step move at the same time = 2 points

Upper body position does not change with pushaway = 1 point

Ball lands in catcher's hands = 1 point

Arm is completely relaxed = 1 point

Your score ___

Timing Drill 4. *Side-by-Side Partner Practice*

In this drill, your partner will take hold of your arm and walk you through the full approach. The goal is to promote a continuous movement of both the feet and the swing. This is an excellent drill in which an experienced bowler who knows the rhythm of good timing can help an inexperienced bowler develop the skill.

At first, practice this drill without a ball. Your partner takes hold of your arm near the wrist. As you begin your approach, your partner helps move the swing at the right time. If the timing is correct, you will initiate the movement, and your partner will not have to do any work at all. Your partner maintains his grip on your arm throughout the approach, helping you maintain smooth progress to the foul line while keeping a long, fluid swing. You should end up in proper finish position as your partner helps the swing all the way through the follow-through.

Remember, the bowler who uses a five-step approach will take an extra cheater step before the movement of the ball.

Your partner should not feel any resistance in the swing movement. If he needs to help the swing at any point, you are not in a free swing or you are not in time with the steps. If your partner has to help your swing, you do not receive any points for the drill.

Perform 10 repetitions, earning up to 5 points each time, then switch roles.

To Decrease Difficulty

- Stop the motion after each step. Your partner makes sure the swing moves to the appropriate location for each step of the approach.
- Your partner counts the steps as the swing location moves.
- Your partner says the swing location aloud ("out," "down," "back," "through") with each step of the approach.
- Gradually increase the speed until you are able to move at a normal walking pace without sacrificing a smooth swing.

To Increase Difficulty

- Use a ball. Your partner walks by your side, holding onto the swing arm just above your wrist as you attempt a complete

97

approach, including the release of the ball. Does the timing and smoothness of the approach change when a ball is used? The addition of the ball should not alter your timing. If it does, you have one of two problems. Either you have no confidence in your ability to hold on to the ball you chose, or you are not yet comfortable with proper timing. Alternate practicing without a ball and with a ball until that confidence is established.

Score Your Success

Ball moves down as first step moves forward = 2 points

Partner feels no resistance in the swing = 1 point

Footwork is smooth and continuous = 1 point

You arrive at the foul line as the swing nears completion = 1 point

Your score ____

Timing Drill 5. *Continuous Swing Motion*

Pendulums gather speed quickly, and you must learn to make your footwork keep pace with the swing. This drill will help you understand the pace of the swing. The objective is to let the swing move back and forth with little hesitation, then just as a new swing starts, to allow the footwork to go with the swing.

From a normal starting position, swing the ball a couple of times without moving your feet. With each practice swing, as the ball comes back to you, return the ball to its starting position, then push it away immediately. On the third pushaway, start the footwork. If using a four-step approach, step with the throwing-side foot. Without hesitating in the swing, complete a full approach, including the release and finish position.

As you go through the drill, talk to yourself:

- First swing: "Push, swing, relax."
- Second swing: "Catch, push, swing, relax."
- Third swing: "Catch, step, swing, and roll."

Practice this routine at least 10 times until the swing and the steps move together without hesitation. If properly executed, there will be no pauses in the motion. The step and the swing motions blend seamlessly together, and you make a quick, smooth movement to the foul line.

Success Check

- You push the ball straight out from your shoulder in a smooth arcing motion = 1 point
- Ball comes back to starting position and is pushed away immediately = 2 points
- At the start of the third swing, you step with throwing-side leg = 2 points
- No hesitation evident in the swing when the steps begin = 1 point
- You complete the approach, exhibiting good timing = 2 points
- You finish in a balanced position = 1 point
- Swing, from pushaway to follow-through, is a smooth and continuous movement = 1 point

Score Your Success

Grade yourself or have someone else grade you based on the point values noted in the success check.

90 to 100 points = 10 points

80 to 89 points = 5 points

70 to 79 points = 1 point

Your score ____

Timing Drill 6. *Assessing the Approach (Without a Ball)*

Have a skilled observer watch your approach from a short distance. The observer stands on your throwing side so she can see where the swing is in relation to each step of the approach. Attempt five shadow approaches, complete with follow-through and finish.

Remember the difference between four- and five-step approaches. Bowlers who use a five-step approach take an extra step (out on two, down on three, and so on).

The observer grades you based on the success checks.

Success Check

- You start from a proper stance = 1 point
- Initial step is smooth and short = 1 point
- Ball moves into swing when throwing-side leg moves = 2 points
- Pushaway moves throwing hand a few inches past the foot after the first step = 1 point
- Ball moves down in a smooth arc = 2 points
- Arm fully extends as ball reaches bottom of backswing = 1 point

- Backswing passes by throwing-side leg before leg moves into third step = 2 points
- Swing reaches top of backswing on next-to-last step = 1 point
- Downswing is a smooth arc from top of backswing until release = 2 points
- Foot enters slide as ball approaches bottom of downswing = 1 point
- Approach finishes and body is in stable position just before the release = 2 points

Score Your Success

70 to 80 points = 10 points

60 to 69 points = 5 points

50 to 59 points = 1 point

Your score ____

Timing Drill 7. Assessing the Approach (With a Ball)

This drill follows the same procedure as the previous drill, only a ball is used. Once the ball is added, many bowlers change the nature of the approach. Some hesitate; others rush the line. Arm tension, abrupt changes in swing direction (pushing down or pulling through), and a bent arm during the swing can all affect the swinging motion. The swing may no longer imitate a smooth pendulum. Changing the shape of the swing makes it difficult to synchronize with the steps.

As with the previous drill, have a skilled observer watch your approach from a short distance. Attempt five approaches with a ball, complete with follow-through and finish. The observer grades you based on the success checks. If your score is more than 3 points lower than your assessment score without a ball, you still need to work on timing. Go back to the previous drills until you achieve a near flawless execution.

Success Check

- You start from a proper stance = 1 point
- Initial step is smooth and short = 1 point
- Ball moves into swing when throwing-side leg moves = 2 points

- Pushaway moves throwing hand a few inches past the foot after the first step = 1 point
- Ball moves down in a smooth arc = 2 points
- Arm fully extends as ball reaches bottom of backswing = 1 point
- Backswing passes by throwing-side leg before leg moves into third step = 2 points
- Swing reaches top of backswing on next-to-last step = 1 point
- Downswing is a smooth arc from top of backswing until release = 2 points
- Foot enters slide as ball approaches bottom of downswing = 1 point
- Approach finishes and body is in stable position just before the release = 2 points

Score Your Success

70 to 80 points = 10 points

60 to 69 points = 5 points

50 to 59 points = 1 point

Your score ____

SUCCESS SUMMARY

Body position is set in the stance and does not change. The initial swing movement is forward and down, and the entire swing movement traces a smooth arc. When the swing moves, the leg on the throwing side moves with it. There are no pauses, hitches, hesitations, or any other disruptions to the smooth progress of the steps and the swing once the approach starts. The slide foot enters the slide just before the ball reaches the bottom of the downswing. The body reaches a stationary and balanced point just as the ball reaches the bottom of the downswing.

Review your drill scores. Record your scores in the spaces that follow and total them. If you score at least 200 points, you are ready to move on to the next step. If you score fewer than 200 points, review the sections that are giving you trouble, then repeat the drills.

Timing Drills

1.	One-Step Swing Away	___ out of 50
2.	Discover the Rhythm	___ out of 50
3.	Partner Drill for Initial Movement	___ out of 50
4.	Side-by-Side Partner Practice	___ out of 50
5.	Continuous Swing Motion	___ out of 10
6.	Assessing the Approach (Without a Ball)	___ out of 10
7.	Assessing the Approach (With a Ball)	___ out of 10
Total		___ *out of 230*

The next step discusses the release, the culmination of a chain of events that starts with the pushaway and concludes with a balanced finish. The release is a difficult skill because so much of what happens before the release influences the result. A consistently effective release occurs only if all the movements and positions leading up to it are correct. For this reason, such a large portion of this book so far has emphasized the basic skills. When the essential movements that lead up to the release are well developed, the chances of a successful release greatly improve. When you feel that all the parts are working together, you can let go of the ball with confidence.

Creating an Effective Release

The release has been described as the moment of truth. At the release point, a bowler's entire effort pays off. The quality of the release is not just a matter of release mechanics; it is also the product of all the movements that have preceded it. If the approach is consistent, the timing correct, and the swing in line, the bowler is ready to send the ball on its way.

The release is a challenging skill involving fine motor control. Slight changes of positioning will dramatically influence how and where the ball rolls. Slight mistakes in movement or hand positioning at the release will have dramatic consequences on the lanes. Bowlers of all skill levels in all situations occasionally find themselves saying, "I missed the release."

Simply holding on to the ball through the approach and then letting go when you are done is not the challenge of the release. At times you will need the ball to roll in different ways, sometimes traveling in a straighter line, other times not. The ability to control and manipulate the release is a prime ingredient for successful bowling.

For most bowlers, problems with the release have nothing to do with the release mechanism itself. The trouble starts at the very beginning of the approach. Improper technique in other skills affects the bowler's ability to release the ball consistently. Take the time to see a reputable ball driller—a properly fitting ball is essential for bowling success.

RELEASE PHASES

The release is a series of events that allows the ball to come off the hand as the force of the swing sends the ball down the lane. Some bowlers mistakenly think of the swing and the release as two separate elements, as if the bowler first swings and then releases. Nothing is further from the truth. Of all the identifiable physical elements of the game, the swing and the release are the two most closely integrated. Remember, the swing applies force through the hand to create the ball's rolling motion, or torque. Ideally, the swing flows through the release point.

There are five phases of the release during the swing: drive, thumb release, turn, extension, and finger release (lift) (figure 8.1).

101

Figure 8.1   Five Release Phases

a

b

c

DRIVE PHASE

1. Feel the ball fall through the downswing
2. Hand feels as though it is pressing against the back of the ball
3. Wrist remains firm; it does not break back

THUMB RELEASE PHASE

1. As the ball nears the bottom of the swing, it starts sliding off the thumb
2. Thumb is relaxed at this point; it does not squeeze the ball
3. You may feel the weight of the ball transfer onto the fingers and front of the hand

TURN PHASE

1. As the ball enters the bottom of the downswing (the swing's lowest point), forearm rotation begins
2. Ball weight has transferred completely to the fingers
3. Fingers remain firmly pressed against the ball, resisting the ball's downward force
4. As the ball drops to the inside toward the ankle, finger pressure works up the side of the ball

The *drive phase* never really ceases to influence the ball until the ball is off the hand. This is the swing's contribution to ball motion. The swing should be a smooth arc. There can be modifications in the direction or shape of the pendulum's arc, but at no time should that movement be hesitant, jerky, or prematurely stopped.

Imagine a bucket full of water. If you swing hard enough, you can swing the bucket in a complete circle over your head and the water will not fall out. Centripetal force keeps the water pressed into the bottom of the bucket. The ball has the same effect on the hand. If the swing continues (no pause at the top of the backswing) and the hand is positioned firmly behind and under the ball, the bowler remains in control of the ball.

The second phase is the *thumb release phase.* As the ball approaches the bottom of the swing, the thumb starts to slide out of the ball. As the ball passes through the bottom of the swing, the bowler feels the ball's swing weight on the fingers. The thumb controls the ball during the backswing; it does little or no work during the downswing. The pressure of the hand against the ball as it falls through the downswing, plus the grip of the fingers, is all that is needed to swing the ball out onto the lane.

Keeping the thumb in the ball too long during the swing will have an adverse steering effect on the ball. There is a tendency to overturn the ball

d

e

EXTENSION PHASE

1. Forearm rotation is complete; continued rotation to a point at which the hand gets on top of the ball is undesirable

2. Swing passes its lowest point, extending out and up

3. Feel the fingers drive through the desired leverage point

FINGER RELEASE (LIFT) PHASE

1. Fingers lift up the side of the ball as the pendulum of the swing starts in an upward direction

2. If the release is correct, the ball is driven into the lane at a shallow angle

if the thumb stays in the ball for too long. Ideally, the thumb will be mostly out of the ball before the *turn phase* begins. If the turn phase starts too early (during the downswing), the thumb will turn downward. This forces the bowler to squeeze the ball to prevent it from dropping off the hand. The downward turn of the thumb causes it to act as a pivot point around which the ball turns, creating an ineffective spin release rather than the preferred rolling or hook release. In addition, the pressure of the squeezing movement prevents a consistent release.

Some bowlers do not squeeze when they start the turn phase early; they have learned not to press forward with the thumb. Although this is correct in terms of grip technique, moving into

the turn phase early may cause them to drop the ball.

The turn phase puts the hand into the desired position for applying torque on the ball. It is used to change the hand position, and thus the application of the swing force, relative to the ball. If there is no change of position (the hand stays directly behind the ball), there is no side roll and therefore no hook.

For some bowlers, the hand will be in the release position throughout the swing. There is no active turning during the swing; the hand has already been turned to the desired position in the setup. The use of this passive, or motionless, release promotes consistency but limits to a certain extent the number of revolutions the bowler generates. Many successful bowlers avoid excessive forearm rotation at the release point. They set the hand in the desired release position for the type of roll desired and keep it there throughout the swing. The release is one of simply swinging through the hand position.

This release is ideal for beginning bowlers. Swinging through the release prevents the difficulty of trying to time an extra movement. Every time an addition is made, an extra link in the chain, the more difficult consistency becomes. If the wrist remains firm and the hand is properly positioned in relation to the ball, a very effective roll can be created without any extra movement.

If the movement is very active, a fast and large movement (ideally late in the swing to take advantage of maximum finger pressure), the revolutions generated can be very impressive. Be careful, though. The forearm may have a large range of motion (radioulnar deviation), but it is not unlimited. An overly exaggerated or premature turning motion, one that occurs too early in the swing, forces the forearm past its natural range. This causes the upper arm to continue the rotation movement. Remember, a true pendulum has only one anchor point around which it swings. The upper arm attaches at the shoulder socket. If the shoulder is rotating within the socket while trying to simultaneously permit the arm to swing back and forth, trouble is brewing. Rotation movements at the shoulder, although easy to accomplish, severely compromise accuracy. In this case, too much of a good thing is bad.

The *extension phase* is the finish of the swing as it drives the ball down the lane. This part of the swing carries the ball through the bottom of the pendulum's arc. Many bowlers tend to relax at this point, allowing the ball to drop onto the lanes. This promotes a weak release in which the ball comes off the hand before the turn and lift phases are completed. There is also the tendency to cut the swing short, sacrificing ball speed and the ability to follow through to the target.

Ideally, you should feel strongest in the extension phase. As you drive the ball out onto the lane, you want to feel in control. As the ball passes the bottom of the swing, feel the weight transfer forward onto the fingers. Now the fingers are in position to resist the ball's downward drop as the pendulum of the swing drives up. This leads to the last phase, and then the ball is on its way.

The *finger release (lift) phase* is the final phase of the release. *Lift* is the fingers' resistance to gravity's effect on the ball. A smooth release drives the ball down the lane. Like a plane landing, the ball glides onto the lane, contacting the surface at a fairly shallow angle. As the swing passes through the bottom of the pendulum, the ball starts to go up. Gravity wants to make the ball fall down. Lift is the pressure on the fingers the bowler feels from these opposing forces. The strength of the lift and where this force is applied to the ball determine the type of roll. Just before the ball leaves the hand, there is a split second in which only the fingers are in the ball. At this point, the fingers are resisting gravity.

With a proper release position, the bowler will feel this split-second kick of the fingers just before the ball comes off the hand. Keep in mind, for most players this is not a deliberate, forceful upward movement. There is no radical alteration to the swing's smooth pendulum feel. Mostly, a feeling of resistance keeps the ball from dropping weakly off the hand.

For a strong release, never relax the fingers. If the mechanics are sound and the fit is correct, the ball will glide off the hand on its own. Just as important, you should not feel as though you need to open up the hand in order to let the ball go, unless your intent is to soften the release.

Sometimes fewer revolutions are preferred (e.g., on a dry lane when the ball will hook easily, or when shooting a spare, when your intent is for the ball to follow a straighter path). In these instances, having less finger pressure at the release moderates the ball's revolutions.

If you look at a side view of the release in relation to the swing, you will notice a flat spot in the pendulum. This occurs not because the swing ceases to be pendular in motion but rather because the body moves the swing forward. The movement of the body forward during the last step elongates the bottom of the pendulum. Essentially, the pendulum flattens out during the drive into the slide step, which gives the bowler a better feeling through the release point.

If the swing pulls up too quickly, there may not be enough time to complete the release motion; the ball will come off the hand too quickly.

If the leg drive is particularly forceful, the acceleration of the body into the slide will press the hand against the back of the ball. The bowler will sense that the swing is being carried along with the body. The feeling of the hand pressing through the back of the ball gives the bowler a sense of power and control through the release point. This feeling of being long and low through the bottom of the swing effectively drives the hand through the ball, helping the bowler maintain ball speed and a feeling of a strong release.

One of the signs that a bowler is not effectively getting the leg into the shot is a weak projection of the ball down the lane. A weak finish with the footwork usually produces a ball thrown with insufficient speed. Many bowlers who have a weak finish because they are not generating enough force through body momentum tend to overexaggerate the hand motion to create a strong roll. The excessive movement makes shot repetition difficult.

Misstep

Bad footwork = bad balance = bad release. The body is not in a centered, balanced position over the slide foot, which would allow the bowler to exert leverage into the shot.

Correction

Keep the body centered over the feet during each step. Keep the footwork straight to the target. The body and the swing stay next to each other during the approach.

If the bowler has balance issues, the body will frequently be in motion at the release point. A consistent release is difficult if the body is not in a stable position. If the accuracy of the swing line is questionable, the hand will not be in proper position to efficiently permit the force of the swing to transfer to the ball. If the footwork is not straight and the body drifts away from the swing, an effective leveraging position will be lost.

Besides the drive of the next-to-last step, a long slide also lengthens the movement of the pendulum. The elongated flat spot at the bottom of the pendulum increases the timing window in which you can manipulate the release (figure 8.2).

Figure 8.2 Strong leg drive lengthens the flat spot, allowing more time for manipulation of the release.

Misstep

Bad timing = bad release. Bad timing on the approach leads to a poor release. The ball is not at the correct place in the swing when the body feels it is time to release it.

Correction

If the approach is not timed properly, the ball will not be at the correct place in the swing when the body is ready to release the ball. Practice timing the approach correctly.

Altering the shape of the pendulum by intentionally flattening it produces the same effect (figure 8.3a). Some bowlers are able to create a dragging effect, as if they are pulling the swing along the length of the approach. This is accomplished by exaggerating the extension through the release point.

Be careful not to overextend when reshaping the pendulum. Using an excessive leaning or twisting motion in the upper body to accomplish this reshaping affects both balance and the ability to keep the shoulders on line to the target.

The shorter the slide, or the more abruptly the pendulum shape of the swing is directed upward, the smaller the timing window for the release (figure 8.3c). The revolutions on the ball can be increased, assuming a proper release position, by redirecting the force of the swing up the side of the ball. Referred to as *hitting up on the ball* or just trying to *hit it,* this modification of the swing is difficult to master and has a limited application on certain lane conditions. This technique is in opposition to the more standard swing–release mechanism that directs the force down through the ball as it is sent along the lane.

Although a high number of revolutions can be applied with this technique, excessive revolutions can sometimes make the ball path hard to predict. The oil on the lane moves and dissipates as play proceeds, and dry or spotty lane conditions make predicting the ball path difficult. A ball that is aggressively hit on, with its accompanying excessive rotations, is very difficult to control in these circumstances. As lane conditions become less consistent, alter your strategy, leaning more toward controllable release techniques.

If the angle of entry into the lane is too steep—known as *laying the ball short*—something went wrong with the mechanics of the release (i.e., the bowler lost control of the ball).

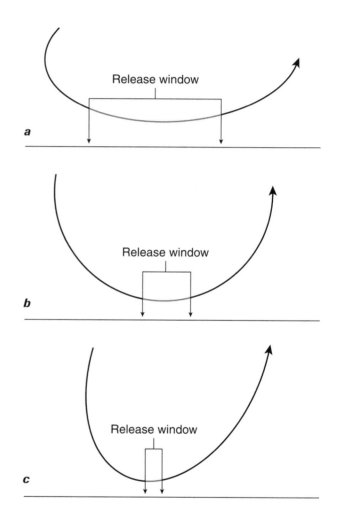

Figure 8.3 Altering the swing to affect release. *(a)* With a flattened swing, there is a long drive phase. Energy is directed through the ball and down the lane. *(b)* A pendulum swing requires a moderate drive and features a moderate release window. *(c)* The angular swing has a very small release window and allows little room for error. The energy of the swing is directed up the ball.

Inefficient transfer of momentum, weak wrist position, or improper grip of the ball might contribute to a weak release. Sometimes setting the ball down early is due to body position. An excessive forward tilt of the upper body angles the swing into the lane (figure 8.4).

Figure 8.4 Excessive body angle at release will cause the bowler to set the ball down early and sweep the swing into the lane.

Figure 8.5 Scooping effect. The hand is under the ball too long, the grip is too strong, and the ball doesn't fit properly.

Excessive loft down the lane means the bowler held on too long. The pendulum started into the upswing before the release of the ball. Excessive loft (more than 3 feet past the slide foot, in most cases) is traceable to three main causes: improper ball fit, poor body position at the release (the bowler pulls the shoulders back at the release), and poor conceptualization of release mechanics. Either the bowler is so early with the motion he is forced to squeeze the ball and doesn't let go, or he is so late the motion is part of the upswing of the follow-through.

If the ball does not fit properly, the ball simply will not release from the hand smoothly. Often the bowler is not confident with the feel of the hand in the ball and squeezes as a reflex.

Poor release position is particularly common for those learning how to hook the ball. The bowler turns the ball either too late or too early. If too late, the hand stays behind the ball and literally scoops it up and throws it out onto the lane (figure 8.5). Ideally, the thumb must be facing somewhat down and in for the ball to release smoothly.

With an early release motion, the bowler has the notion of turning the hand to create the necessary side roll but performs the motion too soon in the swing. If the ball gets to the side of the hand too soon in the swing, it will tend to drop off the thumb. Early release rotation puts the bowler into a drop-and-squeeze pattern. If the thumb points down and in too soon, the ball wants to fall off the hand. On one throw, the ball falls off. On the next throw the bowler, sensing

this loss of control, squeezes the ball to hold on to it. Problems of consistency in ball roll and accuracy result.

Feel for the inside of the arm to pass the hip before starting the release (figure 8.6). During a proper swing, the inside of the arm will brush the hip slightly on the way back and on the way through. In this manner, the hip acts as a guide to a better swing. It is also a checkpoint for the start of the release. Initiating the release motion too early generally causes overrotation, and you will drop the ball. Waiting for the swing to pass the hip will help you learn to start the release at the correct part of the downswing.

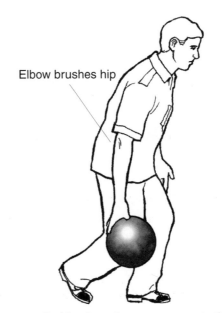

Elbow brushes hip

Figure 8.6 Feel for the swing to come next to the hip. This is the cue to start the release motion.

To visualize when the release occurs, look at the arc of the swing. From different points of the arc, trace tangent lines that point toward the lane. Remember one simple principle—the line of force is tangent to the curve. Imagine now where the ball should land, and trace a line back to the swing arc. The line will be at a slight angle into the lane. By visualizing this point, you can begin to feel for it in the swing. As you sense the swing approaching the ideal release point, put all the phases of the release into motion.

RELEASE POSITIONS

Before discussing the preparation for the different releases, let's discuss how hand position influences ball roll. The position of the hand in relation to the ball dictates how the energy of the swing is transferred through the ball. If the hand is directly behind the ball, all the swing's energy goes through the ball. Offsetting the hand to any degree will redirect some of the swing's energy around the ball, creating a torque motion. When this happens, two different forces influence the ball's movement down the lane. Translational force is the initial direction of the ball down the lane. Rotational force is the direction of its rolling motion, or the orientation of its axis of rotation. The more a ball's axis of rotation is offset from its translational direction, the more potential hook it has.

If you imagine rolling a disc instead of a sphere, the position and motion of the release become clearer. The use of a clock face as a means of picturing the various hand positions has been a traditional method for describing the release. The hand position is depicted at the release point of the ball.

There are two basic release positions, one for the straight ball and one for the hook ball.

Generally, the straight release is a *passive* release—there is no motion by the hand or forearm at the release point. An *active* release is characterized by movement at the release point; in other words, the bowler actively changes the position of the hand relative to the ball as the swing passes through the release phase. The action of this release is meant to increase either the number of revolutions or the degree of side roll. A hook can be created by either a passive or an active release.

Straight Release

The straight release is a passive release (i.e., there is no movement at the release point). The ball is set in position at the beginning of the stance and remains there throughout the swing.

In the straight release, the fingers are aligned in a 12:00 and 6:00 hand position (figure 8.7). The thumb and fingers line up directly behind the ball. This position produces very little side roll. The direction of ball rotation is the same (or almost the same) as the direction it is thrown.

Figure 8.7   Straight Release

HAND POSITION

1. Thumb and gripping fingers are in line directly behind the ball
2. Forearm rotates slightly, enough to line up thumb and fingers with center of forearm
3. Wrist position is straight
4. For some bowlers, the wrist may break back somewhat when they align the hand position with the forearm; this is acceptable

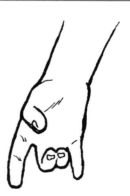

RELEASE

1. Near the bottom of the swing, the ball starts to drop off the thumb
2. Ball rolls forward onto the fingers
3. As the swing extends, ball rolls off the fingers and smoothly onto the lane
4. Fingers come almost directly up the back of the ball

For the straight release, the setup position should not affect the swing. The goal is to create a beneficial ball roll without sacrificing accuracy.

Start the setup by letting your hands hang loosely at your sides. For now, just pretend a ball is in your throwing hand; the bent fingers are locked into the holes and the thumb is straight. Notice that the elbow is closer to the body than the hand is (figure 8.8). This is essential for understanding the position of the swing in relation to the body.

Often, beginning bowlers are told to face the palm to the target when releasing the ball. If the palm faces forward (open position), the thumb points outward. This is especially true if the wrist breaks back. This position would be fine if you wanted to throw the ball at the wall, but I'm guessing you would prefer to throw the ball toward the pins. The thumb has a significant steering effect on the ball. If the thumb faces outward, frequently that is where the ball goes.

With the arms still dangling at the sides, imagine an arrow down the center of the forearm that points toward the middle of the palm. Rotate the forearm very slightly, just until the thumb lines up with the imaginary arrow. Looking down your arm, you will see the thumb over your gripping fingers. Imagine a clock face on the floor under your hand. Align the thumb toward 12:00 and point the fingers down toward 6:00. This is the 12:00 and 6:00 position for the straight release. Maintain this position throughout the swing.

Using this slightly turned initial position has two benefits. First, it is the first step toward learning the hook release. Second, it helps avoid the dreaded backup ball. A release motion in which the hand turns out away from the body creates the backup ball. The ball's roll causes it to fade away from the middle of the lane toward the gutter.

Figure 8.8 Straight release setup.

Put a ball in your hand and repeat the process. From the relaxed hanging position, bend the elbow, raising the ball to a comfortable level. The hand should be directly under the ball. Perform a couple of practice swings without any steps. The swing should glide smoothly back and forth past the hip while the hand stays behind the ball. Now you're ready to bowl.

When using the straight release, keep the wrist straight. You will feel the fingers kick up the back of the ball as the swing sends it out onto the lanes. The heavy end-over-end roll, combined with the stable hand position throughout the swing, allows for accuracy and consistency.

Because it is the easiest to control, this is the beginning bowler's release. Additionally, there is less movement to deal with, so the beginning bowler can concentrate on other aspects of the game. Working with this release initially allows the new bowler to develop accuracy, establish a sound targeting system, and establish a reliable physical game.

The advanced bowler should also have the straight release in her repertoire. It is an excellent hand position for shooting almost any spare. For spare shots, the primary concern (and in some instances, the only concern) is accuracy. Furthermore, the absence of side roll minimizes the effect lane conditions have on the ball. Varia-

tions in the distribution of oil (known as the *lane condition* or *oil pattern*) influence when, as well as how strongly, the side roll changes the ball's direction. On very difficult lane conditions in which the oil distribution is sporadic and unpredictable, the straightest path to the pocket is the best option. Instructors frequently come across students who, having learned how to hook the ball, have forgotten how to throw it straight. This lack of versatility greatly limits a bowler's ability to improve.

Hook Release

The hook can be accomplished with both an active and a passive release. First, the bowler must imagine where the hand needs to be. To create an effective hook, the fingers need to be under the ball and slightly offset from the ball's center. Essentially, the swing drives the hand through then up the side of the ball. The hand is not turning around the ball so much as the ball is turned by the hand. Excessive motion is not necessary for creating an effective hook.

In a hook release, the fingers assume a 10:00 and 4:00 hand position (figure 8.9). The important issue is clearing the ball with the thumb. The ball slides off the thumb before the swing reaches the release position.

Figure 8.9	Passive Hook Release

HAND POSITION

1. Hand is directly under the ball in the setup position
2. Forearm is rotated until palm is facing slightly inward, about a 1/8 turn to the outside of the ball
3. Palm is not turned completely inward (1/4 turn instead of 1/8), nor does it face the ceiling
4. Hand position is maintained throughout the swing

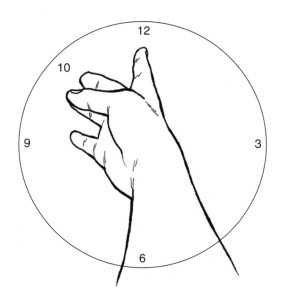

RELEASE

1. Ball slides off the thumb near the bottom of the swing
2. As the ball passes the drive face of the swing, fingers maintain their offset position on the ball
3. As the ball rotates to the inside of the hand, swing continues toward the target
4. Imagine the fingers moving in a straight line through the ball; if the fingers are in an offset position, the ball will rotate

When setting up for the passive hook release, let the hand hang relaxed at the side. Imagine where the hand needs to be in order to be offset from the center of the ball. Offsetting the hand requires a rotation of the forearm. The wrist does not change position; it is firm and straight or perhaps slightly cupped.

Imagine looking down the hand toward a clock face lying on the floor. Rotate your forearm until the thumb points toward 10:00 and the fingers are at 4:00. This is the hook release position (figure 8.10). Bend your arm, bringing the hand straight up (keeping it in line with the shoulder); this is the starting position.

In a more active hook release, the thumb might be pointing more toward 12:00 or 1:00 at the time the ball clears the thumb. As the swing continues and the weight of the ball transfers to the fingers, the fingers rotate to a 4:00 position. They should never rotate past a 3:00 position. A hand that rotates to 3:00 comes directly up the side at the release to create a 90-degree axis tilt (the axis of rotation is turned 90 degrees relative to the initial ball path). Although this may create the strongest potential hook, it is the hardest release to control on dry or variable lane conditions.

Err on the side of caution—keep the fingers in the 4:00 to 5:00 position as you hit the drive stage of the release. The ball will hook in a much more controllable manner.

The preparation for a hook release is not much different from the preparation for a straight release. You never want to greatly disturb the movement of the swing. Too many players are so intent on making the ball hook, they lose sight of the far greater importance of keeping the ball in play.

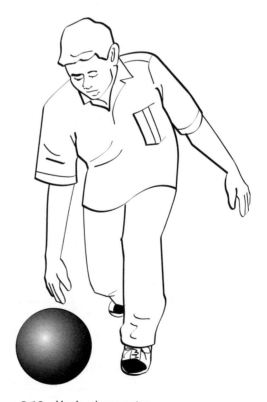

Figure 8.10 Hook release setup.

111

Remember, it doesn't matter how you knock the pins down. Your concern is not how they fall but if they fall. Establishing a "wow" factor, although occasionally useful for intimidating opponents, generally does not pay off in significantly higher scores. If your opponent is smart, he will have learned something from watching the pros. At high levels of competition, many bowlers do not watch their opponents' shots. They keep their focus on their own game to avoid being distracted or discouraged by their opponents' lucky breaks or intimidating actions.

When it is time to release the ball, the ball will slide off the thumb smoothly because it is facing slightly down and in toward the ankle at the bottom of the swing, and the fingers will lift up or be swung up the side of the ball.

Picture smacking a handle with your fingers. There is a bolt attaching the handle to the center of the ball. You want to hit the handle to send it spinning around the bolt, just as hitting up the side of the ball rotates it on its axis. As you drive through the release, be sure the swing stays on line to the target and the fingers remain firm in the ball.

Many bowlers relax their fingers at the release, opening the hand in order to let go of the ball. No! Firm fingers are needed at the release to kick the ball over into its side roll. If timing and release positioning are correct and the ball fits properly, the ball will come off the hand on its own. Do not drop the ball; drive it down the lane.

A passive hook release involves presetting the hand position for the hook at the beginning of the swing and keeping it there throughout the swing. This is the easiest hook release to learn. There is no motion at the release to worry about. The hand position is set at the beginning, and the bowler merely swings through the position.

Even for an active hook release, the hand still finishes with the fingers at 4:00. To create hook, the hand position must be offset to some degree, with the swing driving the fingers up the side of the ball. The greater the hand position is offset (without any breakdown or softening of the wrist position), the stronger the potential side roll (figure 8.11).

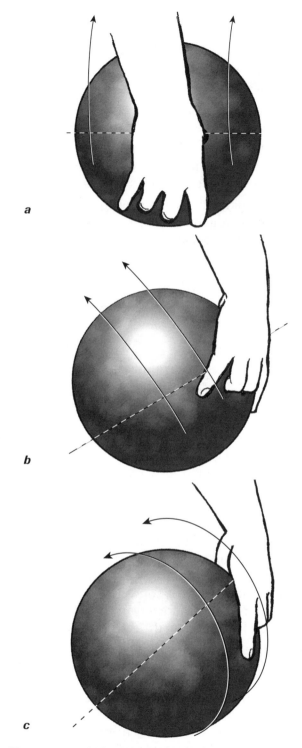

Figure 8.11 (a) Straight. (b) Moderate hook—hand offset from center. (c) Strong hook—strong offset hand position.

The active release is characterized by a change in hand position during the release phase. To imagine what the hand position should be, stand straight up with your bowling hand

112

dangling at your side. Now, using just forearm rotation, turn your hand until the palm faces forward. Point your thumb forward as if it were gripping the ball.

The palm is in this open position during the downswing. By *open* I mean the palm is facing forward or slightly away from the body. This puts the thumb at 1:00. Near the bottom of the swing, the ball starts to slide off the thumb while it is still pointing forward. As the swing continues, the fingers rotate to the 4:00 hook release position. The turn of the hand that repositions the fingers happens after the ball clears the thumb. If the thumb is in the ball as the rotation begins, there is a chance the thumb will hang up in the ball. The thumb will then act as a pivot point around which the hand turns. This creates the ineffective spinner release.

Once it slides off the thumb, the ball will begin to drop off the side of the hand. At this point, the fingers lift up the side of the ball, kicking the ball over into a side roll. Try not to let the fingers follow the thumb. This will cause the hand to come over the top of the ball. Topping the ball—letting the hand rotate to a position on top of the ball—has two negative effects. One, it limits the effectiveness of the hook; the fingers are not applying leverage in the proper direction. Two, it adversely affects accuracy because of the excessive hand motion.

Rolling Release

An active release is one in which the hand moves through and around the ball during the release.

Frequently, the wrist is kept in a stronger cupped position so the fingers can exert leverage from further underneath the ball. As the ball enters the release phase of the swing, the hand usually is directly behind the ball. As the ball begins to slide off the thumb, which allows the weight of the ball to transfer forward onto the fingers, there is an active rotation of the forearm. The movement of the forearm brings the hand into the release position. The active turning of the hand accelerates the ball's rotation.

Frequently, a bowler will try to rotate his entire arm around the ball. The elbow moves away from the body as the upper arm rotates in its socket. This movement usually weakens the release. Instead of working from a strong leverage point that is more behind the ball, the fingers follow the thumb around the ball, which leads to a couple of problems.

First, this type of movement causes a weaker roll. The ball will have a tendency to spin rather than roll. Second, the extra movement of the arm sacrifices accuracy. As the arm rotates away from the body, it no longer stays along a straight swing path. Keeping the elbow close to the body is part of an accurate swing line. Any repositioning of the hand or active rotation during the release should be largely a function of forearm movement.

The simplest of all the active releases is the rolling release (figure 8.12). The release motion is devoid of any aggressive snap or turn of the wrist or forearm. There is no alteration in the smooth flow of the swing.

Figure 8.12   Rolling Release

HAND POSITION

1. Hand is mostly under the ball in the setup position
2. Hand stays in that position during the backswing
3. As the ball nears the top of the backswing, the hand turns slightly outward
4. Thumb faces slightly away from the body

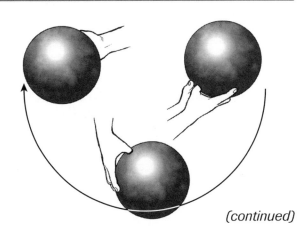

(continued)

(continued)

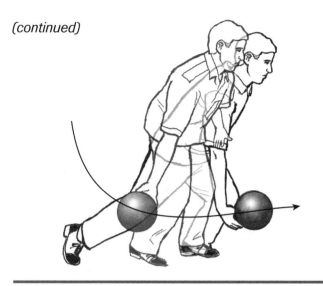

RELEASE

1. At the bottom of the swing, the forearm rotates until the thumb points forward

2. Do not squeeze with the thumb; pressure is maintained with the inserted fingers and the outriggers on the surface of the ball

3. As the weight of the ball transfers off the thumb onto the fingers, fingers drive through the ball toward the target

For this technique, think *open then shut*. Open the hand at the top of the backswing, and close it at the bottom. Simply imagine winding the hand up at the top of the backswing then unwinding it at the release, without an exaggerated twisting motion.

Keep the hand in a neutral position, as with a straight ball release, during the pushaway and backswing. The wrist should be slightly cupped if possible. As the ball approaches the top of the backswing, allow a slight outward rotation of the shoulder. Imagine pointing the thumb toward the wall. Lead with the pinkie as the swing falls toward the release point; this keeps the hand open until the release. At the release, unroll the hand from under the ball. Turn the thumb toward the opposite wall but no further, and roll the hand around the outside of the ball. The swing drives the fingers through the ball as the hand unrolls from under it. Feel for a smooth, rhythmic opening and shutting of the hand position. Count the cadence of the swing and release mechanics in your head—back, open, down, closed.

Misstep

Bad pushaway = bad swing line = bad release. The hand position relative to the ball varies if the swing does not move in a straight line.

Correction

Make sure the pushaway is straight out from the shoulder. Avoid excessive looping motion in the swing. Keep the swing along as straight a path as possible.

A swing that moves away from the body is particularly detrimental. As the swing moves out from the hip, it prematurely shifts the hand to the outside of the ball. This is referred to as *using up the release angle*. With the hand positioned to the outside of the ball, there is nothing left for the release to do.

Variations in wrist position and forearm movement have a strong impact on a bowling ball's direction and type of roll. Remember, the release is the last link in a chain of skill events.

If the preceding links are unreliable, there is little chance for a strong leverage point and a dependable release of the ball.

A lever is simply a segment turning about an axis to transmit force or motion. In bowling, the force is the swing, the segment is the hand, and the leverage is the point at which the force is applied relative to the ball's axis of rotation. Torque is a force that produces rotation. The nature of the torque motion, both its strength and direction of applied force, affects ball roll.

The goal of every serious bowler is to find the wrist position and hand movement that will apply the appropriate torque without sacrificing accuracy or consistency.

A successful active release is smooth and fluid. Try not to squeeze the ball, particularly with the thumb. Relax and let the hand fly through the release point. The release motion is very late and very quick. Tell yourself to wait for the swing. Just as the ball feels heaviest at the bottom of the swing, kick through with the fingers.

You are trying to increase the rotational velocity of the ball. Try to cover as many degrees of the ball's circumference as possible. Remember though, the more movement in the release, the harder it is to be consistent—you give yourself more opportunities for mistakes. Work on hand speed—a small, quick release is just as good as a big, slow one.

Do the math. Covering 60 degrees of the ball's circumference in 1/5 of a second is no better than turning 30 degrees in 1/10 of a second. They both yield the same rotational velocity. The smaller movement, however, reduces the chance of altering the swing to accommodate the exaggerated hand position or of missing the release because you could not get the hand to unload fast enough.

Tell yourself to drive down and through (imagine drilling the ball into the lane) when needing to release faster to get the ball onto the lane sooner. This promotes less skid and an earlier hook, which is useful for bowling on oily lanes when the ball will not hook much.

Swing through the ball to drive it down the lane. Think *out and down the lane* with the swing–release mechanism to promote a longer skid. This is an important adjustment for dry lanes when the ball wants to hook too soon or too much. In some cases, there is no up. Think *out and through* to delay and moderate the hook.

Overrotating the hand to an exaggerated open position will allow for maximum rotation at the release. Imagine leading with your pinkie in the downswing, then flipping from under the ball with the other fingers at the release.

Be careful, however. The swing goes where the thumb goes. For many players, the setup in the stance includes the overrotated hand position. This frequently causes them to push the ball away from the body. After all, the thumb is pointing out. If the pushaway moves away from the body, the backswing ends up behind the bowler. Many wannabe power players give up too much accuracy in order to create a strong release. Largely, that is a bad choice.

All bowlers, as their games develop, will be confronted with the power–accuracy trade-off. With more active releases, a power–accuracy trade-off is inevitable. A cautious, systematic approach to tie the mechanics of the release to the overall mechanics of the game will give you the right answers. Your answer (what you call "my game") may be different from some other bowler's answer, but it will be one with which you can prosper.

WRIST POSITION AND FINGER PRESSURE

Wrist position plays an important role in the type of leveraging position the hand has on the ball. If the wrist breaks back, the hand will be more on top of the ball than behind. This weakens the drive through the ball. Lift no longer comes from under the ball or from behind it; it is more like a pull from the top. In addition, allowing the wrist to bend back causes the fingers and thumb to point downward earlier in the release than is ideal, often causing an early release.

It is difficult to control the ball if it drops off the hand behind the foul line. In most cases,

the hook movement of the ball will be weak and ineffective. The ball comes off the hand before the fingers can finish the work they are supposed to do.

The wrist must stay straight for an effective release. Imagine a straight line from your elbow to your index finger (figure 8.13). This indicates a straight wrist. A straight release allows for a hand position behind the ball. From this position, more of the swing's energy transfers directly through the ball rather than diverts to the side or over the top. Likewise, the fingers are in a

Figure 8.13 A straight wrist position leads to an effective release.

better position to drive and lift the ball. A good wrist position provides for better leveraging from underneath the ball.

View a ball from the side. Draw an imaginary line that cuts the ball into lower and upper halves. A proper wrist position places the fingers below the midline—behind and under the ball—putting them in a strong position to take the weight of the ball at the bottom of the swing.

Many bowlers start the wrist in a weak position from the beginning of the approach, and it stays that way until the release. Others have a tendency to let the wrist weaken sometime during the swing, frequently in the downswing. In either case, controlling the ball is more difficult, and the ability to hook the ball is severely compromised.

The wrist is kept firm by the wrist flexors in the forearm, so adequate forearm strength is necessary to maintain proper wrist position. Think about a wrist curl using weights; the fingers flex inward, closing the grip to resist the weight, and the palm presses upward. Many bowlers do not adequately develop this sense of resistance against the ball. If you simply hang

the ball at your side, letting your hand relax, the weight of the ball will pull down on the thumb. This breaks the wrist back into a weak position. You must try to press back against the weight of the ball using the fingers.

To develop a sense of this resistance, apply pressure with the outriggers, the pinkie and index fingers on the outside of the ball. The two fingers on the inside apply pressure as well. Using the outriggers helps lock the wrist in position. The two fingers not inserted into the holes do not simply rest on the surface. They have important supporting duties for controlling the ball.

With the ball hanging loosely at your side, apply a bit of pressure with your pinkie on the outside of the ball. Now, apply more pressure with the index finger. Keep applying pressure until the wrist straightens out. You want to maintain this finger pressure against the ball's surface throughout the swing. Any relaxing of the wrist flexion during the swing will negatively affect the hand position at the release.

During a strong release, the index finger will feel as if it is driving through the ball to the target. The tendons from the fingers go through the carpal tunnel of the wrist and insert at the elbow. The tension from the application of pressure will draw the carpal bones of the wrist together into a more solid unit. This finger pressure locks the wrist into position. With the wrist in a proper position throughout the swing, the bowler is better assured of the desired release position.

Because of the wonderful range of motion in the wrist, the bowler can lock the wrist in a variety of positions. This change of wrist position (along with variations in the amount and speed of forearm rotation) allows the bowler to create a wide variety of releases. Strong (or cupped) positions, with greater rotation, create a stronger hooking ball. Weak positions (straight or broken back), with little or no rotation, are used to minimize or even eliminate the hook.

Many bowlers have been told, incorrectly, to point their thumbs to the target during the release. Do not point with the thumb. Instead, point to the target with your index finger. Keep the palm up and the wrist firm. Point the index finger (don't let it sag), and shoot for the target as you begin the pushaway.

Wrist and Finger Drill 1. *Wrist Position and Strength Test*

This drill tests for wrist strength and appropriate ball weight. Stand with your arm bent at about 90 degrees. Hold the ball in the palm of your hand without the thumb or fingers inserted in the holes (figure 8.14a). Slowly extend your arm forward and up until it is almost completely extended (figure 8.14b). Do not let the wrist break back. Slowly return to the starting position. Keep a straight wrist position throughout the motion.

If you cannot comfortably complete the movement, the ball is probably too heavy for you. You will have a difficult time controlling the wrist position during the swing.

a

b

Figure 8.14 *(a)* With arm bent to 90 degrees, hold ball in palm. *(b)* Extend arm out and up.

Success Check

- During the setup, keep the wrist straight as the ball rests in the palm.
- Extend the arm from the shoulder; return with a slow, smooth motion.
- At no point should you feel discomfort or sense that the ball will roll off the hand.

Score Your Success

Wrist is straight during the setup = 1 point

Arm extends comfortably from the shoulder = 2 points

Ball is returned to starting position without the wrist breaking back = 2 points

Your score ____

Wrist and Finger Drill 2. *Locking the Wrist*

This drill will help you learn to lock your wrist into position. Let the ball hang freely at your side. Insert your thumb and fingers into the appropriate holes. Relax your wrist, allowing the weight of the ball to pull your thumb down (figure 8.15a). Press up with the fingers in the holes to resist some of the weight. Now press against the surface of the ball, with both your pinkie and index fingers, until the wrist straightens (figure 8.15b).

This technique of locking the wrist into position is useful no matter what the angle of the wrist joint. At times various wrist positions are needed to create different ball rolls. Practice developing a consistent release using a straight wrist first. From there, experiment with different wrist angles (cupped or bent back) to create versatility in your game.

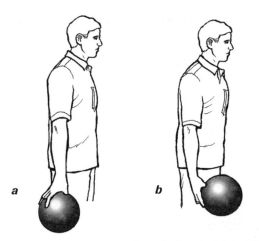

Figure 8.15 *(a)* Ball's weight pulls thumb down. *(b)* Finger pressure causes wrist to straighten.

Intentionally softening the wrist (breaking it back) puts the hand near the top of the ball at the release. This weakens the release, generally making the ball go straighter, a nice option for shooting spares or when bowling on dry lanes. Cupping the wrist keeps the fingers under the ball through the release, creating a stronger side roll and generating a stronger hook. This skill is useful when lane conditions allow for a higher scoring

environment or when excessive oil takes away ball reaction. (The optimal strength angle for the wrist joint is 10 to 15 degrees of flexion.)

Success Check

- Press index and pinkie fingers against the outside of the ball.
- Apply sufficient pressure to straighten the wrist.
- Maintain wrist position throughout the swing.

Score Your Success

Index and pinkie fingers pressed flat on ball's surface = 1 point

Pressure applied with both fingers = 1 point

Wrist straightens out as fingers apply pressure = 2 points

Pressure applied during full swing = 1 point

Little or no wrist position changes during swing = 2 points

Your score ___

Wrist and Finger Drill 3. *Finger Pressure Test*

With the finger pressure test, you will learn what the lock of the fingers in the hole feels like and how the fingers resist the weight of the ball during the swing.

Hold the ball in the palm of your hand. Insert only the fingers in the holes; do not insert the thumb. Allow the wrist to bend back slightly until the ball rolls onto the fingers. Press the fingers against the inside of the finger holes, forcing the ball back onto the palm. Lower the ball until the arm is almost fully extended at the side, cupping the wrist as the ball gets lower. It should feel as if the fingers support all the ball's weight. Remember to apply pressure with the outriggers (pinkie and index fingers) as well. Practice this drill 10 times, earning up to 9 points each time, to develop a sense of finger resistance to the ball's weight.

Success Check

- Ball rests in palm with only fingers inserted.
- Flex (cup) wrist as you extend the arm out and down.

- Press back with the fingers to resist the weight of the ball.
- Maintain wrist position as the fingers support the ball's weight.

Score Your Success

Ball is in the palm of the hand, only fingers inserted = 1 point

As your arm extends down to the side, the wrist flexes to keep the hand under the ball = 2 points

Pinkie and index fingers apply pressure on the ball's surface = 1 point

Inserted fingers press back against the ball = 1 point

Finger pressure prevents the ball from rolling forward = 2 points

Wrist position is maintained while bringing the ball back to starting position = 2 points

Your score ___

Wrist and Finger Drill 4. *Finger Pressure During Setup*

The goal of this drill is to feel for the difference between thumb pressure and finger pressure before swinging the ball. Perform this very simple task before every throw of the ball.

Pressure situations in particular affect the release and swing. In these situations, you may be more likely to tense up or try to control the ball during the swing. You do not want the slight pressure of the fingers to become a tension that moves all the way up the arm. This preparation technique will teach you to feel for the finger pressure and not the thumb squeeze, ensuring a smoother, stronger release.

Assume a normal setup position with a ball, and position your hand for the preferred release. Squeeze very firmly with both the thumb and the fingers. Relax the hand, letting the ball rest in the palm. Do not let the wrist position soften. Again squeeze the ball very firmly. Again relax the hand. Now apply slight pressure with the fingers but not with the thumb. Eventually you will sense the difference between finger pressure and whole-hand squeeze. When the hand is relaxed and the wrist is firm, begin the swing.

Success Check

- Squeeze and relax.
- Note the difference between finger pressure and whole-hand squeeze.

Score Your Success

You assume proper setup position = 2 points

Squeeze, relax, squeeze, relax pattern is followed = 2 points

In relax mode, wrist position does not change = 1 point

After second relax, you press slightly with the fingers only = 1 point

Approach and swing are initiated without any tension in the hand or arm = 2 points

Your score ___

BACKUP BALL

To get a sense of a strong wrist position, imagine letting the ball fall into the palm of your hand as it drops down after the pushaway (figure 8.16). It's like catching the ball in your cupped hand, then relaxing the arm as the weight of the ball pulls the swing back.

A poor hand position behind the ball not only influences the release quality but also exacerbates problems caused by poor wrist positioning. The combination of poor hand positioning (over- or underrotation) and inconsistent wrist positioning causes many errors in the game. It ranks right up there with synchronization (timing) and balance issues on the list of major bowling woes.

Rotating the forearm too early is a frequent mistake. In extreme cases, the entire arm circles around the ball. Once the forearm exceeds its natural range of motion, the remainder of the turning movement comes about by rotation at the shoulder. If the shoulder rotates (no matter which direction), the swing is no longer a true pendulum. Movement is occurring around more than one axis. Release strength (number of revolutions and axis tilt), swing accuracy, and ball control are all negatively affected. This is particularly noticeable in the backup ball.

In a backup ball, the arm rotates to the inside of the ball, with the palm turned away from the

Figure 8.16 The ball falls into the palm of the hand after the pushaway.

body. This is not a natural movement. It is usually accomplished through rotation at the shoulder, which causes the arm swing to pull inside the line of the shoulder. The elbow turns into the hip, and the palm turns away from the leg. This type of motion sacrifices accuracy. The normal rotation of the forearm (called *radioulnar deviation)* allows the palm to turn inward (palm faces the hip). Bowling is most successful when the body is allowed to perform in accord with its natural movements.

A simple task will demonstrate the proper direction and range of movement of the forearm. With your arm hanging down at your side, have someone grab hold of your arm at the elbow to keep you from rotating the upper arm. Start with your palm turned forward. Rotate your forearm inward. Pretty easy, right? This is the intended movement of the forearm. Most people should have close to 180 degrees of movement. In other words, the palm can be turned from a forward-facing position to a position in which it is almost facing directly behind. This is all the movement needed to accomplish any release. Now try to turn the palm away from the body. It is almost impossible, yet this is exactly what backup bowlers try to do.

Backup bowlers accomplish this movement by sacrificing the swing line. They allow the upper arm to rotate outward in the shoulder socket. Often a backup bowler needs to throw the body out of position to accommodate the inward tuck of the swing. With the swing tucking in and the hand (or should we say, the whole arm) twisting out, nothing appears to be working together. Not only are the mechanics faulty, but the amount of reverse hook achieved is also limited compared with more traditional releases. Correct a backup ball release as soon as possible.

Some people are more flexible and may be able to hyperextend at the elbow. Hyperextension frequently permits an outward rotation of the forearm. People with this flexibility (more often found in women) will have a more natural tendency to throw a backup ball. They may be able to accomplish a passive backup ball release without negatively affecting swing accuracy. This passive release, however, does limit the ability to create an effective hook. Any attempt to actively increase hook will bring out the inherent problems of throwing a backup ball.

To correct the backup ball release, begin by emphasizing hand positioning and swing alignment. Hold a bowling bag by the handle using just the fingers. (A suitcase, duffel bag, or backpack will also work.) Slightly overrotate the initial hand position, almost as if you are trying to use a traditional hook release. Take a few practice swings with the bag hanging just from the fingers. After a few swings, feel the bag release off the fingers as you try to slide it down the floor. Imagine the bag has wheels on the bottom and is going to glide to a person in front of you. Avoid excessive upper arm rotation. Imagine an arrow pointing from the crook of your arm where the lower and upper arm meet. Keep the arrow pointed toward the target during the swing.

A more active correction technique may be needed for the determined backup bowler or for a bowler who is strongly ingrained in using the backup ball. Try to overexaggerate the proper release. Just as you are ready to let go, drive the thumb in and flip the fingers around the outside of the ball. Sometimes it takes an exaggerated movement to correct a flaw.

The no-step and one-step practice drills in step 5 (pages 71–72) are excellent for isolating problems in the swing and release. It helps to have an experienced bowler watch your release. It is important that the desired release position be reached at the bottom of the downswing. Also, the chosen release position or motion should not affect the smoothness and accuracy of a true pendulum swing.

Swing and Release Drill. *Evaluating Proper Technique*

Have a coach or experienced bowler evaluate your swing and release technique. Use the following criteria to determine if your swing and release technique are sound.

- Swing is a smooth, continuous arc with no excessive bend at the elbow = 2 points
- Elbow (swing line) remains close to the hip (swing tucked in) = 3 points

- Wrist position is straight throughout the swing = 2 points
- For a stronger hook, wrist position is slightly cupped throughout the swing = 2 points
- Ball slides off the thumb first as the ball enters the bottom of the swing = 3 points
- Hand position behind the ball is stable throughout the swing (passive release) = 3 points
- Forearm rotation starts as the ball passes through the bottom of the swing (active release) = 3 points
- As the swing passes the ankle, the fingers drive through the ball = 2 points
- Swing motion at release is first out (extension) then up (lift) = 2 points
- After release, the fingers are still in a firm position = 3 points

Score Your Success

Excellent = 21 to 25 points

Good = 17 to 20 points

Fair = 12 to 16 points

Poor = 11 points or fewer

Your score ____

ENLARGING THE STRIKE POCKET

After this lengthy discussion of the release, a student of the game might be inclined to ask, "Why go through all the trouble? Why not make the release as simple as possible, taking all changes in position or movement out of consideration, and simply make bowling a targeting game—connect point A to point B?" There is merit in this point of view. In fact, I would recommend that a beginning bowler adopt this perspective when first taking up the game.

Unfortunately, bowlers soon discover the limitations of a straight release. The accuracy required for a ball entering the pins at zero angle is so great that few bowlers can achieve success this way. All good bowlers create an angle into the pins. There are only two ways to create angle.

1. Change position on the lane. Get away from the middle. This should be the first lane strategy all bowlers learn. It is the easiest way to change the ball's entry angle into the strike pocket. You can add more than 1 degree of angle simply by changing your lane position.

2. Create side roll. Learn to hook the ball. Increasing the entry angle greatly improves a bowler's chance to strike. Because the strike pocket enlarges as the amount of hook increases, a bowler can be less accurate and still strike at a high percentage. Keep in mind the trade-off of trying to create increasingly larger hook. Do it intelligently. There is no sense trying to increase the pocket size 50 percent if you end up doubling your error margin.

Researchers at the USBC testing facility used a simple ramp to determine how much increasing the entry angle (hook) increases the

Table 8.1 Strike Percentage Chart

Entry angle	Inches offset from center																	
	-3	-2.5	-2	-1.5	-1	-0.5	0	0.5	1	1.5	2	2.5	3	3.5	4	4.5	5	5.5
0	**76**	**100**	**80**	30	30	18	0	18	30	30	**80**	**100**	**76**	4	2	18	30	6
2	**80**	**76**	62	44	6	4	0	16	48	**88**	**100**	**100**	**82**	16	38	26	60	4
4	**82**	**90**	28	24	0	0	6	4	28	**88**	**100**	**100**	98	88	52	68	30	0
6	60	**98**	**78**	24	20	0	0	0	0	28	88	**100**	**100**	**100**	80	34	**82**	**78**

Negative inches offset are the crossover, or Brooklyn, strikes. Bold numbers indicate the true strike pocket for each entry angle.

size of the strike pocket. Notice the off-pocket strike percentage for the stronger entry angles in table 8.1. At this point, the strike percentage spikes back up even though the ball is farther away from the true strike pocket. Larger entry angles produce greater pin action. Pins will tend to bounce off the sideboards back onto the lanes, and this side-to-side mixing action increases strike potential. Although it does not guarantee strikes in these ranges, there is no doubt about the potential benefit.

If you were to stay with a straight ball, one that has end-over-end roll only, you could never achieve more than about 1.5 degrees of angle.

The strike pocket is approximately 18 inches from the edge of the gutter. Releasing the ball from the very edge of the lane creates an 18-inch displacement (or rise) during a 720-inch run. Performing a basic trig calculation (inverse tangent function) determines the angle. As can be seen in the table, entry angles of less than 2 degrees yield a small strike pocket.

A respectable hook can be produced fairly easily; it does not take tremendous exertion. Many successful bowlers use a small hook. By combining hand position technique with lane position strategy, you can create a very effective entry angle.

SUCCESS SUMMARY

The release is a very touchy movement requiring considerable control and feel for how the ball comes off the hand. There are five phases of the release. In the drive phase, the force of the swing goes through the ball. During the thumb release, the thumb slides off the ball near the bottom of the downswing. At the turn, the hand is positioned (or moves into position) to create the desired ball roll. During the extension phase, the ball passes through the bottom of the swing before leaving the hand. At the finger release (lift), the fingers resist the ball's weight as the swing continues upward into the follow-through.

To ensure a proper release, keep the hand behind the ball during the swing, and maintain a firm wrist throughout the swing. The swing is a straight, relaxed, loose pendulum. Do not change the nature of the swing to accommodate different types of releases.

Review your drill scores. Record your scores in the spaces that follow and total them. If you score at least 120 points, you are ready to move on to the next step. If you score fewer than 120 points, review the sections that are giving you trouble, then repeat the drills.

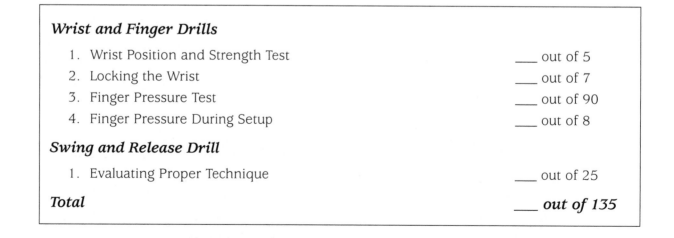

Wrist and Finger Drills

1. Wrist Position and Strength Test   ___ out of 5
2. Locking the Wrist   ___ out of 7
3. Finger Pressure Test   ___ out of 90
4. Finger Pressure During Setup   ___ out of 8

Swing and Release Drill

1. Evaluating Proper Technique   ___ out of 25

Total   ___ *out of 135*

Not everybody's game fits within a standard performance model, so a cookie-cutter approach does not work when it comes to skill development. The descriptions and practice regimens described in the previous steps outline the basic skills. Bowlers should strive to perform these movement patterns as closely as possible to the way they were described.

Keep in mind that every bowler is unique. Everybody has a distinct body structure and a distinct method of processing information. No two athletes, even if they are trained in exactly the same way, are exactly alike. To be success-ful, an athlete must find a way to adjust basic skill techniques to fit his own unique qualities. Although you cannot stray too far from the basics without sacrificing skill development, there is a range of acceptable adjustments that allow each athlete to maximize her potential.

Some adjustments have been alluded to already. Changing the starting height of the swing and adjusting the size of the steps are two examples. The next step discusses the variations in basic skill development that allow bowlers to develop their games properly while still establishing a game to call their own.

Adjusting the Stance, Swing, and Release

The previous steps introduced the essential physical skills of bowling. Within a number of these steps, ideas were given on how to modify the physical game. All athletes need versatility if they wish to be successful under a variety of competitive situations. For bowling, the versatility aspects are very subtle and precise. Make sure you are confident in your basic physical game before adopting too many alterations. With practice, you will be able to play from different positions on the lane and adjust for changes in the lane conditions with confidence.

In this step, you will learn to add versatility in three broad areas—the stance, the swing, and the release—thereby broadening your set of skills and giving you opportunities for success under a wider range of playing conditions. With each of these adjustments come opportunities to manipulate the game, either to fit your unique physical characteristics or to make strategic adjustments as you find yourself in various competitive environments.

Lane conditions change constantly. The distribution of oil on the lane surface varies from one bowling center to the next. In addition, each time a bowler throws a ball, oil is picked up by the ball and moved to a new location. Over a period of time, the oil completely moves from the lane's surface. The great variety of lane conditions requires a bowler to be comfortable with adjusting his or her basic game.

No successful bowler in the modern game throws the ball the same way from the same location over the same target every time. Once a basic set of skills is developed, adjustment strategies must follow quickly. One-dimensional bowlers may be successful under very specific situations, but when taken out of their comfort zones, they tend to struggle terribly. Most experienced bowlers know individuals who carry high averages in a particular bowling center, often referred to as a house mouse, yet do not bowl particularly well in other venues. Don't be a house mouse! Strive to be a lion on the lanes everywhere you bowl.

ADJUSTING THE STANCE

A bowler does not stand on the same spot of the approach for every throw. As the position on the lane changes, adjustments in the setup are necessary in order to stay on line to the target. For the most part, simply turning the whole body and facing the target is all that is needed. The position of the ball doesn't change, nor does the stance setup. The bowler simply realigns the starting position relative to the target. In some instances, however, changes in the stance actually help the mechanics of the approach.

Playing the Outside Line

Beginning bowlers must be convinced to move away from the middle of the lane. The farther they move away from the middle, the better angle they will have into the strike pocket (figure 9.1). This is an essential adjustment until they learn how to hook the ball. The common complaint is, "Every time I move over, I throw the ball down the gutter!" This indicates that the angle was not closed; the bowler needs to reorient the whole body.

Under certain conditions, such as a large amount of oil spread across the lane, even hook throwers may find the ball is not hooking. These players, too, will need to move toward the edge of the lane to make up for the angle lost because of a decrease in ball reaction.

The farther one moves toward the edge of the lane, the more likely that the visual target will be to the inside of the swing shoulder. For a right-handed bowler, the target will be to the left of the shoulder. This positioning creates a right-to-left angle on the lane. Trial and error will tell the bowler which starting position in relation to a particular visual target will create the desired line to the strike pocket.

For a small adjustment, turning the body may be sufficient; the stance positioning does not need to change. When setting up, the bowler simply turns everything and faces the preferred target. This means the bowler will not face straight up the lane. The setup and the line of the footwork once the bowler starts moving will be at an angle to the lane. The bowler need concern herself only with walking toward the target.

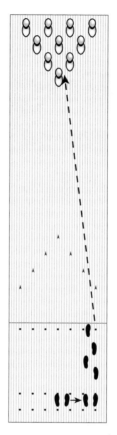

Figure 9.1 Moving away from the middle of the lane will give you a better angle into the strike pocket.

If the adjustment to the side is fairly large, a staggered position of the feet may prevent this alignment, so some bowlers may be more comfortable with adjusting the standard setup position. For those who employ a small hook, less of a preset in the body's angle (feet, hips, and shoulders) is necessary. Reducing the preset may give these bowlers a better sense of the proper alignment at an angle to the lane toward the target.

Bring the foot on the throwing side even or almost even with the opposite foot (figure 9.2). Bringing the foot forward closes the angle of the hips. The ball will be slightly closer to the midline of the body, so move the ball position slightly inward as well. The best way to do this is by closing the shoulders. Remember, both the upper and lower body have the same alignment to the target. The middle of the ball will be in front of the inside of the shoulder. This will change the swing line to a slight out-to-in movement. It will feel as if the ball is moving away from the body on the backswing. The swing, as it goes to the target, will come back next to the hip.

| Figure 9.2 | **Adjusting to Play the Outside Line** |

1. Throwing-side foot is even with opposite foot
2. Ball is moved slightly inward
3. Shoulders are closed
4. Upper and lower body are aligned to target

In the finish position, the shoulders will be closed and the balance arm will be pulled back slightly. The back leg will kick back only to the 6:30 position. If the nonthrowing arm is too far forward or the back leg is kicked around too far, the body will be thrown back into an open position at the finish. The bowler will have a hard time swinging to the target. He will need to pull the swing across as the body faces away; this is not recommended.

If the target is closer to the middle of the lane than to the shoulder position, the body must close up. The bowler cannot be expected to walk straight down the approach and then suddenly yank the swing across the body in order to hit the target. Align everything—feet, hips, shoulder, and swing line—in the setup. You will have a better chance of getting everything to work together.

Playing the Inside Line

Bowlers who throw a substantial hook expect to move across the center of the lane as the lanes dry out. Every time a ball is thrown, the ball picks up oil from the lane. Some of this oil rubs off the ball and is deposited in a new location farther down the lane. Much of it, however, is removed entirely from the lane's surface. Over a period of time, the depletion of oil increases ball traction. Without the layer of oil, the ball's surface comes in direct contact with the lane's

surface. If the bowler has any kind of side roll, the ball will hook sooner and stronger than it did at the beginning of the bowling session.

At this point, an open setup position is required to create enough angle across the front of the lane to keep the ball from hooking too soon (figure 9.3).

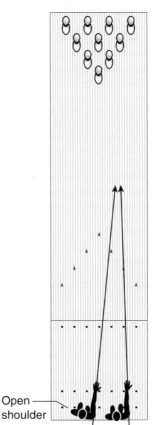

Open shoulder

Figure 9.3 A more open setup will create more angle and keep the ball from hooking too soon on lanes that are getting dry.

To play the inside line, preset the hips by dropping the throwing-side foot a few inches more than normal (figure 9.4). Set the hips and shoulders in an open position. Adjust the ball so it aligns with the outside of the shoulder.

Figure 9.4   Adjusting to Play the Inside Line

1. Throwing-side foot is dropped back farther
2. Ball is aligned with outside of the shoulder
3. Shoulders are open

The pushaway will feel as though it is moving slightly away from the body. Consequently, the backswing will feel slightly behind the back. The swing line will run from inside to out, and the downswing will tuck in next to the hip (inside, close to the body) and then swing out from the shoulder to the target. It will still be close to the ideal 90-degree swing alignment of the shoulder.

The shoulders will be open in the finish position. The balance arm will be slightly forward, and the back leg will kick behind to a 7:30 or 8:00 position.

When playing an extreme inside line, learn to walk down the edge of the lane. This will feel awkward at first. The approach goes one way, but at the release, the shoulders open to face another direction. Learn to sidestep. Steps that cross over slightly will keep the feet straight on the approach even though the idea is to play a strong angle across the lane.

Right-handed power players in particular need to learn this technique (figure 9.5). The right side of the lane breaks down faster than

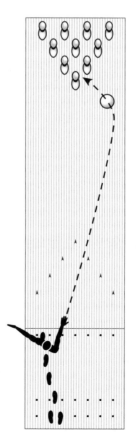

Figure 9.5 Right-handed power players should learn to walk left and throw right.

the left side. Finding a target left of center is not unusual for a right-handed power player. If a right-handed bowler is bowling on an even-numbered lane, the ball return may become a problem. A bowler can move only so far left before running into the ball return.

Some bowlers teach themselves a shortened approach. They stand in front of the ball return when playing an extreme inside line and try to shorten their steps enough to allow for a full approach in a very short space. This is not easy, particularly for a tall bowler.

Other bowlers take fewer steps. They teach themselves to move the ball into the downswing before they start walking. Essentially the first

step is imaginary (only the swing is moving), and then they take just three steps. Some people are quite successful with this three-step approach adaptation. Neither of these techniques is easy to learn. Many bowlers are uncomfortable with drastic changes in the natural rhythm they have developed for the game.

For others, adjusting the line of the approach as the footwork proceeds may be the answer. Because the ball return is in the way, the standard adjustment of moving the feet and the target will not work. Once against the ball return, moving the feet farther is not an option. Learning to walk left and throw right is an important technique for power players to develop.

Footwork Drill 1. *Outside Line*

The purpose of this drill is to practice a different stance position. The goal is to start near the edge of the approach and walk a straight line to a point inside the starting position. This would be a right-to-left approach line for a right-handed bowler.

Get into setup position using a reverse stagger of the feet. For a right-handed bowler, the right foot will be slightly (1 to 2 inches) ahead of the left foot. Position the ball to the inside of the swing shoulder. Use an outside-in swing. Note what board is between your feet at the start of the approach. Place a marker at the end of the approach, two to three boards to the left of the starting position for the feet. Identify the specific target you are aiming for. The target at the arrows should be four to six boards to the left of the swing-side shoulder's starting position.

Practice this approach line 10 times, earning up to 2 points each time.

Success Check

- Swing follows outside-in pattern.
- Feet are in reverse stagger in setup.

Score Your Success

Approach finishes in front of marker = 1 point

Throw rolls ball over identified target = 1 point

Your score ____

Footwork Drill 2. *Straight Down the Lane*

The purpose of this drill is to practice a normal stance position and approach line. The goal is to walk straight down the approach toward a target directly in front of the swing shoulder.

Get into setup position using a normal stagger of the feet. For a right-handed bowler, the right foot will be slightly (about 2 inches) behind the left foot. Position the ball directly in front of the swing shoulder. Use a straight swing. Note what board

is between your feet at the start of the approach. Place a marker at the end of the approach on the same board as the starting position for the feet. Identify the specific target you are aiming for. The target at the arrows should be directly in front of the swing-side shoulder's starting position.

Practice this approach line 10 times, earning up to 2 points each time.

Success Check

- Swing is straight.
- Feet are in normal stagger in setup.

Footwork Drill 3. *Inside Line*

The purpose of this drill is to practice a different stance position. The goal is to start near the middle of the approach and walk a straight line to a point outside the starting position. This would be a left-to-right approach line for a right-handed bowler.

Get into setup position using a larger stagger of the feet than normal. For a right-handed bowler, the right foot will be 3 to 4 inches behind the left foot. Position the ball to the outside of the swing shoulder. Use an inside-out swing. Note what board is between your feet at the start of the approach. Place a marker at the end of the approach, two or three boards to the right of the starting position for the feet. Identify the specific target you are aiming for. The target at the arrows should be four to six boards to the right of the swing-side shoulder's starting position.

Practice this approach line 10 times, earning up to 2 points each time.

Success Check

- Swing follows inside-out pattern.
- Feet are in larger stagger than normal in setup.

ADJUSTING THE SWING

Adjustments to the swing are considered from two different perspectives. One perspective is to view the swing from the side, which lets us look at the shape of the pendulum as the ball swings back and forth. Adjusting the shape of the pendulum as the swing nears completion allows the bowler to redirect the energy of the swing, sometimes more down the lane and other times more up the side of the ball.

The other point of view is from the top down, allowing us to see the lateral movement of the swing. Becoming aware of a swing's side-to-side motion helps us understand how far it may deviate from a truly straight line. It also gives the bowler a sense of how tight the swing line is to the side of the body.

From a side view of the swing, you can see the adjustment of the shape of the pendulum. By changing the shape of the swing's arc, you can redirect the force of the swing. Directing the force of the swing more upward increases ball revolutions. On the other hand, the force can be directed more outward to promote a greater drive down the lane. Release leverage can be adjusted this way without disturbing the smooth pendulum motion.

The three basic arc shapes are pendulum (half circle), flattened, and V-shape; each has

130

its place in the bowling arsenal. However, with the advent of the modern, high-tech game, the V-swing is not as favored as it once was. Many of the newer balls on the market feature very aggressive cover stocks with high flair potential, which causes them to read the midlanes early—the ball's surface interacts with the lane's surface more easily. Even with oil on the lanes, modern ball technology allows the current generation of bowling balls to dig through the oil and create traction with the lane's surface. There is such a thing as too much hook! Toning down the position of the release, and promoting a swing that goes through the ball rather than aggressively up the side, moderates the strong hook tendencies of certain types of bowling balls. Technological developments have reduced the need for an aggressive swing style.

Essentially, a bowler takes the energy of the swing and redirects it. Sometimes the direction of the swing is more down the lane in order to reduce the hook and add control to the ball's movement. Other times the energy is directed up through the ball, adding acceleration to the release.

Half-Circle (or Pendulum) Swing

The half-circle, or pendulum, swing (figure 9.6) is the traditional swing taught to all beginners. All players should first learn to bowl with this type of swing, which is modestly aggressive. The most versatile swing, it can be used with almost any release type to create a variety of ball reactions.

The swing is based on a pendulum motion. Once the bowler gets the ball into the swing, the ball will swing along its natural path without any effort from the bowler. There is nothing to alter. The inherent consistency and accuracy of the swing make it an important part of a bowler's development. Because of the muscle-free and reliable movement, it is the easiest for novice bowlers to learn.

| Figure 9.6 | Half-Circle (or Pendulum) Swing |

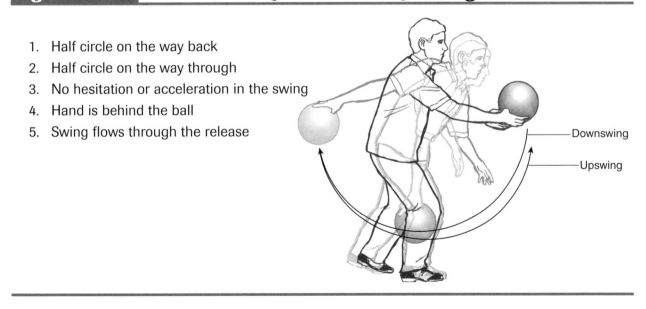

1. Half circle on the way back
2. Half circle on the way through
3. No hesitation or acceleration in the swing
4. Hand is behind the ball
5. Swing flows through the release

Imagine making a half circle with your swing—trace a half circle on the way back and a half on the way through. Relax and allow the swing to complete its full motion without any hesitation or acceleration. Notice that gravity acts on the arm and the swing with the same force. The arm and the ball fall through the downswing at the same rate.

Feel for the hand behind the ball. Do not press forward against the ball as the swing comes down. Applying pressure might cause an acceleration that will disturb the continuity of the swing.

As the swing continues up, feel the fingers lift up the back of the ball. The swing provides the force; the finger leverage position provides the resistance. Allow the swing to flow through the release. You should feel no sense of gripping and throwing the ball out to the target. The swing

will carry the ball out onto the lane. A loft of 12 to 18 inches past the slide foot is typical.

Flattened Swing

Imagine stretching out the arc of the swing, essentially creating a long flat spot at the bottom of the arc. This is a flattened swing (figure 9.7), the least aggressive of the swing types.

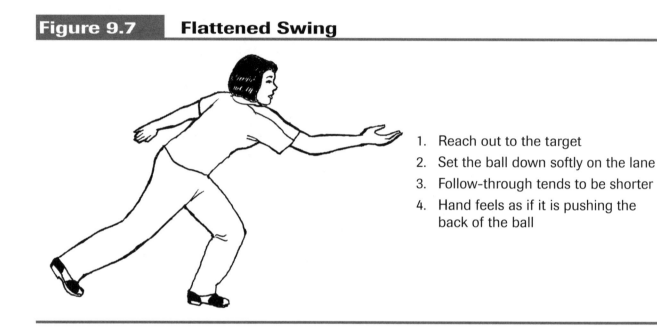

| Figure 9.7 | Flattened Swing |

1. Reach out to the target
2. Set the ball down softly on the lane
3. Follow-through tends to be shorter
4. Hand feels as if it is pushing the back of the ball

The flattened swing has been described as a drag shot because it feels as though the swing drags the ball along the floor. Generally, the follow-through is shorter. Think about reaching out to the target rather than bringing the hand up and through the shot. With a flattened swing, it will feel as if the hand is pushing through the back of the ball, as if you are trying to reach through the ball toward the pins. Direct the energy of the swing down the lane.

The flattened swing causes very little loft. The ball does not drop onto the lane but is set down softly. For a bowler of average height, the ball will contact the lane 6 to 10 inches past the slide foot. For some bowlers, the ball will just barely clear the foul line.

The goal of a flattened swing is to push the ball down the lane. Typically, not a lot of release motion is involved. The whole idea is to promote

a straighter, more controllable ball movement. This swing type goes best with a softer wrist position. Together the two provide a nice drive down the lane with minimal hook. The flattened swing is a solid technique to use on dry lanes or to shoot most types of spares, when the prime concern is accuracy rather than power.

V-Swing

The V-swing (figure 9.8) features a sharp angle of descent from the top of the downswing toward the release point, followed by an aggressive upward redirecting of the follow-through. This is known as *hitting up on the ball*. The redirected force of the swing accentuates the leverage force during the release. There is noticeable lift at the release point.

Figure 9.8 | V-Swing

1. Press against the back of the ball as it goes into the downswing
2. Ball rolls forward onto the fingers at the bottom of the downswing
3. Kick the fingers up from under the ball
4. Press with the fingers only, not the thumb
5. Follow-through moves upward

As the ball falls through the downswing, press against the back of the ball. This is not a quick, jerky downward drive. Imagine pressing against a large spring or squeezing the air out of a bag. The constant pressure will accelerate the downswing.

As the swing approaches the bottom, feel the ball roll forward onto the fingers. Some bowlers soften the wrist position slightly. This tilts the hand forward, promoting the ball's transfer onto the fingers.

As you feel the weight of the ball on your fingers, kick the fingers up from under the ball. Pull the fingers closed by pressing them toward the palm. Do not press forward with the thumb, only the fingers.

Just as the ball comes off the fingers, redirect the follow-through upward. Reach for the ceiling. Imagine trying to kick the ball over into a heavy roll.

The release is late in the swing, and the hand movement is very quick. If the release is very late, the ball will come off the hand just as the pendulum of the swing moves upward.

This swing type sometimes promotes a loft that goes farther down the lane than usual, perhaps as much as 24 to 36 inches. Particularly lengthy loft distances (more than 36 inches) indicate excessive squeezing with the thumb, not just the fingers. The release becomes less effective and usually less consistent.

Misstep

Your swing sends the ball more than 36 inches down the lane.

Correction

Make sure that only finger pressure is applied at the release. The thumb does no work.

Some players are capable of driving the ball down into the lane while accomplishing an aggressive release and follow-through technique. They may be able to impart considerable revolutions of the ball while setting the ball down quickly.

Caution: The V-swing, in conjunction with a strongly offset hand position, generates tremendous ball revolutions and a very strong axis tilt. Although the entry angle is potentially very large (8 degrees or more), ball reaction is very difficult to control. The ball will tend to overskid where there is oil (imagine a car spinning its tires on ice) and overreact or flip as soon as it touches a dry part of the lane. As lane conditions deteriorate and become less predictable, the use of this release is ill advised.

The timing window in which to complete the V-swing release is very small, and it is a relatively easy release to miss. The upward redirecting of the swing must work perfectly with the finger lift. Because there is little extension before the finger lift, the turn and lift phases of the release are close together.

Loop (or Inside-Out) Swing

The shoulder is a complex joint with a wide range of motion. The goal is to create a swing that accommodates the natural movement of the arm without compromising the accuracy of the swing. Notice that a true pendulum is not continuous. It has a stopping point (technically not a true pause) at the top of its arc at which it changes direction. Wouldn't it be nice to have a smooth, powerful swing that uses the natural rolling motion of the arm in the socket but is still a dependable, accurate swing?

The loop, or inside-out, swing (figure 9.9) is the power player's swing.

What are the advantages of this type of swing? First, it is a continuous, fluid stroke. The footwork has no pauses, so why should the swing? This type of movement keeps the swing moving smoothly as well. Second, the inward tuck of the swing puts the hand in a better leveraging position behind the ball. Once the hand is behind the ball, the bowler has options—loft or roll, hook or straight, passive or active, drive

through or swing up. Without options, there is no versatility. Third, many find the mechanics of this swing to be less stressful than a true pendulum motion. The loop swing works well with the natural movement expected from the ball-and-socket structure of the shoulder.

Is this swing as accurate as a true pendulum-type swing? Probably not. However, the body structure of many bowlers (particularly those whose hips are wider than their shoulders) prevents the development of a true back-and-forth pendulum swing anyway. Why not develop something that works with the body's natural movement?

The benefits of a well-practiced loop swing far outweigh the slight sacrifices of overall accuracy. By no means does the swing incorporate a large, dramatic loop. It is a very small adjustment from a straight line, no more than an approximate 4-inch total deviation, 2 inches out and 2 inches in.

The backswing may not be in a perfectly straight line, but the downswing is. The swing will loop back into position at the top of the backswing. From the top of the backswing to the release, the entire downswing movement will be on line to the target.

A common error is an outside (away from the body) loop. Although an inside loop is desirable, an outside loop should be fixed as soon as it is recognized. Luckily, it is easily detected. The backswing is usually fairly straight, but the swing moves away from the body in the downswing, usually because of one of these two factors:

1. Pushaway. Some bowlers are not comfortable letting the swing pass next to the hip. Others, in an attempt to keep the hand behind the ball, overexaggerate the open hand position. In either case, the initial ball movement is away from the hip. If the pushaway goes out, the swing path of the backswing will end up behind the back. The bowler must then send the downswing back around the hip to provide clearance for the ball.

2. Footwork. Some bowlers walk in front of the swing, forcing a swing realignment. It is particularly noticeable among bowlers who play the inside line and walk back

Figure 9.9	Loop (or Inside-Out) Swing

a   *b*   *c*

PUSHAWAY

1. Starts a little to the inside of the shoulder line

BACKSWING

1. As the ball swings back, clearing the hip, it will feel as if it is away from the body
2. The swing will brush past the hip on the way back
3. At the top of the backswing, the bowler will feel the swing loop back in line with the shoulder

DOWNSWING

1. As the back leg kicks out of the way, the swing tucks in
2. Think of the ball filling the space or hole where the back leg has just been
3. Feel the inside of the arm or the elbow brush past the hip during the downswing
4. At the bottom of the swing, the ball is directly under the shoulder or slightly inside the shoulder line
5. The swing drives through the ball and reaches out from the shoulder

toward a target closer to the middle of the lane. Remember, the line of the footwork and the line of the swing do not cross during the approach.

Whatever the cause of the outside loop, it needs to be corrected immediately. An outside loop is detrimental for a number of reasons. Accuracy is considerably diminished, and the movement of the ball away from the body pulls the bowler off balance. As the swing moves away from the body, the ball shifts the center of gravity away from the balance line. For most

people, the farther a weight gets from the body, the harder it is to hold on to it or control it. Additionally, as the arm moves away from the body, it becomes more difficult to keep the hand in position behind the ball for an effective release. Frequently, the hand turns around the ball early in the swing because of the outward movement. Release inconsistencies such as dropping the ball are bound to happen. An outside loop swing will occasionally send the entire arm around the ball as the swing enters the release phase. This is known as *circling the ball,* and it promotes a weak release.

135

Make sure the ball is properly aligned with the shoulder during the setup. Position the elbow directly above the hip at the side of the body. The pushaway is straight forward, allowing the swing to pass along the side of the body. Avoid an outward movement during the pushaway; this will cause the swing to wrap around behind the body.

Keep the footwork in a relatively straight line. The only crossover step is the slide step. This crossover movement is small, just enough to position the slide foot directly under the body. Do not let any step cross over in front of the line of the swing.

Swing Drill 1. *Outside-In Swing*

This exercise helps you develop a feel for a swing line that is slightly different from one that is straight back and forth. Stand in finish position with a practice partner behind you.

Have your partner position his hand slightly to the outside of your shoulder. (To the right, if you are right handed.) The goal is to swing the ball back so it touches your partner's hand near the top of the backswing.

Set your shoulders in a closed position. Start the pushaway to the inside, and let the ball swing back toward your partner's hand. The ball should touch your partner's hand at the top of the backswing. If the ball swings back to the wrong location, your partner will catch the ball in the backswing and reposition it so you can feel where the correct location should be.

Practice 10 outside-in swings, earning up to 1 point per swing.

Success Check

- Feel for the correct location.
- Each swing should be separate, with a distinct pushaway, backswing, and pause.

Score Your Success

Swing touches partner's hand and does not need repositioning = 1 point

Your score ___

Swing Drill 2. *Straight Swing*

This exercise helps you develop a feel for a swing line that is straight back and forth. Stand in finish position with a practice partner behind you.

Have your partner position her hand directly behind your shoulder. The goal is to swing the ball back so it touches your partner's hand near the top of the backswing.

Start the pushaway straight out from the shoulder, and let the ball swing back toward your partner's hand. The ball should touch your partner's hand at the top of the backswing. If the ball swings back to the wrong location, your partner will catch the ball in the backswing and reposition it so you can feel where the correct location should be.

Practice 10 straight swings, earning up to 1 point per swing.

Success Check

- Feel for the correct location.
- Each swing should be separate, with a distinct pushaway, backswing, and pause.

Score Your Success

Swing touches partner's hand and does not need repositioning = 1 point

Your score ___

Swing Drill 3. *Inside-Out Swing*

This exercise helps you develop a feel for a swing line that is slightly different from one that is straight back and forth. Stand in finish position with a practice partner behind you.

Have your partner position his hand slightly to the inside of your shoulder. Set your shoulders slightly more open than normal. Start the pushaway slightly to the outside, and let the ball swing back toward your partner's hand. The ball should touch your partner's hand at the top of the backswing. If the ball swings back to the wrong location, your partner will catch the ball in the backswing and reposition it.

Practice 10 inside-out swings, earning up to 1 point per swing.

Success Check

- Feel for the correct location.
- Each swing should be separate, with a distinct pushaway, backswing, and pause.

Score Your Success

Swing touches partner's hand and does not need repositioning = 1 point

Your score ___

ADJUSTING THE RELEASE

Changes in wrist position at the release alter the leveraging position of the fingers. The three basic wrist positions are bent, straight, and cupped. Adjusting wrist position, in combination with adjusting the hand's position behind the ball, allows you to create a number of different releases. Mastering these different releases will give you the ability to adjust the ball reaction to changes in lane conditions. Do not limit the conditions in which you can successfully perform by limiting your arsenal to only one or two releases.

The bent wrist position (figure 9.10) is the weakest. Use this position when you want very little or no hook. It is a good technique for dry lanes and spare shooting.

When setting up in the stance, prepare for the bent-wrist release by laying the wrist back. The wrist will remain bent during the swing. As the swing enters the release phase, the fingers will be near the top of the ball. With the wrist laid back, the thumb will point down during the release. The tendency will be to roll the ball off the hand early, which typically sets the ball down just over the foul line.

This release works well with a relaxed, extended follow-through. An active release can be used with this wrist position. The result will be a softly arcing, modest hook.

Unfortunately, bowlers often use this release unintentionally. It is the main reason beginning bowlers cannot generate an effective hook. Develop a straight wrist position for your typical release before modifying the position to create various types of ball roll.

The straight wrist position (figure 9.11)—the basic wrist position all bowlers should strive to develop—creates a modest to strong hook, depending on whether the release is active or passive. If the release is somewhat late in the swing, an effective hook can be created through strong extension, good leverage, and an aggressive follow-through.

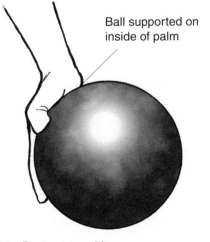

Ball supported on inside of palm

Figure 9.10   Bent wrist position.

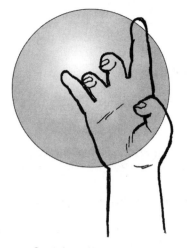

Figure 9.11 Straight wrist position.

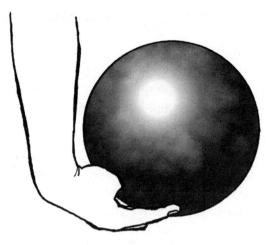

Figure 9.12 Cupped wrist position.

In the straight wrist position, imagine a straight line from the elbow to the tip of the index finger. Lock the gripping fingers in place. Feel the pads of the fingers pressing against the inside of the finger holes. Firm pressure against the surface of the ball with the outside fingers locks the wrist in position. This helps maintain wrist position throughout the swing. The palm presses against the back of the ball as the swing enters the release phase. Feel the fingers drive through the back of the ball as the release is finished.

The straight wrist position is the most versatile. You will be free to do just about anything you want to at the release. You can change hand positions, depending on how much side roll you want, or change the aggressiveness of

the release motion, depending on the number of revolutions you want to impart on the ball.

The cupped wrist position (figure 9.12) is the most difficult wrist position, and it may even cause injury. Not everybody is capable of using a strongly cupped wrist during the release. Problems with the fit of the ball (which prevents a smooth, quick release) or an overly exaggerated release movement will accentuate the already considerable stress on the wrist.

With the wrist cupped, the ball feels as though it is resting on the heel of the palm. As the flex angle of the wrist becomes greater, turn the hand inward slightly. The fingers will point in (toward 9:00), and the thumb points out (toward 3:00).

Misstep

Flexing the wrist straight up. Merely flexing the wrist without an offsetting turn puts considerable stress on the wrist.

Correction

Point the fingers toward the wall. Imagine a line from the middle of the wrist to the index finger. This is the line of support positioned underneath the ball.

As the ball enters the release phase, imagine driving the back of the hand under the ball as the release motion is performed. It is almost like scooping the ball up as it is released. Feel the fingers drive up from underneath the ball.

Caution: In the cupped wrist position, some bowlers have a tendency to bend at the elbow as the swing enters the release phase, particularly if they are using a strongly cupped wrist position. There is a lot of tension in the wrist if

138

it is cupped at a strong angle. Bending the arm puts the hand under the ball in the same way as cupping the wrist. This allows the bowler to use less of a cupped position, taking away the stress on the wrist.

Some power players will increase the angle of the wrist as the ball enters the downswing. This is often accompanied by a bend at the elbow. Unconsciously, the bowler is trying to position the hand as far under the ball as possible before entering the release phase of the swing. Some bowlers have used this technique of bending the arm while cupping the wrist with success. (This technique is particularly noticeable among those who use the thumbless grip. Bending the arm is the only way they can keep the ball on top of the hand without dropping it.)

Ideally, the wrist cup should not be so great you feel the need to bend the arm. Bending the arm puts the hand under the ball without the need for a strong wrist angle. This is a compensation movement, increasing the angle of one joint in order to reduce the angle of another.

If the bend is slight, and there is no alteration of the swing line, this is acceptable. Bending the elbow does position the hand under the ball for a potentially stronger leverage position. It is important, though, that the swing line remain straight.

Unfortunately, an excessively bent arm sacrifices power—it is a shorter pendulum—and accuracy. The elbow will tend to fly away from the hip. Most bowlers who have a bend at the elbow during the swing have a hard time keeping the swing close to the body. The tendency is for the elbow to drift away from the body (called *chicken winging*) during the downswing. This sends the swing off from a straight line as well as promotes a premature rotation around the ball. Generally speaking, avoid bending the elbow during the swing. Release strength should be a function of the swing and the hand position.

Misstep

Chicken winging, or flying elbow syndrome. Flying elbow syndrome is most likely to occur during an aggressive release motion. As the forearm rolls through the release motion, the rest of the arm tends to follow it around the ball.

Correction

Cup the wrist only as much as is comfortable. Keep your arm straight throughout the swing. After the pushaway, feel the arm fully extend at the bottom of the backswing. Make sure the swing line is next to the hip and on line to the target. Put only as much release motion into the shot as will still allow for consistency and accuracy. Err on the side of caution.

Softer Wrist, Stronger Release

An interesting characteristic of a powerful release is the backward bend of the wrist at the release point. The wrist does not collapse completely; if it did, the release would be ineffective. Instead, the very slight softening tilts the ball forward onto the fingers. The wrist recovers its position just as the fingers pull through the ball.

The flex-and-recover mechanism is very difficult to adopt. Frame-by-frame video review reveals this technique in many of the game's extreme power players, and many of them developed this release unintentionally. For the most part, they are unaware of the subtle wrist movement. Their goal was to drive down into the ball then pull back up through the release.

Release Drill 1. *Under the Bar*

The goal of this exercise is to learn how to get the ball down on the lane sooner. The objective is to minimize the lift and to emphasize swinging down the lane.

While using a normal approach, practice a flattened swing and a longer extension to the target. You may choose to use a weaker wrist position, as well.

If bowling with a partner, use a bar or long handle about 3 feet long. Have your partner get in position by the foul line, holding the bar across the lane at a height of about 10 inches. Your partner should hold the bar far enough out past the foul line that your hand will not hit the bar on the follow-through.

If you are practicing by yourself, support the bar using two boxes placed in the gutter on either side of the lane. The bar must be long enough (45 to 48 inches) to reach across the lane. Alternatively, cut a large hole in opposite sides of a large box. The hole should be large enough to allow the ball to pass through. The height of the hole should be no more than 10 inches.

The objective of this drill is to drive down and through the ball, using a flattened swing and a follow-through that extends down the lane rather than in an upward arc. Try to minimize finger lift and ball loft.

Execute 10 consecutive throws, earning up to 4 points per throw.

Success Check

- Use a flattened swing.
- Extend the follow-through down the lane.
- Minimize finger lift and ball loft.

Score Your Success

Wrist is in a straight or weak position at the release = 1 point

Ball passes under the bar without touching (or goes through the hole in the box) = 2 points

Ball is not released behind the foul line = 1 point

Your score ____

Release Drill 2. *Clear the Towel*

The purpose of this exercise is to develop a later and stronger release. The idea is to learn a faster release from a strong position under the ball for increased ball revolutions. This drill will be particularly helpful to a bowler who sets the ball down early because of a weak hand position or insufficient swing momentum.

Place a towel on the lane 12 to 15 inches past the foul line. The objective is to allow the momentum of the swing to send the ball past the towel. Have a partner watch to see where the ball lands. If you are squeezing too hard, the ball will have excessive loft. If there is excessive loft, the partner should hold a bar or his hand over the lane to indicate where the ball should land. Getting the ball over the towel but under the bar requires precise release mechanics. Practice either a pendulum swing or V-swing. The wrist position should be straight or cupped.

Execute 10 consecutive throws, earning up to 7 points per throw.

Success Check

- Use a pendulum swing or V-swing.
- Wrist position is straight or cupped.

Score Your Success

Swing is smooth, with no jerky motion at release = 1 point

Finish position is held; body does not pull up = 1 point

Wrist position is straight or cupped at release = 2 points

Ball is projected past the towel = 2 points

Ball lands smoothly, with no loud thump from excessive loft = 1 point

Your score ____

SUCCESS SUMMARY

This step emphasizes basic ways you can modify the standard set of skills. The purpose of the modification is to broaden your skill set. All bowlers who progress to higher levels of involvement in the game will be confronted with a variety of environmental conditions, specifically variations in lane conditions. To maintain the desired scoring level, they must develop adaptive skills.

The variations in the swing, the approach, and the release discussed in this step will give you a larger set of tools. Changing the nature of the ball movement (more or less hook), as well as the spot on the lanes at which a target line may be established, provides opportunity to adjust to changing lane conditions. You must be confident in your ability to throw the ball in different ways and play all parts of the lane. Once basic skills are firmly established (the initial steps of this book), modifying the basic skills creates a more complete game.

Review your drill scores. Record your scores in the spaces that follow and total them. If you score at least 170 points, you are ready to move on to the next step. If you score fewer than 170 points, review the sections that are giving you trouble, then repeat the drills.

Footwork Drills

   1. Outside Line   ___ out of 20

   2. Straight Down the Lane   ___ out of 20

   3. Inside Line   ___ out of 20

Swing Drills

   1. Outside-In Swing   ___ out of 10

   2. Straight Swing   ___ out of 10

   3. Inside-Out Swing   ___ out of 10

Release Drills

   1. Under the Bar   ___ out of 40

   2. Clear the Towel   ___ out of 70

Total   ___ *out of 200*

This step is the last one to specifically discuss physical skills. The following steps will give insight into some of the strategic elements of bowling. As you worked your way through the preceding steps, the complexity of the game should have become apparent.

Do not be too hasty to experiment. Be confident in your basic skills—footwork, timing, balance, swing line, and release—before attempting any of the more-advanced techniques. Every alteration to a basic element requires the creation of a new motor program. Even if the new program is not greatly different from the basic program, learning is still taking place. Be patient!

On the other hand, don't be too cautious. As you develop a greater command of basic skills, try new things. Expect to make mistakes.

Occasionally you will be frustrated, but don't be discouraged. Establish reasonable goals, ones that push you to work without seeming insurmountable. Once you reach a goal, determine a new one.

Think through problems. A careful step-by-step analysis will lead you to the issue that may be holding you back. Once you identify it, conquer it. Seek advice. Others' observations may lead you to an insight into your own game. Sometimes the mere notion that another person supports your efforts may be all you need to confidently pursue higher levels of performance. Finally, persevere. Nothing worthwhile comes easy. In the words of coaching legend John Wooden, "Nothing works unless you do."

Adjusting the Line to the Strike Pocket

The goal of bowling is to find the strike pocket, and this step presents some of the basic systems for adjusting the strike line. The physical skills bowlers develop allow for shot repetition and effective ball roll. Once you find the strike pocket, you want to throw the ball there consistently. Once you can hit the strike pocket, you want to have enough angle and ball drive to actually throw strikes.

Finding a path to the strike pocket is a matter of targeting strategy, but no targeting strategy works if you cannot hit your target. This is where physical skill comes in. However, the actual line to the target is discovered through an understanding of the lane dimensions. Paying attention to the starting position on the approach, what target on the lane the ball rolls over, and where the ball contacts the pins gives you all the information needed to determine a line to the pocket.

Assuming that diligent practice of the skills emphasized in previous steps has yielded a consistent and effective physical game, it is now time to apply those skills toward actually throwing strikes. Even if you have the best physical game in the world, if you throw the ball on the wrong part of the lane (and have no system in place for adjusting for miscalculation of the line

to the strike pocket), then you will have little chance of bowling success.

The two basic strategies for adjusting your target line to the strike pocket rely on an understanding of the distance on the lane. The first system allows for the change of the ball location by simply adjusting the starting position on the approach. This is a *pivot system*. The entire target line rotates around a central point, or pivot. The second system is an *angle shift system*. You can change the angle at which the ball enters the pocket without changing where the ball hits. If you maintain a specific relationship between how much the visual target on the lanes is changed relative to how much the starting position on the lanes is changed, the entry angle to the pocket can be increased or decreased at will. Entry angle can be altered without changing the ball's final location.

All bowling lanes are built to specified dimensions. Bowlers need to know the distance from the starting position on the approach to the foul line, the distance from the foul line to the targeting arrows on the lane, and the distance from the targeting arrows to the pins. Knowing the relationship of the distance for each section of the lane allows the development of adjustment strategies based on simple ratios.

For any targeting strategy to pay off, you must pay careful attention to every point of the target line. This is not the time to lose focus. Know exactly where the approach starts and finishes. Know exactly where your intended target is and whether the ball rolled over it or not. If you missed the target, by how much did you miss it? Watch the ball hit the pins. Was the pinfall what you expected?

The pins that remain standing are clues as to the quality and accuracy of the shot. Pins stand for a reason. The intelligent bowler knows, solely through pinfall observation, whether the problems are physical or strategic. Many bowlers blame bad luck for their lack of pin carry. They get it into their minds that nothing can be done about it. Without analyzing the problem and implementing a revised strategy, they are bound to repeat the same mistake and get the same result.

PRIMARY AND SECONDARY TARGETS

The two primary target points on the lane are the starting position on the approach and the target arrows on the lanes (figure 10.1). These two points define the target line to the pins.

When setting up on the approach, pay attention to the location of your throwing-side shoulder. Because you swing from the shoulder, you should aim from the shoulder. The position of the shoulder relative to the position of the visual target determines both the nature of the stance (open or closed) and the direction of the footwork. In many situations, you do not walk straight down the lane; instead you walk toward the target.

Three sets of dots, usually five or seven dots per set, are spread across the approach in a direct line with the arrows on the lane. One set of dots is 12 feet from the foul line, another is 15 feet, and the last set of dots is at the end of the approach, just in front of the foul line.

Knowing which dot the throwing shoulder is initially positioned over, relative to the arrow the bowler has identified as the visual target, lets the bowler know something about the angle he is creating on the lane. This angle will naturally influence the direction of the footwork. By comparing the dot you started at with the dot you finished in front of, you can determine whether or not you walked in the correct direction.

Primary Points of the Target Line

The two primary points of the target line are the bowler's starting position on the approach and the visual target on the lane. The arrows about 15 feet out on the lanes are the preferred visual targets for most bowlers. Some bowlers may choose to look at a point between two arrows. In either case, the visual point is fairly close to the foul line.

The pins are not the primary visual target. Learn to be a spot bowler rather than a pin

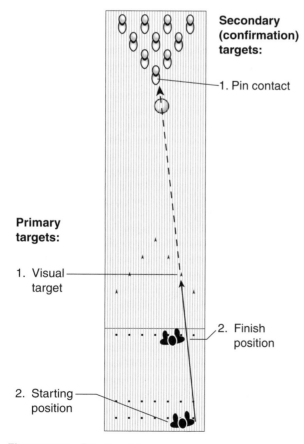

Secondary (confirmation) targets:

1. Pin contact

Primary targets:

1. Visual target

2. Finish position

2. Starting position

Figure 10.1 Target points.

bowler. Pick a spot on the lanes that is close and easy to focus on. Although not all bowlers use just the arrows, the arrows are the obvious targets to start with. Good bowlers do not look at the pins until the ball hits them. If the starting position is correct and the ball rolls over the intended target, the ball's path is inevitable. It doesn't matter if the pins are 60 feet away or 600.

Why look at the pins at all? Because the pins are a secondary target. Where the ball makes contact and how the pins fall (or don't fall) are clues to how effective the shot was. Always take the time to learn from each shot.

Secondary Points of the Target Line

The secondary points of the target line are the finishing point of the approach and the ball's contact point at the pins.

Compare the finishing point on the approach with both the starting point and the visual target on the lane. This tells whether the footwork was straight toward the target. If the approach is not straight, one of two things happens. Either the bowler is unable to hit the desired target, or she hits the target from a different angle than was originally intended. In either case, the ball path will not be along the desired target line.

Develop the habit of looking down at the slide foot after each shot. The final position of the footwork will tell you if you walked in a straight line to the target. The finish position should split the difference between the start position and the visual target. For instance, if the visual target is 4 inches to the right of the starting position, expect the finishing point on the approach to be 2 inches to the right of the original starting point.

Where the ball contacts the pins is the final point of the target line. Verification of your choice of target line comes from hitting the desired strike pocket. If the ball does not end up where it was supposed to go, you need to determine the problem. Either you had poor technique and didn't throw the ball the way you were supposed to, or you used an incorrect strategy—your choice of starting position or target was incorrect.

As you become more consistent in your physical performance, you can begin to eliminate physical factors as a cause for poor results. To be more precise, sensitivity to your physical game will allow you to determine more readily what caused an errant shot. Once you are satisfied that a physical problem is not to blame, you can concentrate your efforts on adjusting targeting strategies.

USING STRIKE ADJUSTMENT SYSTEMS

The two basic strike adjustment strategies (3-1-2 and 3-4-5) rely on the relationships between three reference points—the pins, the arrows, and the starting position on the approach. The third system, the 1-to-2 system, is a variation of the 3-4-5 angle shift system. The relationships are in 15-foot increments, and the adjustments are a matter of bowling math. Ratios are in multiples of 15.

3-1-2 Pivot System

Of the three reference points that define the strike line, the visual target will not change. The target is the pivot around which the strike line moves (figure 10.2). It's like a seesaw—as one

end goes down, the other end goes up. As the starting position is moved farther right, the ball location at the pins moves left.

It is 45 feet (three sets of 15 feet) from the arrows to the pins and 30 feet (two sets of 15 feet) from the arrows to the starting position. This 3-to-2 ratio allows you to change where the ball ends up by making careful changes in your starting position on the lane.

Remember the ratios 3 to 2, 6 to 4, 9 to 6, and so on. Adjustments are made as multiples of 3 to 2.

Move two boards to the right from your initial starting position. Make sure to turn the body enough to face the same target. If you walk to that target, the approach will end up one board

145

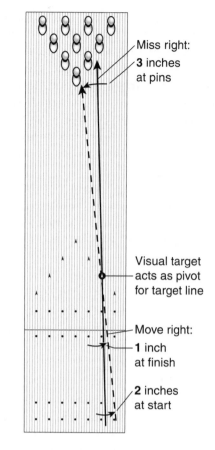

Miss right:

3 inches at pins

Visual target acts as pivot for target line

Move right:

1 inch at finish

2 inches at start

Figure 10.2 3-1-2 pivot system.

to the right of the original path. The ball will be three boards left of the original contact point at the pins. Move in the direction of the mistake. For instance, if the initial throw sent the ball too far to the right, moving right will steer the ball left.

This is a basic adjustment strategy for bowling: Move in the direction of the mistake. If you miss right, move right. If you miss left, move left.

The 3-1-2 system has its limits. A very large movement to the right without moving the target may cause a right-handed bowler to walk away from the swing. Be sure that adjustments are made to body alignment. Turn your body to face the target, or adjust the amount of preset angle used in the setup (as described in step 9) to avoid footwork drifting away from the swing.

Likewise, large moves to the left may cause a right-handed bowler to walk in front of the swing. Careful preparation of the stance will help avoid this problem as well.

If the bowler is not attentive to the alignment of the body or the preset angle in the setup, problems may occur. The swing line and the approach line will tend not to be parallel, resulting in potential for either a convergence or a divergence on the approach. In either situation, swing accuracy or release consistency will be sacrificed.

In general, you should expect to be close to the strike pocket by the second adjustment when using the 3-1-2 system. If the second adjustment of the starting position still does not get the ball near the strike target, it is unlikely you are hitting the intended target each throw. No targeting system will work if you can't hit the target.

3-4-5 Angle Shift System

Figure 10.3 illustrates the 3-4-5 angle shift system in which the entry angle is changed without changing the ball's contact point. When the initial shot is close to the strike pocket, only subtle changes in ball path are needed. The pin

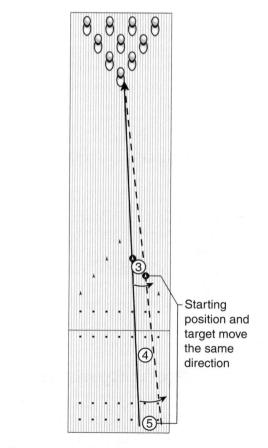

Starting position and target move the same direction

Figure 10.3 3-4-5 angle shift system.

contact point remains the same. Adjust the starting position and the visual target in the same direction. Moving closer to the middle of the lane reduces the angle. Moving closer to the gutter increases the angle.

It is 45 feet from the pins to the target arrows (three increments of 15 feet), 60 feet from the pins to the foul line (four increments of 15 feet), and 75 feet from the pins to the starting position at the back of the approach (five increments of 15 feet). Be precise! Move the target 3 inches at a time with every 5-inch change in the starting position. (The approach will finish 4 inches from the original strike line.) An adjustment in anything other than a 3-to-5 ratio changes the ball's final position.

The 3-4-5 angle shift system works in any multiple. Instead of standing in the middle of the lane and using a target in the middle of the lane, move 10 inches with the feet and 6 inches with the eyes. For even more angle, try moving 15 inches at the start and 9 inches at the arrows. Keep in mind, when the position and the target move in the same direction, they should not get in each other's way.

For a straight ball thrower, this system can be used to find a line to the pocket knowing nothing else but where the strike pocket is. The bowler merely has to work her way back from the strike pocket. The ratio of the distances will identify the visual target, the release point, and the starting position on the lane.

The perfect strike pocket is 2 1/2 inches offset from the center of the lane. The center of the lane is the middle of the 20th board. Boards are counted from the edge of the gutter (the 1 board) to the center. The boards are slightly more than 1 inch wide. This will put the strike pocket at about the 18th board. Working back from the 18th board, you can now figure out everything else about the target line.

For the sake of convenience, we will use a 3-board deviation for every 15-foot increment the target line is away from the pins.

- The arrows are three sets of 15 feet (45 feet) away from the pins. 3×3 boards = 9 boards. 18 (strike pocket) – 9 (board shift) = 9. The visual target is the 9 board.

- The foul line is four sets of 15 feet (60 feet) away from the pins. $4 \times 3 = 12$. $18 - 12 = 6$. The release point at the foul line is the 6 board.

- The starting position at the beginning of the approach is five sets of 15 feet (75 feet) away from the pins. $5 \times 3 = 15$. $18 - 15 = 3$. Start on the approach in a position that puts the swing over the 3 board.

To sum it up: If your swing starts on the 3rd board and the ball is released over the 6th board and it rolls over the 9th board, you will have created a straight line that ends up at the 18th-board strike pocket.

You could use a smaller increment (2-board deviation for every 15 feet away from the pins), but it would yield a smaller and potentially less effective angle to the pocket. A larger increment (4-board deviation) would put the release point close to the edge of the lane, which would make for a larger angle. Unfortunately, the ball return on certain lanes (odd-numbered lanes for the right-handed bowler) would most likely interfere with the bowler's starting position.

1-to-2 Ratio Angle Shift Variation

The 1-to-2 adjustment is a variation of the 3-4-5 system. Essentially, the 3-to-5 ratio is cut in half. Cutting the ratio in half yields a 1 1/2 board move with the eyes (visual target) for every 2 1/2 board move with the feet (starting position on the approach). Most bowlers don't calculate for the change at the approach; they assume a straight line from start to finish. However, if you want to be sure the approach is straight, the adjusted position should be 2 boards over from the previous finish.

Experienced bowlers round off this adjustment. It is commonly referred to as the 2 and 1—2 boards with the feet and 1 board with the eyes (figure 10.4).

Although 2 and 1 are not as mathematically exact, they are easy to remember and have practical application. For example, a right-handed bowler's ball hooks too much and hits high on the headpin. He does not want the ball to hit the

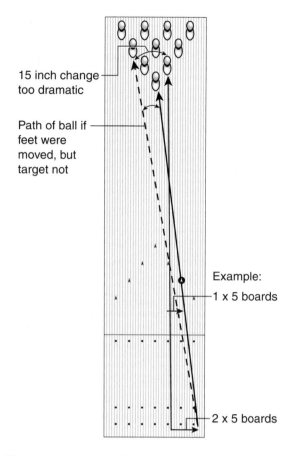

15 inch change too dramatic

Path of ball if feet were moved, but target not

Example:

1 x 5 boards

2 x 5 boards

Figure 10.4 1-to-2 adjustment.

same spot again. (Remember, any adjustment related to the 3-to-5 ratio changes the angle but not the location.) The ball missed the pocket to the left, so the bowler should move left. Remember, miss left, move left. Because 2 to 1 is a greater ratio than 3 to 5, the ball will end up slightly farther right if the move is to the left.

The bowler accomplishes two things when applying the 1-to-2 system. First, he changes the ball's final position at the pins using the 1-to-2 ratio in the same way as the basic 3-1-2 adjustment. This is possible because the 1-to-2 system is not an exact equivalent of the 3-to-5 system. Changing the target line (relative to the starting position) in anything but a 3-to-5 ratio

will cause the ball to end up in a different location. The 1-to-2 system allows for a fine-tuning of the location; the basic 3-1-2 system is somewhat less precise.

Second, the bowler has made a practical adjustment for changing lane conditions using a very simple angle adjustment system. He is now playing on a different part of the lane. This differs from the pivot system, which keeps the target the same.

Bowling on the same part of the lane, throw after throw, will wear down the oil in that particular area. This will change ball reaction. Often, a ball will hook too much because the oil on that part of the lane is used up. At some point, changes in lane conditions will become dramatic enough to force the bowler to change her physical game or play another part of the lane. Most bowlers are more comfortable making small moves on the approach rather than subtle changes in mechanics. The 1-to-2 ratio changes the target as well as the starting position. With a new target comes a fresh part of the lane. The new oil line allows the ball to travel down the lane more easily.

The 1-to-2 adjustment also works going the other way. Oil pushed down the lane from ball movement (called *carrydown*) prevents the ball from hooking in time to get back to the strike pocket. Most bowling centers have less oil near the edges of the lanes than they do in the middle. Moving the feet and the target closer to the edge of the lane allows for both an increase in angle and a ball path that is on a dryer (and therefore more hooking) part of the lane. Both benefits are useful if the bowler is looking for a stronger angle to the pocket.

Because it is easy to remember and has practical application for the way lane conditions change under normal circumstances, the 1-to-2 system is the adjustment used most often among experienced bowlers.

UNDERSTANDING PINFALL

For a perfect strike (figure 10.5), the ball hits only four pins. All the other pins fall as a result of pin-to-pin contact. This requires that the ball

strike the targeted pins in just the right location to initiate the proper chain of pinfall.

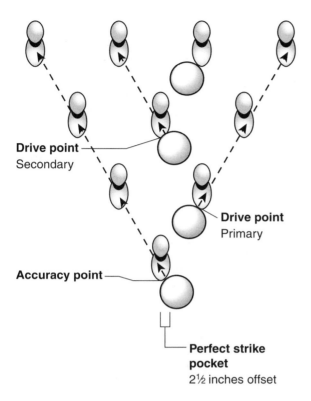

Drive point
Secondary

Drive point
Primary

Accuracy point

Perfect strike pocket
2½ inches offset

Figure 10.5 Ball path of a perfect strike.

The line from the headpin to the 7 pin is called the *accuracy line*. First and foremost, you must be able to roll the ball to this location, but merely throwing the ball is not enough. The ball must have sufficient drive to push through to the 3 pin after contacting the headpin. The line from the 3 pin to the 10 pin is called the *drive line*. If the ball does not have enough drive (it deflects too much), it will not contact the 3 pin in the correct location. A number of factors influence drive, including ball weight, ball velocity, traction between ball surface and lane surface, ball location at contact (accuracy), and entry angle.

Pins that remain standing tell you something about how the ball hit the pocket. Many throws appear to hit the strike pocket yet leave pins standing. This is not a matter of bad luck. Pins stand because they are supposed to stand. As frustrating as this may seem, pins stand because you made a mistake.

Swallow your pride, take a deep breath, and make an intelligent adjustment. When determining what adjustment to make and how large the adjustment should be, visually estimate the size of the error. Usually it will be obvious if contact

was slightly left or right of the ideal strike pocket. Determining the size of the error, and subsequently the size of the appropriate corrective action, takes practice.

Light (or Low) Hit

On a light hit, the ball is wide of the strike pocket. For a right-handed bowler, a light hit goes wide to the right of the strike pocket.

The corner pins (the 10 pin for a right-handed bowler and the 7 pin for a left-handed bowler) are the first indicators the ball did not make it to the pocket. If the ball is a little to the right, the headpin pushes the ball to the side. The ball then strikes the 3 pin a little too head-on. As the 3 pin is cut straight back, it will slice the 6 pin around the 10 pin.

The error margin for contacting the headpin is larger for heavier balls and sharper entry angles. Shallow entry angles (ball thrown straight down the lane) and lightweight balls are more easily deflected. The perfect contact point for the ball is 2 1/2 inches offset from center. To throw a strike, a bowler with an average hook has about a 2-inch range of contact (error margin) at the pins—from 1 1/2 to 3 1/2 inches offset. The error margin drops to about 1 inch for the bowler with no entry angle. If a ball makes contact to the right of the error margin (light hit for the right-handed bowler), the 10 pin will often be left standing.

The 5 pin indicates an obvious light hit. Leaving the 5 pin is a blatant error. There is an expression in the game—no drive, no five—that applies to this situation. Using a ball that is too light, or using a shallow entry angle, frequently causes the 5 pin to remain standing.

A right-handed bowler who throws a light hit will usually leave one of the following pin combinations:

- Single pins: 10, 5, 7, 2, 8 (the 8 pin is somewhat rare)
- Two-pin combinations: 5-7, 5-10, 5-8, 2-8, 2-10, 8-10, 7-10 (also known as the swishing 7-10)
- Other multipin combinations: 2-8-10, 2-4-5-8 (bucket), 1-2-10 (washout), 1-2-4-10 (washout)

If your shot is consistently coming up light, first make the most obvious adjustment: Move your feet, your target, or both. Change the angle, the location, or both. Remember, miss right, move right.

Experienced bowlers try to change the roll of the ball. One trick is to move the visual target closer, an almost unconscious adjustment. Looking closer on the lane creates a slight forward tilt of the upper body. With the upper body tilted slightly more than usual, incline of the downswing into the lane is somewhat sharper. The net result is that the ball is driven down into the lane. This is a great way to get the ball rolling a little earlier and hooking sooner.

Another trick some bowlers employ is moving back on the approach. If you have room, move your starting position back a bit. A couple of inches back at the start means the ball will hook a couple of inches sooner on the lane.

Other tactics include changes in the release and the ball speed. Try to create a stronger hook. Adjust your hand position by using a stronger wrist cup, or position your hand more on the side of the ball at the release to increase the axis tilt and create a sharper entry angle into the pocket. Slowing down the ball's speed gives the ball a chance to grab the lanes, decreasing skid and increasing potential hook. Lower the ball position in the stance, or slow down your feet.

Heavy (or High) Hit

A ball that hits more toward the middle of the headpin is said to be *high*. For a right-handed bowler, this is a miss to the left of the strike pocket. Adjust the location, or reduce the entry angle. For a right-handed bowler, the 4 pin gives the first indication the ball is too high; for a left-handed bowler, it's the 6 pin. With many light

hits, the pins left standing allow for fairly easy spares. Conversely, hits that are progressively higher on the headpin get the bowler closer to splitsville. That is a road best not taken.

A right-handed bowler who throws a high hit will usually leave one of the following pin combinations:

- Single pins: 4, 6, 9 (the 9 pin is more commonly left by those with a very strong hook)
- Two-pin combinations: 3-6, 6-10, 3-10 (baby split); many types of splits including 4-9, 4-10, 7-10
- Other multipin combinations: 4-6-7-10 (big four), 4-6-7-9-10 (Greek church), 4-6-7-8-10 (Greek church)

The basic adjustment for the high hit is to move in the direction of the mistake. If you miss left, move left. If the ball is only a little bit high—in other words, you are hitting the pocket but not striking—use the 3-4-5 method (moving both the feet and the target closer to the middle) to reduce entry angle.

Another adjustment is increasing ball speed, which delays or reduces the hook. Moving the visual target farther down the lane helps accentuate a longer and flatter swing, creating more of a drive down the lane rather than up the ball, which also delays or reduces the hook.

If the ball seems to make a rather sharp turn at the hook point, the release might be too strong. Soften the wrist position so the fingers are not lifting from under the ball from such a strong leverage position. Avoid a strong hand position change at the release as well. Keep the hand more behind the ball. Staying behind the ball reduces the axis tilt; the ball will have more of an end-over-end roll and less side roll.

ESTIMATING THE SIZE OF THE MISS

Knowing the direction of the miss is only one part of the solution. You must figure out how large the miss is in order to know the size of the appropriate correction. Figure 10.6 shows the distances within the pin setup.

Going down the side of the pin triangle, it is 6 inches from the center of one pin to the center

of another. You can visually recognize the space between any two adjacent pins. This space is called a *pocket*. For strike adjustment, the main concern is the strike pocket. A pocket cuts the 6-inch space in half. That means as the ball location moves from pocket to pin or from pin to pocket, it is changing 3 inches at a time.

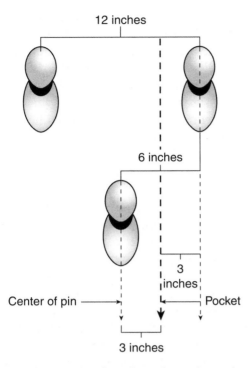

Figure 10.6 It is 3 inches from the strike pocket to the center of the pins on either side of the pocket.

You now have a visual tool for estimating the size of the miss. Simply compare where the ball hit (a particular pocket or pin) with the desired strike pocket. Estimate errors in multiples of 3 inches. This works very well with the 3-1-2 adjustment system (page 145). That system allows for 3-inch changes in ball location based on 2-inch adjustments with the feet. The technique for estimating the size of the error coincides nicely with the system for adjusting ball location.

What should you do when the ball appears to hit the pocket but a strike does not happen? First, congratulate yourself on a good throw. Second, remember that nobody strikes all the time. You may have missed the strike pocket, but it was by only a small margin. For instance, leaving a 10 pin on a good pocket hit usually indicates a miss of less than an inch. Leaving a 5 pin usually shows a miss of about an inch or so. One pin standing is what happens when the ball is thrown well, just not well enough to strike.

In this case, a radical change in ball location is not required. If you apply the 3-1-2 adjustment system, in which the target stays the same, the movement of the starting position will be in fractions of an inch. Small misses require small, precise adjustments. Adjustments on the approach of half an inch at a time are meaningful for the good bowler.

If you use the 3-4-5 angle adjustment system, expect to follow the same procedure. You may have to cut the 3-to-5 ratio into smaller increments in order to fine-tune the entry angle. Adjustments should be small and precise.

MAKING OTHER ADJUSTMENTS

For those who throw a hook, particularly a large hook, simply changing the angle on the lane may not be enough. Hook throwers play lane conditions, not just angles. The game becomes more complex as the interaction between the ball and the ever-changing lane surface becomes more dramatic. It is important to develop the proper adjustment tools. Ideally, the strategy for surmounting challenges should be in place before the challenges present themselves. (Adjusting to lane conditions is discussed in more detail in step 12.)

Too many bowlers get comfortable with only a certain area of the lane. This limits opportunities to create a scoring advantage when lane conditions change or are different. Many bowlers start the day scoring well, but as lane conditions change, their scoring pace declines. As oil pattern shifts, you need to move with it.

The feast-or-famine approach, in which a bowler is great on only one condition and struggles on others, is very frustrating. Instead, become a hunter. Learn to play all parts of the lane. Find the area of the lane that presents a playable line and an optimal attack angle to the pocket. Then you will feast, no matter when or where you bowl.

Parallel Move

In the angle adjustment strategies discussed earlier, the ball is projected at an angle in relation to the lane. The ball path will cross boards. When moving toward the middle, for instance, the ball will end up closer to the gutter as it gets

151

farther down the lane. If the ball is hooking too much, sending it out wider on the lane gives it more room to hook. If the size of the hook and the accompanying adjustment are both judged accurately, the ball will hook into the pocket instead of in front of it.

In some bowling centers, the outside parts of the lanes have considerably less oil than the middle. As a result, the wider you send the ball, the more it hooks. You will not get anywhere with standard adjustments. In some situations, the dry part of the lane is so dry the ball loses rotational energy. The ball will roll out—it will hook early and abruptly, then quit hooking altogether. Frictional drag will cause the ball to precess too soon; the rotational direction and the translational direction become the same long before the ball reaches the pins. The outside part of the lane appears unplayable. Now is the time for a parallel move.

The feet and the target move the same distance in the same direction. You are playing a new part of the lane up front where the ball crosses through the head of the lane. The ball travels on a new part of the lane farther down as well. The entire line has been moved. Use this adjustment until a controllable ball reaction is established, then use one of the two basic systems to fine-tune the line to the strike pocket.

Change of Visual Target

One way to compensate when the ball hooks without having to change the target line is to move the visual target up or down the lane. Most bowlers are comfortable with moving the target left or right, but it takes some practice to learn how to look closer or farther down the lane. Many bowling centers have synthetic lanes with no distinguishing characteristics. The targeting arrows may be the only visual attention-getter. The inconsistencies of natural wood's coloration can be helpful when targeting on the lane based on something other than the arrows.

Some manufacturers of synthetic lanes imprint alternating light and dark boards. One manufacturer (Brunswick) puts short lengths of dark coloration on specific boards at a point farther down the lane. In either case, these irregularities will help you find different areas to use when determining a target line.

Looking down the lane means to move your visual target down the lane as a way to delay the hook of the ball. This technique tends to change upper body position. The farther the target is down the lane, the more upright the body tends to be at the finish, which usually increases the loft of the ball. (Be careful not to create excessive loft.) The longer the ball is in the air, the less time it spends on the lane. Therefore, it will not grab the lane as soon. Also, bowlers who look farther down the lane tend to accentuate the follow-through, swinging through the ball rather than hitting up on it early. The exaggerated extension drives the ball to a later break point. This technique is useful when the lane begins to dry out. You may not want to abandon your current line to the pocket, but the ball is not holding the line as well as it was. The slight delay in the hook may be just enough to keep the ball in the pocket.

Looking short on the lane, moving the visual target in front of the arrows, will have the opposite effect. You will tend to lay the ball down early. If the ball is on the lane longer, it will have more time to get into a roll. On oily lanes, the ball stays in a skid longer; it does not move into the hook and roll soon enough. Looking short causes a slight increase in the forward tilt of the upper body. You will feel as if you are swinging down into the lane rather than swinging along it. In addition, bowlers tend to throw where they are looking. If the target is close, they will throw down into the lane. The release motion starts when you try to drive the hand down through the ball. Overall, the release is quicker and the loft minimal.

ACCURACY DEVELOPMENT

Table 10.1 lists performance characteristics of bowlers at different skill levels. As skill increases, improvements become evident in accuracy, velocity, speed consistency, and revolutions.

Table 10.1 Performance Based on Skill Level

Average	Initial velocity (mph)	Velocity variance (mph)	Target range (inches)	Entry angle (degrees)	Initial rotation (rpm)
139 or lower	15.5	1.10	6.8	1.4	77
140 to 149	15.5	0.85	5.9	2.2	118
150 to 159	17.3	0.97	4.8	2.3	133
160 to 169	17.0	0.79	4.6	2.6	156
170 to 179	16.9	0.77	4.1	3.1	177
180 to 189	17.2	0.76	3.9	3.7	210
190 to 199	17.7	0.75	3.5	3.6	235
200 to 209	18.1	0.71	3.5	4.2	272
210 to 219	18.2	0.58	2.5	4.4	285
220 or higher	18.5	0.60	2.1	5.2	374
Professional	18.9	0.47	1.7	5.9	385

The information in this table represents data collected from participants in the Computer Aided Tracking System (CATS) program. The CATS program is a setup of sensors and cameras installed on the lanes to measure characteristics of both the bowler and the ball. Various training institutes have this system in place. At certain times, CATS programs have been available at national tournaments; the ABC/WIBC headquarters in Greendale, Wisconsin, has a permanent installation. The goal of the program is to guide the development of an athlete's abilities based on empirical data, comparing the characteristics in the bowler's current game with the skill level he would like to achieve. Not everybody develops at the same rate. Certain elements of bowling may come easily for an individual even as he struggles with other elements.

Initial velocity is the ball's speed at release, an indicator of swing efficiency and footwork. Velocity variance is the ball speed variation from shot to shot. Target range accuracy is determined by noting the left-and-right error margin (at the arrows, 15 feet from the foul line) where 95 percent of the shots were thrown. Arguably, this is the most important characteristic. Accuracy is affected by footwork, swing line, timing, and body alignment.

Both the number of revolutions and the axis tilt play a part in the entry angle. Axis tilt, a product of the hand position at the release, is the most important. Revving the ball quickly will do no good if all the rotational movement is straight forward.

To track the initial rotation, tracer tape is put on the ball. Videotaping the release reveals just how far the tape moves for each frame on the video. This rotational velocity (angular movement per amount of time) is converted into revolutions per minute (rpm).

Improvement in a skill is noticeable from one level to the next. For example, initial velocity jumps from 15.5 in the average range of 140 to 149 to 17.3 in the range of 150 to 159. These thresholds come at different times for different characteristics, which is typical of skill development. Early in the learning process, you establish a consistency of footwork and rhythm. This naturally leads to ball velocity increases and speed consistency. Later on, the more difficult elements—body position control and release efficiency—begin to fall into place.

Whenever possible, use additional targeting aids on the lane. These attention-getters will confirm your accuracy and help you improve.

Purdue Target Practice

During one Purdue University team practice, I used targeting tape to lay out a line on the lane. After a few unsuccessful attempts to hit the tape let alone the pocket, one team member turned to me and said, "This isn't my line." My response was, "You only have one?" If you are willing to play only one line to the pocket, you will not be successful at higher bowling levels. That bowler did not bowl for Purdue the following year.

Often where you think you see the ball going is not where the ball actually goes.

Eye dominance plays a factor when determining what target the ball is rolling over. For instance, a right-handed bowler with left-eye dominance will miss the target more than it appears compared with a right-handed bowler who is also right-eye dominant. The eyes are watching from an angle that differs from the angle of the throw. When the brain processes the visual information, you may think you are hitting the target; in reality, you are not. To get around this problem, have a helper get in position directly behind your swing and tell you where the ball rolls.

Another solution is to place targets on the lane that give both visual and auditory feedback. Placing targets on the lane is solely a coach's prerogative, but the bowling center manager or proprietor must give permission. Not just anybody is allowed to stroll down the lane, dry off an area of oil, and place a target on the lane. Generally, only employees of the bowling center are allowed past the foul line. Ask permission before modifying the lane surface. From a liability point of view, do not be surprised if permission is denied.

As an instructor, I have had great success with medical tape. Be sure to use thick water-proof medical tape. This durable tape will not break down from the oil on the lane and stays in position despite balls rolling over it repeatedly. Generally, it will not leave a residue on the lane like other types of tape. In particular, avoid using masking tape, clear adhesive tape, or cloth medical tape.

The thickness of the medical tape makes quick removal and replacement easy. More important, the ball will make an audible "tha-dumb" sound as it rolls over the tape. This sound confirms that the ball has gone over the intended spot. If you don't hear it, you didn't hit it!

Less-experienced bowlers may have trouble distinguishing the sound of the ball rolling over the tape from the considerable background noises in a typical bowling center. Using a double thickness of tape will make the sound more distinct. When doubling the tape, do not put one piece directly over the other. Instead, stagger the placement to create a mini-ramp over which the ball passes (figure 10.7). Pay attention to where you place the tape; the glare of the lights or the masking units may obscure the marker.

Adhesive note pads also work well. Fold the piece at the adhesive line so it stands up (figure 10.8). The only problem with the note sheets is that they have height. The ball may hit them without necessarily rolling right over the spot.

A product on the market called the Accu-Wedge is a foam rubber wedge with an adhesive on the bottom. As the ball rolls over the pad, the pad flattens out. You will hear it roll over the wedge, but the pad is not thick enough to deflect the ball off course.

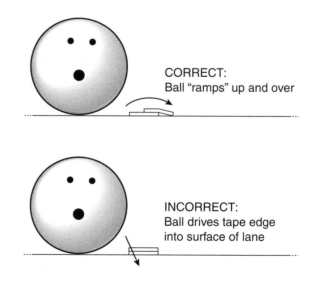

CORRECT:
Ball "ramps" up and over

INCORRECT:
Ball drives tape edge into surface of lane

Figure 10.7 Staggering tape on the lanes to create a mini-ramp.

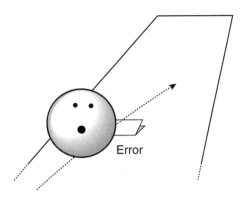

Figure 10.8 Use an adhesive note sheet as a marker.

When you are trying to focus on a particular spot on the lane, one extra target is usually enough. Remember, the arrows on the lane are permanent targets. The temporary target can be placed either in front of or past the target arrow. The placement of the extra target will influence the nature of the swing and the approach.

Two points define a line. As soon as possible, try to visualize target lines rather than just a target spot. Slight changes in the approach or the swing will change the angle to the target. If you find yourself thinking, *Hey, I hit my target! Why can't I get good results?* remember you may be hitting the target from a slightly different angle each time. Therefore, the ball ends up making contact with the pins at a different location each time.

Two targets on the lane allow for the line of the approach to match the target line down the lane. These two lines working together promote better footwork as well as a better swing. The first target usually is near the arrows; the second is farther down the lane. When setting up on the approach, your body alignment should be toward the first target. As you start into the motion, your focus should move up the line to the second target. This spotting down the lane reinforces a vision of the target line and promotes a better sense of a relaxed, free swing that extends out from the shoulder to the target.

A variety of games can challenge you to develop targeting skills or learn to play different parts of the lane. Pull your attention away from the actual score on the score sheet; be concerned only with the task.

Accuracy Drill 1. *Wiedman's Target Game*

This game is a test of accuracy.

Place two pieces of tape on the lane. The length of each piece of tape and the spacing between them vary depending on your skill level. If you are a beginner, each piece of tape should be 1 1/2 inches long, and the pieces should be placed 3 inches apart. This will give you an error margin of about 6 inches. Intermediate bowlers should place two 1-inch pieces of tape 2 inches apart on the lane. Skilled bowlers should use two 3/4-inch pieces of tape, set 1 1/2 inches apart.

Roll the ball between the pieces of tape. At this point, do not be concerned with pinfall or lane conditions. Your main objective is to establish concentration and targeting skills. Do not worry about shooting spares; with every throw of the ball, the primary goal is to throw between the tape. This drill focuses on the first 15 or 20 feet of the lane.

One game variation consists of 10 consecutive throws. If the ball rolls between the tape pieces and you do not hear it hit the tape, score the throw as a *strike*. If the ball hits one of the pieces of tape, meaning you were a little left or right of the target, score the throw as a *9 and a spare*. This error was small enough that you might have left

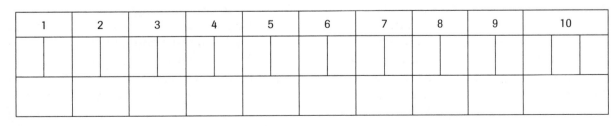

1	2	3	4	5	6	7	8	9	10

Figure 10.9 Scorecard for Wiedman's target game.

an easy spare to pick up. Score throws outside the range of the tape as an *8 and a miss.* Throws this inaccurate leave difficult spares. Record your scores in the scorecard shown in figure 10.9. Give yourself a bonus—add 3 pins to your final score—if you hit the target and throw a real strike.

Once you are consistently scoring "excellent" or "very good," make the spacing between the tape pieces smaller, or make the tape pieces themselves smaller.

Be creative, and always pursue a challenge. As certain tasks become easy with increased skill, find ways to push yourself to a new level.

To Increase Difficulty

- As skill improves, make the location and size of the targets more challenging. Once you can score 185 or better, decrease the spacing between the pieces of tape.

- If you are a skilled bowler, change the location of the tape as well. Putting the tape at different places on the lanes lets you practice lane play as well as accuracy. Two 1/2-inch pieces of tape separated by 1 1/2 inches yields an error margin of only 3 inches. Aim small, miss small.

- Try moving your starting position on the lane without moving the tape. This helps you practice different angles on the lane.

- Once you are hitting the space consistently, start paying attention to where the ball hits the pins. Try to adapt to lane conditions. Find a line to the strike pocket while still trying to throw through the predetermined spot.

Success Check

- Setup is properly aligned to the target.
- Focus on the space between the tape pieces.
- Watch the ball roll through the space.
- Listen for the sound of the ball rolling over the tape. This indicates inaccuracy.

Score Your Success

Excellent: 210 or more = 10 points

Very good: 185 to 209 = 8 points

Good: 160 to 184 = 6 points

Average: 135 to 159 = 4 points

Below average: 110 to 134 = 2 points

Beginner: 109 or lower = 1 point

Your score ___

Accuracy Drill 2. *Mark Roth's Target Practice*

I attribute this game to professional bowler Mark Roth, one of bowling's all-time greats. He was one of the dominant players on the tour during the late 1970s and early 1980s. In a bowling article, he indicated that this was his favorite practice drill.

In this very simple drill, you get to practice on all parts of the lane. The oil on a lane is not evenly distributed, so each part of the lane gives a different ball reaction. The goal of the drill is to learn the correct combination of release, speed, and ball selection that keeps the ball in the pocket no matter what line is played on the lane.

Line up using the first arrow. Attempt 10 throws, making small adjustments on the approach or with the release until you hit the pocket. Keep playing only the first arrow for all 10 throws.

After 10 throws, line up over the second arrow. Repeat the drill. Continue moving to a new arrow every 10 throws.

After 10 throws over the fourth arrow, go back to the first arrow and start again. Keep track of your first-ball average, recording your scores on the scorecard shown in figure 10.10.

To calculate your first-ball average on each arrow, divide the total number of pins for that arrow by 10. A good first-ball average for a beginner is 6.5, for an intermediate player is 7.75, and for a skilled player is 8.75. Go back and practice over the arrow where you scored your lowest first-ball average.

Throw	First arrow	Second arrow	Third arrow	Fourth arrow
1				
2				
3				
4				
5				
6				
7				
8				
9				
10				
Total				
	÷ 10	÷ 10	÷ 10	÷ 10
Average				

Figure 10.10 Scorecard for Mark Roth's target practice drill.

To Increase Difficulty

- Set a particular criterion for moving from one arrow to the next. For example, do not move to the next arrow until you hit the pocket four times in a row.

- If you have more than one ball, do not change balls. Instead, find the correct combination of speed and release that allows the ball to work from any line.

Success Check

- Focus on the target.
- Watch the ball roll over the target.
- Pay attention to body position and footwork direction each time you adjust for a new target line.

Score Your Success

For each arrow played, rate your skill.

Excellent: first-ball average of 8.5 or higher = 10 points

Very good: first-ball average of 7.75 to 8.49 = 8 points

Good: first-ball average of 7.0 to 7.74 = 6 points

Average: first-ball average of 6.25 to 6.99 = 4 points

Below average: first-ball average of 5.5 to 6.24 = 2 points

Needs work: first-ball average lower than 5.5 = 0 points

Your score ___

Accuracy Drill 3. *Swedish National Team Drill*

The Swedish national team has enjoyed considerable success in international competition. Because lane maintenance practices vary so much around the world, international competition presents a unique challenge for the experienced bowler. Even within the same city you can find considerable variation in lane conditions from one bowling center to the next.

This drill emphasizes keeping the ball in play. The goal is to make quality shots. Lucky strikes are just that—luck! And luck eventually runs out. On the other hand, a quality shot is something you can depend on. It is only a matter of time before quality shots pay off. Strikes are nice but useless if open frames follow them.

The scoring system is very easy. You can keep track of how you are doing without writing anything down. If you hit the strike pocket and strike, you score 2 points. If you hit the strike pocket and spare, you get 1 point. If you miss the strike pocket, regardless of whether you strike or spare, you score zero points. An open frame, whether you hit the pocket or not, is worth minus 1 point. Missing a single-pin spare is worth minus 2 points. Play a 10-frame game.

One of the ideas of this game is to not reward lucky strikes. Somebody who is throwing the ball all over the map and still scoring well is not reliable. Strikes can happen in all sorts of unusual ways. Just because somebody is scoring well

157

does not mean she is bowling well. This practice scorekeeping system helps discern, to a certain extent, the quality of the performance.

I have used this scoring system when coaching my high school team. In our conference, seven players are on the roster, but only five bowl during the game. If a few bowlers are struggling, I need to determine who sits out the next game. It can be difficult, amid all the distraction of intense competition, to remember 50 frames. This simple plus–minus system allows me to recognize who is making the quality shots. I would rather use a player who is keeping the ball close, even if his score is not very high. This player may be only one small adjustment away from a great game. The player who has as many minus frames as he does plus frames is just as likely to start throwing splits as he is to throw strikes.

Success Check

- Swing is relaxed and smooth.
- Maintain unwavering focus on the target.
- Adjust for changing lane conditions.
- Use practical spare-shooting strategy.

Score Your Success

Perfect: 20 = 15 points

Outstanding: 16 to 19 = 12 points

Excellent: 12 to 15 = 10 points

Good: 8 to 11 = 8 points

Average: 4 to 7 = 6 points

Needs work: 0 to 3 = 4 points

Weak: –4 to –1 = 2 points

Poor: –5 or lower = 0 points

Your score ___

Accuracy Drill 4. *Call Your Shot*

This drill requires you to hit your target as you bowl a regular game. If you do not hit your target, subtract pins from the total. If you do hit the target, add pins to the total. You must identify the target you intend to roll over before every shot.

Having a partner who will watch each throw makes it easier to confirm that you are rolling over the intended target. An exact board number identifies a target. Allow one board error left and one board error right. This creates a three-board area in which to roll the ball.

Bowl a regular 10-frame game. Keep track of targeting for the first ball (strike throws) only. If you miss your called target, subtract 3 pins from the throw. If you hit your called target, add 3 pins to the throw. Perfect targeting will add 30 pins (perhaps as many as 36) to your final score. If you mark in the 10th frame, you get one extra throw. If you strike in the 10th frame, take two extra throws.

Success Check

- Use good judgment when determining your target.

Score Your Success

Add 30 pins or more = 10 points

Add 25 to 29 pins = 8 points

Add 20 to 24 pins = 6 points

Add 15 to 19 pins = 4 points

Add 10 to 14 pins = 2 points

Your score ___

SUCCESS SUMMARY

Successful strike targeting requires the following:

- Focus. See the target, hit the target.
- Assessment or evaluation. Did you achieve your goals? If not, what was missing?
- Strategy. What changes should you make, physically or on the lane, to make the next shot better?
- Implementation. Trust yourself to do what needs to be done. No second-guessing on the approach.

The important element for finding a strike line is shot consistency—you must have a reliable physical game. Targeting systems work only if you can hit the target. The inability to throw the ball the same way over an identified target is what makes making adjustments (and judging changes in lane conditions) so difficult. You cannot determine with any assurance what the problem might be. It could be the chosen line to the pocket (which requires strategic changes), or it could be your technique (which requires identifying and correcting performance errors).

As you develop a more consistent physical game and can reliably throw the ball the way you want and where you want, the targeting systems will start to pay off. This step describes two basic systems: the 3-1-2 pivot system and the 3-4-5 angle shift system.

The 3-1-2 system allows the bowler to change the location of the ball. The bowler needs to accurately assess the size of the error (how far the ball was from the desired strike pocket when it contacted the pins) before making any adjustments to the starting position.

The 3-4-5 system allows the bowler to change the angle of the ball as it enters the strike pocket without changing where the ball makes contact with the pins. This is an important fine-tuning element. With this system, adjust the visual target and the starting position in the same direction. For every three-board adjustment of the target, move the starting position five boards.

The 1-to-2 system, a simple variation of the 3-4-5 system, is a rough approximation of the 3-to-5 ratio. This easy-to-remember system allows for precise adjustments and can also be applied to adjust for changing lane conditions.

Review your drill scores. Record your scores in the spaces that follow and total them. If you score at least 40 points, you are ready to move on to the next step. If you score fewer than 40 points, review the sections that are giving you trouble, then repeat the drills.

Accuracy Drills

1. Wiedman's Target Game	___ out of 10	
2. Mark Roth's Target Practice	___ out of 10	
3. Swedish National Team Drill	___ out of 15	
4. Call Your Shot	___ out of 10	
Total	___ *out of 45*	

It would be nice to strike every time you throw the ball, but nobody is perfect. The sport of bowling is too challenging for this to happen. Sure, some highly skilled (and maybe just a little bit lucky) bowlers manage to throw 20, 25, or even more strikes in a row, but this is rare. At some point, they stop throwing strikes.

Most of us do not strike in even half the frames. That means almost every bowler will have to shoot at a spare in a majority of his or her frames. Even for the most elite bowlers, spare shooting is a critical part of consistently high scores. The ability to fill frames is the earmark of the highly skilled bowler. In fact, when asked, most elite professional bowlers confess that they did not reach their level of success until they developed reliable spare-shooting strategies. Simply put, you cannot throw enough strikes to make up for the lost pin count that results from poor spare shooting. In the long run, poor spare shooting holds back a bowler's improvement. We all want to roll high scores; spare shooting is a critical part of consistently scoring well. Strategies for shooting spares when the bowler rolls a less than perfect first ball is the topic of the next step.

Using a Spare-Shooting System

Every time you don't strike, you will be presented with a spare opportunity. Strikes are difficult to achieve. Even at the professional level, almost half of all frames include spare chances. Because relatively few frames have strikes, spares become very important for a bowler's success.

To put it another way, open frames negate the positive effects of strikes. Every time there is an open frame in the middle of a game, the bowler will need to throw two strikes in a row (a double) twice or three strikes once to have a chance of shooting a score of 200. Once three or four open frames occur, there is almost no chance of rolling a respectable score.

On the other hand, a decent score is achievable from nothing but spare shooting. An all-spares game can be as high as 190. A score of 190 is considerably above what the typical bowler scores. For many of the simpler spares—single pins or two pins next to each other—the error margin is much greater than for a strike ball. Generally, spares are easy, strikes are tough. It makes sense to put a lot of practice time into what's easy. It is very rewarding and more likely to have an immediate positive impact on your game.

This step covers two basic spare-shooting systems. One is a pivoting system. Remember

the pivot (3-1-2) system described in the previous step for strike adjustments? This is simply an expansion of that system. Instead of correcting for an errant shot, use the system to intentionally throw to the left or right at the remaining pins in order to make the spare.

The other system is a modification of the pivot system, and it applies to those who may have a nonstandard strike starting position. For bowlers whose normal strike position starts very far left or right on the approach, adjusting from the strike starting position as a means of shooting spares may not be altogether practical.

As with all targeting systems, it is critical to know exactly where the footwork starts. When adjusting the starting position, movements must be very precise. Counting boards is as important for shooting spares as it is for throwing strikes.

These basic systems apply to most players in a majority of playing situations. However, they are only a starting point. You may very well develop your own unique system. As you become more serious about the game and bowl on a wide variety of lane conditions, you may find it necessary to alter the basic systems to fit your needs. Do not be afraid to tweak these strategies.

3-6-9 AND 4-8-12 PIVOT SYSTEMS

Spare shooting is a variation of the pivoting system used for strike adjusting. If moving right can correct an errant strike throw, steering it back to the left, moving to the right can be used to intentionally throw further left to pick up a spare.

Why intentionally throw to the right or left? Most spares are not in the middle of the lane. To improve your score, you must learn to throw left or right of center. Once you establish a line to the strike pocket, adjustments from the strike line (figure 11.1) allow you to shoot any spare.

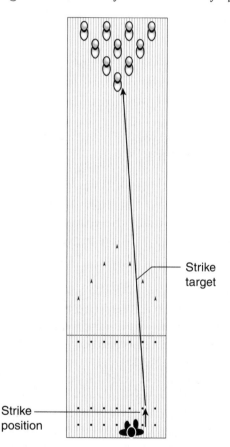

Figure 11.1 Strike line for a right-handed bowler. Spare adjustments will be made based on this strike line and the strike target.

There are six basic adjustments, three to the right for left-side spares (figure 11.2) and three to the left for right-side spares (figure 11.3). For spares in the center, there is no adjustment. For a right-handed bowler, here are the seven basic spare positions:

- Left corner, 7 pin (9-board adjustment to the right)
- Left, 4 pin (6-board adjustment to the right)
- Left center, 2 pin and 8 pin (3-board adjustment to the right)
- Center, 1 pin and 5 pin (no adjustment; use strike line)
- Right center, 3 pin and 9 pin (4-board adjustment to the left)
- Right, 6 pin (8-board adjustment to the left)
- Right corner, 10 pin (12-board adjustment to the left)

Focus on one pin only. For a group of pins, identify the key pin, usually the one in front, and adjust for that pin. Remember, always walk toward the target. After setting up on the approach, turn the body—not just the shoulders—and face the target. The line of the approach should be oriented toward the target, not straight in relation to the lane.

Why move only three boards when adjusting to the right but four boards when going left? The right-handed bowler has already established an angle from right to left because of the hook of the ball or the starting position on the lane. When throwing with your natural angle, moving in three-board increments should be enough. When throwing against your natural angle, four-board moves are needed.

The illustrations shown in figures 11.1, 11.2, and 11.3 are from a right-handed bowler's perspective. Left-handed bowlers must reverse the numbers. You will still move left for a right-side spare, just not as far. You will still move right for a left-side spare, but more than a right-handed bowler would. Figure 11.4 shows the left-handed bowler's strike line and target.

A left-handed bowler can also make six basic adjustments, three to the left for right-side spares (figure 11.5) and three to the right for left-side spares (figure 11.6). For spares in the center, no adjustment is needed. For a left-handed bowler, here are the seven basic spare positions:

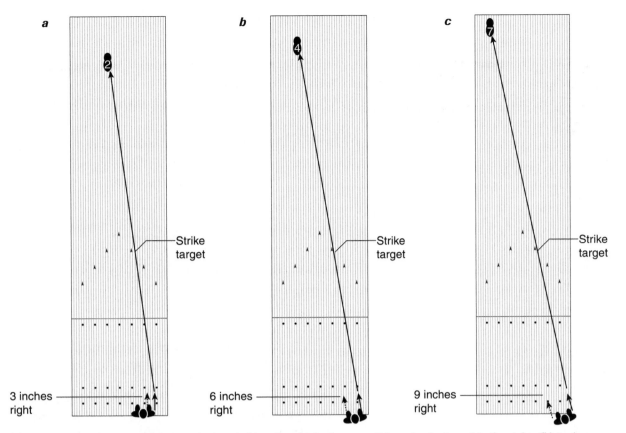

Figure 11.2 Left-side spares for a right-handed bowler: *(a)* 2-pin spare, 3-board adjustment to the right; *(b)* 4-pin spare, 6-board adjustment to the right; *(c)* 7-pin spare, 9-board adjustment to the right.

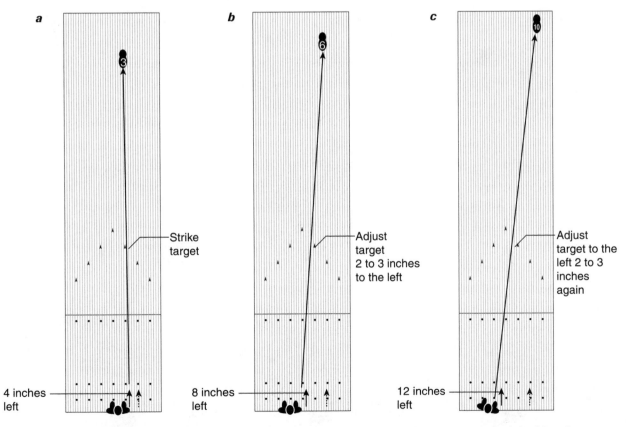

Figure 11.3 Right-side spares for a right-handed bowler: *(a)* 3-pin spare, 4-board adjustment to the left; *(b)* 6-pin spare, 8-board adjustment to the left; *(c)* 10-pin spare, 12-board adjustment to the left.

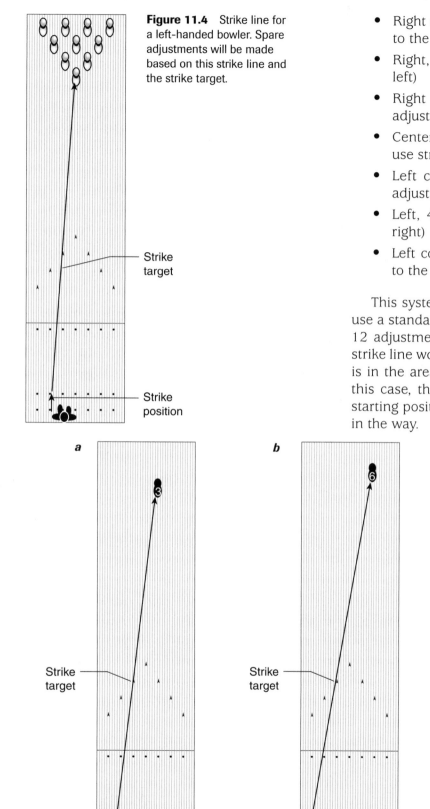

Figure 11.4 Strike line for a left-handed bowler. Spare adjustments will be made based on this strike line and the strike target.

Strike target

Strike position

- Right corner, 10 pin (9-board adjustment to the left)

- Right, 6 pin (6-board adjustment to the left)

- Right center, 3 pin and 9 pin (3-board adjustment to the left)

- Center, 1 pin and 5 pin (no adjustment; use strike line)

- Left center, 2 pin and 8 pin (4-board adjustment to the right)

- Left, 4 pin (8-board adjustment to the right)

- Left corner, 7 pin (12-board adjustment to the right)

This system will work well for bowlers who use a standard strike target. The 3-6-9 and 4-8-12 adjustments from a previously established strike line work best if the bowler's strike target is in the area of the second or third arrow. In this case, there is enough room to move the starting position without the ball return getting in the way.

a Strike target

3 inches left

b Strike target

6 inches left

c Strike target

9 inches left

Figure 11.5 Right-side spares for a left-handed bowler: *(a)* 3-pin spare, 3-board adjustment to the left; *(b)* 6-pin spare, 6-board adjustment to the left; *(c)* 10-pin spare, 9-board adjustment to the left.

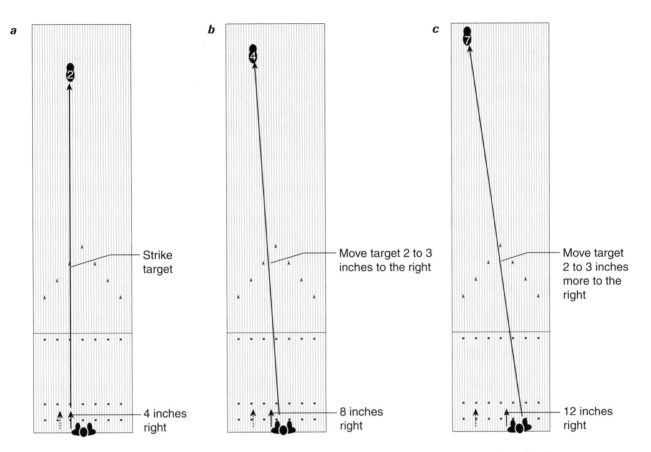

Figure 11.6 Left-side spares for a left-handed bowler: *(a)* 2-pin spare, 4-board adjustment to the right; *(b)* 4-pin spare, 8-board adjustment to the right; *(c)* 7-pin spare, 12-board adjustment to the right.

For players who use less-common strike targets (such as first or fourth arrows), this spare system may not always work. If you find the ball return consistently getting in the way when making the standard adjustment for spares, you may need to adopt a spare-shooting system completely independent of your strike line.

SECTIONING THE PIN SETUP

One spare-shooting system that works independently of the strike line is to section the pin setup. With this system, the pin triangle is broken into three sections—right corner, left corner, and middle. The left-corner and right-corner spare lines have nothing to do with the strike line (figure 11.7).

For a right-corner spare, find a line to the 10 pin. Play as much angle across the lane as you comfortably can. Take lane conditions out of the equation by letting the ball cross through the area with the heaviest oil. Use a straight ball release. (Learn one if you don't have one!)

Anticipate targeting somewhere near the fourth (middle) arrow. Adjust four boards to the right from the 10-pin starting position to shoot for the 6 pin.

For a left-corner spare, find a line to the 7 pin. Once again, throw much less hook than normal, and keep the ball on the oil. Adjust four boards to the right from the 7-pin starting position to shoot for the 4 pin.

For a middle-of-the-lane spare, use the already established strike target. Unless you have a very strong hooking ball, a normal release can be used. Adjust four boards to the right from the

165

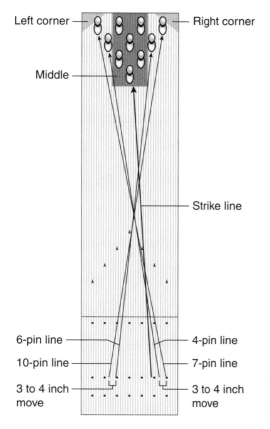

Left corner — Right corner

Middle

Strike line

6-pin line — 4-pin line

10-pin line — 7-pin line

3 to 4 inch move — 3 to 4 inch move

strike starting position to shoot the 2 pin. Adjust four boards to the left from the strike starting position to shoot the 3 pin.

Be careful about back-row spares. Because the pins are farther away, the ball will need to roll farther on the lane before making contact with the pins. For example, a ball that hooks into the 2 pin is likely to hook past the 8 pin. Based on the spacing of the pins, the 8 pin is almost 21 inches farther away than the 2 pin. For most spare-shooting scenarios, a straighter ball is usually the best choice. Learn to tone down a strong hook ball.

Figure 11.7 Right-corner, left-corner, and middle spare lines. The spare lines for left- and right-corner spares are independent of the strike line.

FOCUSING ON A KEY PIN

For all spares, there is a particular place the ball must be thrown in order to convert the spare. If you focus on a particular pin—the key pin—you can reduce almost all spare setups to one of seven basic positions. There are 1,024 possible spare combinations (most of which are never seen); you cannot have 1,024 different strategies.

Using the seven key pins is a way of limiting potential confusion. Simply think of where you want the ball to end up, determine which key pin is closest to that position, and then make your spare-shooting adjustment for that pin.

This is particularly useful when faced with difficult spares or splits. In these situations, it is unlikely you will be able to make the ball hit all the pins. You need to put the ball in a place that will cause it to deflect one pin into another. Chances are, that place is close to one of the key pins.

Now you won't have to panic—you have a strategy for making almost all spares. Think of

a split as a variation of a single pin. You know the strategy for any single pin; therefore, you have a strategy for every spare.

Figures 11.8 and 11.9 illustrate examples of using certain key pins for making spares. Do not be too concerned if you do not make these spares all the time. Many of the difficult spare attempts—splits and washouts—have error margins of less than half an inch. The more extreme splits, such as the 6-7 or 4-10, have error margins of about 1/4 inch. The placement of the ball must be very precise. Focusing on a key pin gives you an idea of where the ball needs to go. You will not be able to throw the ball exactly where you need to every time. The key-pin strategy will get you close, though. Be confident. Every once in a while, you will make a difficult spare that will be the highlight of the day. Every year the USBC presents award patches as recognition for the thousands of 7-10 splits made by league bowlers.

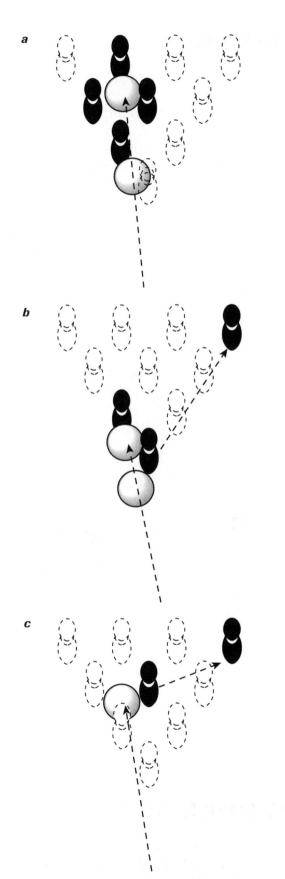

Do not let the disappointment of an errant first shot keep you from focusing on your second one. Every spare is makable! Put the last shot out of your head. Focus only on the task at hand:

- Determine where you want to put the ball.
- Identify what key pin is closest to that location.
- Relax; take a deep breath.
- Make your adjustment based on your spare-shooting strategy.

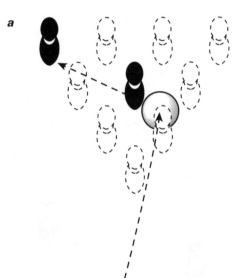

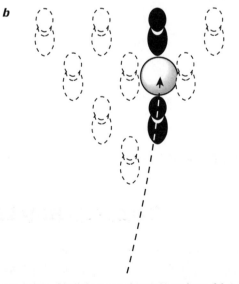

Figure 11.8 Variations on the 2 pin as key: *(a)* 2-4-5-8 bucket; *(b)* 1-2-10 washout; *(c)* 5-10 split.

Figure 11.9 Variations on the 3 pin as key: *(a)* 5-7 split; *(b)* 3-9 double wood.

SHOOTING SPLITS

When shooting at a split, you may need to roll the ball at an imaginary spot. The key pin you want to throw at may not be one of the pins standing. The location of the ball is what is important.

First, determine where you want the ball to go. For most splits, you need to hit the outside of the pin in order to slide it over into the other pin. Once you know where you want the ball to end up, determine what key pin is closest. Make your adjustments on the approach as if you are throwing at that pin, whether or not it is actually standing.

Some splits are almost impossible to make; the standing pins are directly across the lane from each other, and a considerable distance separates them (figure 11.10). The 7-10 and the 4-6 splits come to mind. With these splits, make sure you knock down at least one pin. This is called *saving count*. In some nearly impossible splits, such as the 4-6-7-10 (called the big four) and the 4-6-7-9-10 (Greek church), several pins remain standing. Unless you are in a desperate do-or-die situation, get as many of the remaining pins as possible.

It is amazing how many needless pins of count are thrown away because of inane attempts at nearly impossible spares. The bowler ends up getting no pins at all, which is particularly hurtful after a strike. On occasion, you will hear savvy bowlers reminding less-experienced teammates that one is two when shooting at a spare. What this means is, after a strike, the pins on the spare attempt count twice. The pins count in the frame they are knocked down in as well as back in the frame with the strike. In this situation, every pin missed on the spare attempt is two pins lost from the final score.

Unless you are near the end of the game and making the spare is absolutely critical for determining the outcome of the match, you are better off being conservative in your spare attempts. Far more matches are lost because of needless loss of pin count during the game than are won by someone converting an almost impossible split.

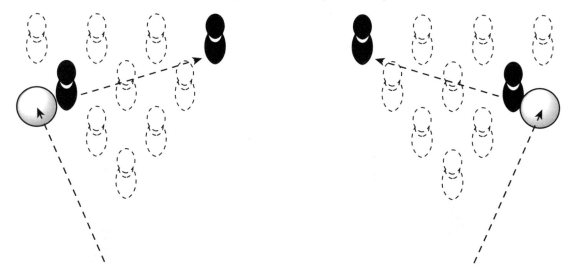

Figure 11.10 On nearly impossible splits, practice the corner pins: *(a)* 4-10 split; *(b)* 6-7 split.

SPARE-SHOOTING PRACTICE

Many bowlers are so concerned with throwing strikes they do not take the time to practice spare shooting. Over time, even bowlers with very high averages strike only 55 to 60 percent of the time. That means they have to shoot spares in 40 to 45 percent of their frames. An average bowler can expect to deal with spares much more frequently.

Spare-Shooting Drill 1. *Corner Pin Game*

This classic game of targeting and concentration goes by other names (lo ball, the 7 and 10 game). The basic premise of the game is to bowl the lowest possible score without throwing the ball in the gutter.

The goal is to pick off just the 7 pin and the 10 pin out of the entire set of pins. Try for the lowest possible pinfall on each throw. Gutter throws are assessed a penalty. Some versions of the game assign a particular pin count to gutter balls, such as 10 pins a gutter ball on any first throw, and 5 pins for missing all of the remaining pins on any second throw. Other versions of the game score marks for any gutter ball: a strike if the first ball is in the gutter; a spare if the second throw gets no pin count.

Whether you keep score by hand or use the automatic scoring found at most bowling centers might influence what version you play. Some automatic scoring systems are programmed with a version of the lo-ball game.

Bowl a 10-frame game. Throw twice in each frame, one ball at each corner. The lowest total after penalties are assessed wins. For each zero count on a first ball, add 10 pins to the final score. For each zero count on a second ball (missing all of the pins that remain standing), add 5 pins to the final score. (Automatic scoring will take care

of adding strikes and spares; don't worry about penalties for these.)

Example: You get a 7 on the first ball then miss all of the remaining three pins on the next ball. That frame is worth 12 points (7 pins plus a 5-point penalty). The scoring system would record the 7 as usual; you just have to remember to add 5 more to the final total at the end of the game.

Success Check

- Apply corner-pin spare-shooting strategies.
- Make sure the adjustments are large enough to get the ball to each corner.
- Be conservative! Keep the ball on the lanes.

Score Your Success

Perfect game: 20 = 20 points

Excellent: 21 to 50 = 15 points

Very good: 51 to 80 = 12 points

Good: 81 to 100 = 10 points

Average: 101 to 120 = 8 points

Below average: 121 to 140 = 6 points

Needs work: 141 or more = 0 points

Your score ___

Spare-Shooting Drill 2. *Bowling Golf*

The goal of bowling golf is to shoot below par. Par for the game is 70.

Sometimes pins roll around and knock over other pins, giving you a higher score in a lo-ball game than you would otherwise deserve. In this version of a low-score game, pinfall is not considered at all. The bowler need only recognize which pin is contacted first. There are seven key pins the ball could hit—1, 2, 3, 4, 6, 7, or 10.

Start with a score of 170. Subtract the numerical value of the pin first contacted from the total. For example, if you take out just the 7 pin on one throw and the 10 pin on the other, you would subtract 17 for the frame. Shooting 10 frames of –17 would bring you down to zero. Do not subtract any points for any ball that ends up in the gutter or does not hit any pins at all. The goal is to hit some pins but as few as possible with every throw.

Every first throw of a frame is a corner-pin practice. Make sure there is a full line of pins down the side you are throwing at when attempting your second ball.

Strikes and spares are not recorded. Hitting the headpin allows you to subtract 1 from the total. If you throw a strike on the first throw, a second throw in the frame must be taken anyway.

A good strategy for a low score in this game is to play for the 4 pin and the 6 pin. Hitting close to each corner yet staying well away from the gutters gives you –10 for each frame. After 10 frames of –10, your score would be down to 70.

From a practical point of view, throwing a ball in a location that hits the 6 pin first would also take out the 10 pin in a normal game situation. The same is true for the 4 pin and 7 pin on the other side. How challenging is it to pick a corner pin out of a full rack of pins? You have only about a 2 1/2-inch margin between the gutter and the next pin over. This is about the size of the strike pocket. It takes considerable discipline and concentration to achieve this on a consistent basis.

Success Check

- Know what your strike line is.
- Make adjustments based on one of the spare-shooting systems.
- If not getting to the corners consistently, modify your starting position or adjust your target on the lane.

Score Your Success

Perfect score: 0 = 20 points

Golfing god: 1 to 49 = 15 points

Below par: 50 to 64 = 12 points

Par: 65 to 79 = 10 points

Over par: 80 to 94 = 8 points

In the rough: 95 to 109 = 6 points

Bunker buddy: 110 to 124 = 4 points

Gutter duster: 125 or more = 2 points

Your score ___

Spare-Shooting Drill 3. *Playing for Both Pockets*

It is not always easy to practice other types of spares. For example, learning how to intentionally throw at the other strike pocket is a very useful skill. For a right-handed bowler, this would be the 1-2 pocket. Learning to put the ball in this area is good practice for shooting the 2-8 spare, the 2-4-5 spare, and the 2-4-5-8 bucket spare as well as washouts such as the 1-2-10.

One simple practice drill is to throw the first ball at the 3-6 pocket. If you are successful, you will leave the 1-2 or the 1-2-4 standing. Your second throw is at these remaining pins.

Bowl 10 frames. Keep track of your score on a sheet of paper.

- Hit the 3-6 pocket on the first ball (+5)
- Hit the 1-2 pocket on the second ball (+3)

If you miss the 3-6 pocket on the first ball, the best you can do is break even for the frame. You must knock over all the remaining pins, for a real spare. This is worth 0 for the frame.

If you hit the 3-6 pocket on the first ball, the rest of the pins should be knocked over if you hit the 1-2 pocket on the second ball. If you hit the 3-6 pocket on the first ball and pins remain standing after the second ball, subtract the number of pins left standing from your total.

Score Your Success

Perfect: 80 = 20 points

Excellent: 70 to 79 = 15 points

Very good: 50 to 69 = 10 points

Average: 30 to 49 = 8 points

Below average: 0 to 29 = 6 points

Needs more work: –1 or lower = 0 points

Your score ___

Spare-Shooting Drill 4. *Modern-Day Kingpin*

More than 150 years ago, the most common form of bowling was ninepins. The pins were set in a diamond shape. In one version of this game, the objective was to knock down all the pins except the one in the middle—the kingpin.

This spare-shooting drill uses the modern triangular pin setup. The headpin is the kingpin, and the goal is to leave just the headpin standing. This requires knowing where to aim in order to hit the 3-6 pocket and the 2-4 pocket. Proper practice of this skill improves your chances of hitting both left-side and right-side spares.

Bowl a 10-frame game. If you leave just the headpin after two throws, you earn 5 points. If you hit the headpin on the first throw, subtract 5 points. If you hit the headpin on the second throw, subtract 3 points.

If you hit the headpin on the first throw and pins remain standing, you will have a chance for a saving throw. To save the frame after hitting the headpin on the first throw, you must knock down all the remaining pins. The saving throw is worth 2 points.

If you throw a strike on the first throw, there is no chance for a saving throw. For a strike, subtract 3 points.

Score Your Success

Spare-shooting royalty: 50 = 20 points

The king is pleased: 30 to 49 = 15 points

Commoner: 10 to 29 = 10 points

Call the guards: –10 to 9 = 7 points

Spare-shooting serf: –23 to –11 = 5 points

Throw 'em in the moat: –24 or lower = 0 points

Your score ___

Spare-Shooting Drill 5. *Roll-of-the-Dice Kingpin*

This game involves a pair of dice, a little bit of luck, and a lot of strategy. Your goal is to leave one pin—the kingpin—standing. The pin that is named king for any given frame depends on a roll of the dice.

Roll a pair of dice. Whatever the dice add up to is the kingpin for that frame. If you leave just the kingpin after two throws of the ball, score 1 point for the frame. If the kingpin is standing but other pins remain standing as well, the frame is a wash. Do not add or subtract any points. If the kingpin is knocked down on either the first or second throw, subtract 1 point for the frame. If you roll an 11 or 12, there is no kingpin for that frame. All the pins must be knocked down in order to record 1 point. Shoot 10 frames with 10 rolls of the dice.

Score Your Success

King for the day: 10 = 20 points

Spare-shooting knighthood: 7 to 9 = 15 points

Royal guard: 4 to 6 = 10 points

Invitation to the castle: 2 to 3 = 7 points

Squire duties: 0 to 1 = 5 points

The king disapproves: –3 to –1 = 3 points

Off with the head: –4 or lower = 0 points

Your score ___

Spare-Shooting Drill 6. *Beggar Thy Neighbor*

Spare practice can involve more than one bowler. Here is a bowling version of the card game beggar thy neighbor.

Each person bowls the first throw of his or her opponent's frame. The first bowler attempts to leave the most difficult spare possible. The opponent takes the second throw of the frame in an attempt to pick up the remaining pins. The goal of the game is to leave enough difficult spares that the opponent's score is kept low. Gutter balls are not allowed. Switch leadoff bowlers every frame. Remember, you throw your opponent's first ball, and your opponent throws your first ball. The winner is the one with the highest score.

A leadoff bowler who is especially daring could try to take out just the 7 pin or 10 pin, leaving as many pins as possible. On the other hand, the leadoff bowler could try to hit the headpin head-on, leaving a nearly impossible split for the second bowler. This tactic may backfire, though. Hitting the headpin could result in a strike! If the leadoff bowler inadvertently throws a strike, it is awarded to the opponent; the opponent will not need to shoot at a spare. Hitting the headpin might also result in a high pinfall for the second bowler.

Score Your Success

You win the game = 5 points

Your score ___

SUCCESS SUMMARY

For the beginning bowler, spare-shooting is the best way to improve scores. Strikes are difficult. The size of the strike pocket is a few inches at best. For those who throw a straight ball, the strike pocket is barely 1 inch across. On the other hand, most single-pin spares have better than a 13-inch error margin—the width of the ball (8.59 inches) plus the width of a pin (4.776 inches).

For corner-pin spares, the gutter does take away a few inches from the outside. Even then, the error margin for a corner-pin spare is about 9.4 inches. It makes sense to spend a decent amount of practice time on an easier aspect of the game that, for most bowlers, has the most immediate positive impact on scoring.

Without a doubt, as your strike ball becomes more accurate, the spares you leave will become easier. You will have more one- and two-pin combinations as opposed to the near endless variety of the more difficult spares. Although strike practice is always a prime concern, it should not be done to the exclusion of sound spare practice.

Most spares can be made by adjusting from an already established strike line. Start with what you are comfortable with. Most spare attempts are based on six adjustments—three to the right (the 3, 6, and 10 pins) and three to the left (the 2, 4, and 7 pins).

Review your drill scores. Record your scores in the spaces that follow and total them. If you score at least 90 points, you are ready to move on to the next step. If you score fewer than 90 points, review the sections that are giving you trouble, then repeat the drills.

Spare-Shooting Drills

1. Corner Pin Game   ___ out of 20

2. Bowling Golf   ___ out of 20

3. Playing for Both Pockets   ___ out of 20

4. Modern-Day Kingpin   ___ out of 20

5. Roll-of-the-Dice Kingpin   ___ out of 20

6. Beggar Thy Neighbor   ___ out of 5

Total   ___ *out of 105*

The last two steps discuss spare-shooting and strike-throwing strategies. These basic strategies are applicable to many situations. Bowling, however, has some unforeseen complexities. The most important of these is lane conditions.

Bowling presents an ever-changing environment. Every throw of the ball changes the lane conditions. The best bowlers are those who can modify their basic strategies to accommodate for the wide variety of lane conditions the sport presents.

You cannot overlook versatility in physical performance. That is why a large portion of this book concerns itself with physical skill development. It is the combination of physical skills, versatility, and strategy that makes for successful performance.

The stage on which you bowl is the lane surface. Your ability to recognize variations and potential changes in lane conditions and then modify your skill set to adjust to the changes defines you as a bowler. The variety of conditions a bowler must learn to recognize and the means to adapt to those conditions is the topic of our next step.

Adjusting to Lane Conditions

Lane conditions are constantly changing. The great challenge in bowling is to recognize the changes and devise a strategy to overcome them.

Bowling alleys put a thin layer of oil on the lanes to protect the lane surface against the friction of the ball. In reality, the oil also can be used to manipulate scoring, sometimes to the bowler's benefit and sometimes not.

Every bowling center oils the lanes differently, so every bowling center presents a unique performance environment. Few standards have been established to dictate the amount of oil and how it is distributed down the lanes. The USBC uses a standard called a *unit of oil,* a specific volume of oil spread over a certain square footage of area. The USBC mandates that a minimum depth of three units of oil must be on every board that oil is applied to.

What does this mean for the average bowler? Almost nothing! Bowlers are not allowed to reach out and touch the lanes to test how much oil is out there. In fact, three units represents a very thin film of oil. How does one judge how much oil is on the lanes? Trial and error.

Some centers run the oil for only 20 to 25 feet past the foul line. A few others choose a conditioning pattern in excess of 40 feet, as long as the boards have at least three units. The depth

of the oil is also subject to the discretion of each individual center. Some leave their lanes relatively dry, causing the ball to hook nearly as soon as it touches the lane. Others apply so much oil to the lanes the ball has almost no chance to hook at all.

The pattern of distribution must also be considered, not just how far down the lane the oil goes but also how it is distributed from left to right. There is no requirement that the oil be applied evenly from gutter to gutter. As you move left to right across the width of the lane, you will find variations in the depth of the oil (figure 12.1). Looking at an oil graph is like looking at a topographic map. The bowler's goal is to negotiate the terrain and find the best path to the pocket.

Some bowling centers and specific tournaments allow bowlers to look at the graph of the lanes. In fact, some tournaments publish their lane graphs on a Web site. This allows other bowling proprietors to download the oil program into their own lane machines and replicate the competition shot in their own bowling centers. Bowlers can then practice a specific tournament's lane conditions before going to that tournament.

In general, the more evenly distributed the oil, the more difficult the lane conditions. If the lane graph shows a very large amount of oil in the middle of the lane compared with a relatively

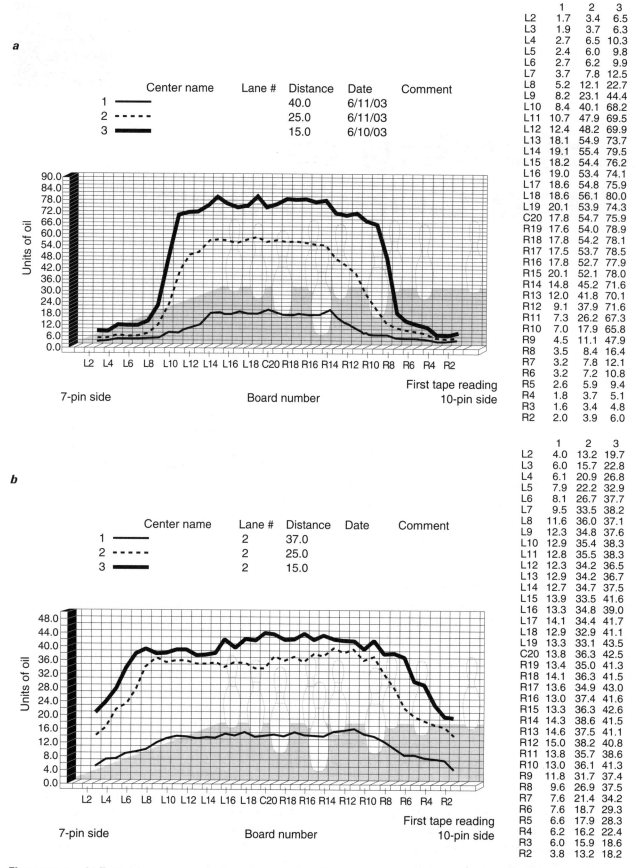

Figure 12.1 *(a)* Typical house lane conditions have a ratio of 8 to 1 to approximately 10 to 1. Significantly more oil is in the center of the lane. *(b)* Sport bowling patterns have a ratio of 2 to 1 or lower. No more than twice the amount of oil is in the center compared with the outside at 15 feet, 25 feet, and 2 feet before the end of the pattern.

Data for figure (a):

	1	2	3
L2	1.7	3.4	6.5
L3	1.9	3.7	6.3
L4	2.7	6.5	10.3
L5	2.4	6.0	9.8
L6	2.7	6.2	9.9
L7	3.7	7.8	12.5
L8	5.2	12.1	22.7
L9	8.2	23.1	44.4
L10	8.4	40.1	68.2
L11	10.7	47.9	69.5
L12	12.4	48.2	69.9
L13	18.1	54.9	73.7
L14	19.1	55.4	79.5
L15	18.2	54.4	76.2
L16	19.0	53.4	74.1
L17	18.6	54.8	75.9
L18	18.6	56.1	80.0
L19	20.1	53.9	74.3
C20	17.8	54.7	75.9
R19	17.6	54.0	78.9
R18	17.8	54.2	78.1
R17	17.5	53.7	78.5
R16	17.8	52.7	77.9
R15	20.1	52.1	78.0
R14	14.8	45.2	71.6
R13	12.0	41.8	70.1
R12	9.1	37.9	71.6
R11	7.3	26.2	67.3
R10	7.0	17.9	65.8
R9	4.5	11.1	47.9
R8	3.5	8.4	16.4
R7	3.2	7.8	12.1
R6	3.2	7.2	10.8
R5	2.6	5.9	9.4
R4	1.8	3.7	5.1
R3	1.6	3.4	4.8
R2	2.0	3.9	6.0

Data for figure (b):

	1	2	3
L2	4.0	13.2	19.7
L3	6.0	15.7	22.8
L4	6.1	20.9	26.8
L5	7.9	22.2	32.9
L6	8.1	26.7	37.7
L7	9.5	33.5	38.2
L8	11.6	36.0	37.1
L9	12.3	34.8	37.6
L10	12.9	35.4	38.3
L11	12.8	35.5	38.3
L12	12.3	34.2	36.5
L13	12.9	34.2	36.7
L14	12.7	34.7	37.5
L15	13.9	33.5	41.6
L16	13.3	34.8	39.0
L17	14.1	34.4	41.7
L18	12.9	32.9	41.1
L19	13.3	33.1	43.5
C20	13.8	36.3	42.5
R19	13.4	35.0	41.3
R18	14.1	36.3	41.5
R17	13.6	34.9	43.0
R16	13.0	37.4	41.6
R15	13.3	36.3	42.6
R14	14.3	38.6	41.5
R13	14.6	37.5	41.1
R12	15.0	38.2	40.8
R11	13.8	35.7	38.6
R10	13.0	36.1	41.3
R9	11.8	31.7	37.4
R8	9.6	26.9	37.5
R7	7.6	21.4	34.2
R6	7.6	18.7	29.3
R5	6.6	17.9	28.3
R4	6.2	16.2	22.4
R3	6.0	15.9	18.6
R2	3.8	13.2	18.2

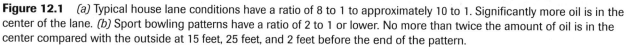

shallow depth of oil near the edges, the lane conditions will play easier.

To add another layer of complexity to the concept of lane conditions, consider oil migration. The oil on the lane is not stationary. As the ball moves across the lane surface, it picks up oil. Some of the oil rubs off farther down the lane, and some stays on the ball. (Be sure to wipe oil off the ball when you pick it up from the return.) The rolling action of the ball dries out the oily parts of the lane and makes the dry parts of the lane oilier, changing how the ball rolls. You must learn to adjust.

In this step, we will discuss three factors of the performance environment:

1. Ball motion. How does the ball perform as it is rolling? What can be done physically and technologically to manipulate the ball's performance?

2. Lane changes. How does the oil move? What does the bowler need to do to adjust to these changes?

3. Lane patterns. What types of oil patterns are typically found in bowling centers?

BALL MOTION

Visualize the lane in three sections: head, midlane, and back end (figure 12.2). The head is the front part of the lane where the heaviest oil is found. How heavy that oil is—its depth—will determine how soon the ball makes the transition to a midlane motion. As the oil tapers out, the ball starts to hit the midlane.

In the midlane, the ball stops skidding and starts moving in the direction of the side roll. This is not an abrupt change. The ball skids less and less as it starts to pick up increasingly more side roll, giving the ball a smooth arcing (hook) motion on the lane rather than a sharp angular change in direction.

Ideally, the ball stops skidding entirely in the back end. It is now in a full end-over-end roll. If there is excessive oil or if the ball was thrown too hard, the ball might still be skidding at this point. If the ball is in a skid, it will tend to deflect when it hits the pins. When the ball is in a true roll, it maximizes the traction effect between the lane surface and the ball surface. The friction between the two surfaces keeps the ball from deflecting off the pins. It will drive (hold line) all the way through the pins.

As the ball passes through each section, it moves smoothly through three phases: skid, hook, and roll. With the advent of newer ball technology, three distinct elements can be used to manipulate these movement phases: surface, construction, and balance.

Although the surface of the ball is always in contact with the lane, and thus always influences

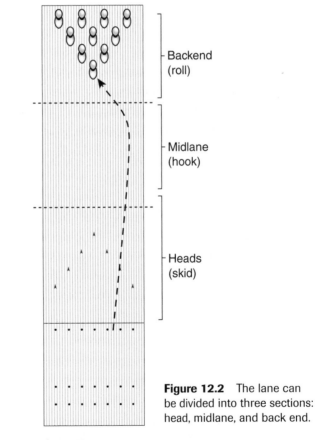

Figure 12.2 The lane can be divided into three sections: head, midlane, and back end.

the nature of the ball's movement, it is easier to consider each technological element as influencing just one part of ball motion. This section gives you an idea of the complexity of the relationship between the ball in your hand and the lanes you are bowling on. We discuss the influence of technology in more detail a little later in the step.

175

Skid Phase

The amount of oil on the lane and the velocity of the ball largely dictate the length of the skid phase. The more oil, the less traction the ball has. Likewise, if the ball is thrown very fast, it will tend to hydroplane on the oil (similar to driving too fast on icy or wet roads).

The technological element that influences the skid is ball surface. If there is too much skid, the ball will not move into the hook phase soon enough to bring the ball back to the pocket. In extreme situations, the ball will skid as it hits the pins and will deflect more easily than normal. The friction between the ball's surface and the lane surface helps resist deflection.

When confronted with too much skid, you have a few options:

1. Move away from the center. During the setup, move toward the edges of the lane. Releasing the ball from a wider position will compensate for the angle lost from the reduction in ball reaction.

2. Reduce ball speed. Being on a lane with lots of skid is like being stuck on ice. Revving the engine only spins the tires in place. Give the ball time to dig into the lane and establish traction.

3. Use a ball with higher surface friction. Get rid of those racing slicks and put on the studded tires. In other words, try using a ball with a rough surface. Many balls on the market have a high coefficient of friction. Try one! It will grab the lanes better.

4. Change your release. Try to get the ball down onto the lane sooner. A high rev rate will only make the ball hydroplane on the oil. Instead, use a heavy roll.

Some bowling centers choose not to put a lot of oil on the front part of the lane. This is noticeable when the ball moves into its hook and roll phases much sooner than expected. Sometimes the bowler himself causes this to happen.

Drying out of the lane heads is a natural phenomenon of the game. As a bowling session progresses, more and more of the oil is removed by the action of the ball. In particular, if many bowlers roll the ball over the same area, they will wear out the oil on that part of the lane. One of the key elements of lane adjustment strategy is to pay attention to where other bowlers are playing the lane. Expect changes on those parts of the lane soonest. Using very aggressive equipment—a ball with a dull or textured surface—with a high degree of friction will also cause the lane to change more rapidly.

If there is too little skid, use the opposite strategies:

1. Move the setup position more toward the center of the lane. This increases the launch angle to the target, sending the ball wider before it starts to hook. In addition, the center of the lane frequently has more oil.

2. Increase speed or loft. Letting the ball travel through the air longer is a way to preserve ball energy. The less time the ball is on the lane, the less opportunity it has to create friction.

3. Switch to a ball with a smoother surface.

4. Use a drive release. Keep the motion passive. Reduce hand action.

Hook Phase

As the ball comes off the oily part of the lane, it starts to generate friction and slow down. As it slows down, it will start to move in the direction of its side roll. The stronger the side roll (or axis rotation), the sharper and more abrupt the change of direction. In addition, if the transition from the oily part of the lane to the dry part of the lane is very distinct in the midlane region, the change of direction will be abrupt. Some centers have a very defined line between where the oil stops and the dry part of the lanes begins. For certain types of bowlers, this radical change of direction makes it hard for them to control the ball's movement. Other bowling centers allow the oil to taper off gradually (called the *buff zone*), which permits for a smoother transition from skid to hook.

Adjust ball speed to alter the hook point. Increasing or decreasing ball velocity has an important effect on how soon the ball starts to hook. Greater speed drives the ball farther down the lane, delaying the hook. Slower speed allows for an earlier transition into the hook.

An early transition will help the ball create an angle to the pins, which is important on oily lanes when ball reaction is minimized. A sharp late hook, though somewhat unpredictable for the less-skilled bowler, has benefits. The longer a ball skids, the more energy it retains because it is not losing as much energy to friction. Balls such as these will move into the roll phase very late; much more of the ball's energy will be put to use at the pins. A late-hooking ball has the potential to come in at a sharper angle. As discussed in a previous step, the more entry angle a ball has going into the pins, the larger the strike pocket and the error margin.

Ball construction also affects the hook point. Bowling balls have two basic types of internal construction based on their center of mass (the point at which the mass of the ball is concentrated). If the center of mass is positioned away from the geometric center of the ball, the ball is said to be surface heavy (figure 12.3a). The center of mass makes large, slow circles, which allows the ball to retain energy. This is an excellent ball to switch to as the lanes dry out.

Balls that have their center of mass concentrated in the middle are said to be center heavy (figure 12.3b). Instead of big, slow circles, the center of mass makes small, quick ones. These types of balls rev up. They are an excellent choice for lanes on which the ball is a little hesitant to hook.

Roll Phase

The ball is in a true roll when the rotational direction and the translational direction are the same. Ideally, the ball should be in a roll just before it hits the pins. When the ball makes contact with the pins, it is at the point of maximum surface contact. The interaction between the lane surface and the ball surface will help the ball hold the line. In addition, all of the ball's energy is directed forward. This, too, decreases deflection. If the ball is still hooking when it hits the pins, then it is still skidding.

If the ball starts rolling too soon, friction will cause it to bleed energy. Watch the ball's movement to ensure it enters this final transition at the correct place. Ideally, you want to see no

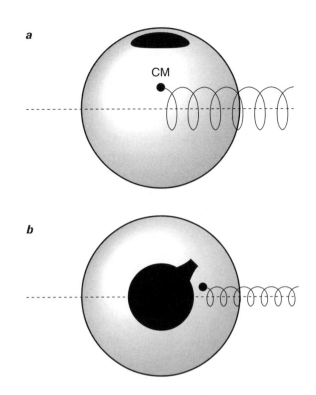

Figure 12.3 *(a)* A surface-heavy ball makes big, slow circles and is a good choice for a dry lane. *(b)* A center-heavy ball makes small, fast circles and is a good choice if the lane is preventing the ball from hooking.

more than three full end-over-end rolls just before the ball contacts the pins.

The degree of side roll affects how quickly the transition occurs. If the ball hooks and rolls too soon, tone down the release. If the ball is not getting to a roll at all, find a part of the lane that has more friction and less oil, or reduce ball speed.

The balance of the ball influences how soon the hook turns into a roll. Both dynamic and stable drilling layouts are available. Dynamic drillings (figure 12.4a) are essentially imbalanced. The core of the ball wobbles, and the ball's effort to find a stable rotation point creates a stronger ball reaction. These balls read the midlane sooner, and the transition into the hook and roll happens sooner. Dynamic balls are great on medium-dry to medium-oily lanes. The ball's reaction, and subsequent angle to the pocket, is strong and predictable.

Stable drillings essentially eliminate core wobble. They are designed to create a smooth arcing motion. When the lane is fairly dry and the ball hooks more uncontrollably, or when the lane conditions are spotty and less predictable and you want a ball that will behave itself, a stable drilling helps restore a measure of control. A surface-heavy ball with stable drilling is useful for very dry lanes, especially dry back ends when the bowler needs to get the ball down the lane and still have a predictable hook. A center-heavy ball with stable drilling performs well on an oily or spotty lane when the bowler wants a strong, predictable arc to the pocket.

If the lanes are dry, the transition into the hook and roll happens too quickly. The hook becomes uncontrollable, and the ball loses energy before it hits the pins. If the lanes are very oily, no amount of dynamic imbalance will change the movement of the ball in time. There is no sense forcing the ball to hook if that's not how the lanes are playing. On extreme lane conditions, stable drillings (figure 12.4b) are your best option. Choose stable, surface-heavy drilling layouts for dry lanes and stable, center-heavy layouts for oily lanes.

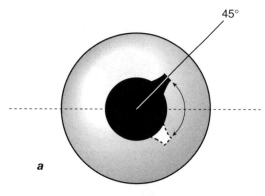

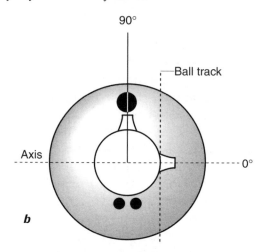

Figure 12.4 *(a)* A ball with dynamic drillings is a good choice on a medium-dry to medium-oily lane. *(b)* A ball with stable drillings is a good choice on a lane that is either extremely dry (surface-heavy ball) or extremely oily (center-heavy ball).

LANE CHANGES

With every throw of the ball, the lanes undergo subtle changes. Eventually, the cumulative effect is enough to alter ball movement. One of bowling's great challenges is to recognize these changes and make the correct adjustments. Adapting to varying lane conditions, not just from bowling center to bowling center but from shot to shot, is what separates the average bowler from the skilled bowler.

Lanes go through three basic phases: fresh shot, carrydown, and breakdown. The fresh-shot lane condition (figure 12.5) occurs just after the lane machine runs. When the ball comes off the oil and enters the dry area of the lane, the ball reaction is usually sharp and consistent. For those with a strong release, the hook can be more difficult to control in this phase.

This phase does not last very long. Several factors influence the rate of change into the other phases. For example, the number of bowlers determines the overall wear and tear on the lanes.

In addition, the area of the lane the bowlers are using influences the lane change. If many bowlers are using the same line to the pocket, that area of the lane will change quickly. The adjustment to the strike line will be small and consistent. It is not difficult to find the oil line and move when it moves. If a group of bowlers is playing all over the lane, the transition will be sporadic and less predictable. As you adjust your line to accommodate lane changes, you may end up running into somebody else's line. Small adjustments on the lane are often followed by jumps to larger adjustments.

Ball selection also affects the transition of the lane. Balls with aggressive cover stocks (surface texture) pick up and remove oil more readily than other ball types. Certain makes of balls—reactive resin and particle balls—are oil sponges. The surfaces of these balls absorb oil. They are designed to create traction, even on heavily oiled lane conditions. These types of balls change the lanes very quickly and very dramatically.

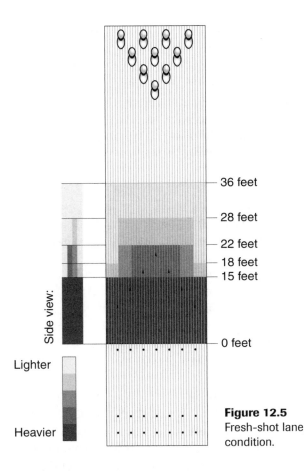

Lighter

Heavier

Side view:

— 36 feet
— 28 feet
— 22 feet
— 18 feet
— 15 feet

— 0 feet

Figure 12.5
Fresh-shot lane
condition.

up. From the very first practice ball, the lanes begin to change. Within the first few frames of the first game, you may need to adjust your line to the pocket.

The easiest adjustment is with the feet. Move in the direction of your mistake. If the ball comes up light—wide of the headpin and too far right for a right-handed bowler—move the starting position on the approach wider. Remember, miss right, move right. In many bowling centers, the amount of oil decreases as you get closer to the edges of the lane. Making the starting position wider changes the angle on the lane, and you may also find an area of increased traction. This will allow the ball to hook and roll before it is affected by the carrydown.

Choosing a different ball is another option. A more textured ball surface will create traction on the oil. A dynamic drilling layout causes the ball to move into the hook sooner (called *turning over*). This allows the ball to set up its attack angle sooner and drive through the carrydown.

As the game progresses, the oil depletes (figure 12.7). Some of the depletion is caused by simple evaporation, but most is caused by

The lane surface influences how quickly the lane changes. Wood lanes change at a different rate than synthetic lanes. Oil tends to pool in the grain of the wood. The wood lane may appear to dry out a little faster, but the condition will stabilize. On a synthetic lane, the oil sits on the smooth, hard surface, waiting for a ball to come by and take it away. With synthetic lanes, there is a perception of a stronger wet or dry condition, what bowlers refer to as *skid/flip ball reaction*. Because of the nature of the synthetic material, the ball skids wherever there is oil, and it really grabs the lane wherever the lane is dry. Lane conditions change quickly and abruptly on synthetic lanes.

Temperature and humidity also affect the lane. The atmosphere in the bowling center affects the thickness of the oil on the lane and its rate of evaporation.

The first transition from the fresh-shot phase is carrydown (figure 12.6). Oil picked up from the head of the lane is deposited farther down. Ball reaction becomes weaker. A line to the pocket that was leading to strikes now comes up light. Carrydown starts to occur during warm-

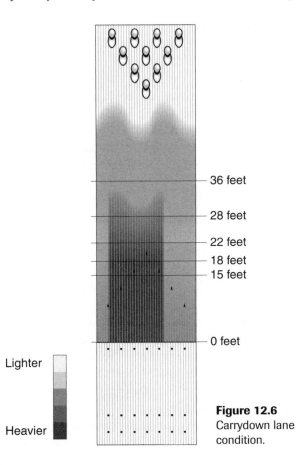

Lighter

Heavier

— 36 feet
— 28 feet
— 22 feet
— 18 feet
— 15 feet

— 0 feet

Figure 12.6
Carrydown lane
condition.

179

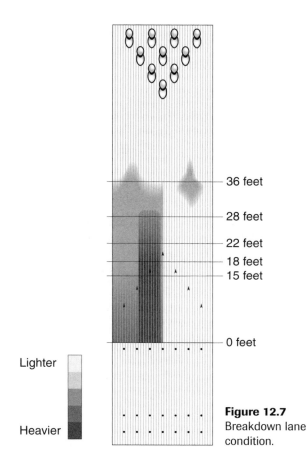

36 feet

28 feet

22 feet

18 feet
15 feet

0 feet

Lighter

Heavier

Figure 12.7
Breakdown lane
condition.

the lane is used up, an oil line develops. Right next to the section of dry lane, you will find an oily section. Move your starting position (and sometimes your target as well) in order to catch a part of that oil line. If you don't move enough, the ball will hit the dry area too soon and hook early. An early-hooking ball may go through the middle of the pins, leaving a split or another difficult spare.

If the adjustment is too large, the ball will be on the oil too long for it to recover back to the strike pocket. If the ball stays too wide or if you leave pins that indicate light hits (see step 10), you may have adjusted too much.

Once you find the optimal area for a controllable ball reaction, stop moving. After playing on this line for a while, the oil will deplete here also. Now you must move your feet and target again. The 1-to-2 adjustment discussed in step 10 (page147) works very well under these circumstances.

An observant bowler is well attuned to the motion of the ball. The slightest deviation from the expected ball path tells the bowler the lanes are changing again. Great bowlers anticipate the changes and make slight preemptive moves. They do this not to keep throwing strikes, though it is nice when that happens, but rather to avoid bad frames. Bowlers who wait too long to adjust are taking a chance. Do not wait until a bad frame before moving. Try to determine what the lanes are doing before a split or other difficult spare clues you in to the need to move. Great bowlers adjust after strikes or spares and learn from their successes. Average bowlers adjust after open frames, learning only from their mistakes.

Ball choice is critical in a lane breakdown condition. A ball with a low-friction surface will clear the heads cleanly. Definitely stay away from dynamic balls. A smooth, controllable arc movement is preferred when the lane gets squirrelly. Stable drilling patterns, which generally create less angle to the pocket, produce more predictable movement on unstable lane conditions. When the conditions become erratic, do not choose a ball with an extreme reaction on the lanes. Save that ball for when the lanes are wide open and strikes are coming fast and easy. When the lanes get tough, a smart bowler chooses a ball that is easy to keep in play.

ball action. In the long run, balls remove oil from the surface. Once the oil on the lane starts to break down, it will continue to do so for the remainder of the session. Nothing will restore the oil to the lane. A ball that was barely making it back to the pocket just a few frames earlier will suddenly start hooking too much. To stay near the strike pocket, you must make very quick decisions about ball selection and target line on the lane.

Balls with high-friction surfaces and dynamic drilling layouts cause the breakdown effect much more rapidly than any other type of ball. Back in the old days, when every bowler used very hard plastic and rubber balls, lanes did not change as much as they do today. The technology intruding into the sport (particularly during the last 20 years) has given bowlers an opportunity to strike like never before, but there is a price to pay. Lane conditions change more rapidly today than they ever did. A bowler who is not willing to learn to adjust to these rapidly changing conditions is in for some trouble on the lane.

So what do you do about breakdown? First, chase the oil line. As the oil on a certain area of

LANE PATTERNS

With the current generation of lane machines, the conditioning patterns are almost infinite. Your goal is to determine the general lane pattern and then fine-tune your line, using sound adjustment strategies, based on that unique lane condition.

Try to find the wall. The wall is the dry area of the lane just outside your intended target (figure 12.8). You will find an oil line just to the inside of the intended target. Playing this line creates an error margin—if you miss in a little, the ball will hold the line; if you miss out a little, the ball will recover. Sometimes the wall is very hard, and the ball will react as soon as it touches it. Other times it is soft; when the ball touches the drier area, its recovery is moderate. If you have a strong release, you will want the ball to touch the wall farther down the lane. If you have a weak release, roll the ball along the wall. Earlier contact with the wall allows more time for the ball to recover.

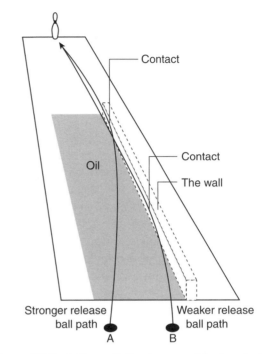

Figure 12.8 At the wall, the dry area of the lane just outside the target, a stronger ball reaction is noticed.

Misstep

The ball reacts too much.

Correction

Too much reaction is a result of hitting the dry part of the lane too soon. Reduce the side roll of the ball, or move your feet to change the ball's point of contact with the wall.

Misstep

The ball doesn't react enough.

Correction

Not enough reaction results when the ball hits the wall too late or hits it at the wrong angle to recover to the pins. Increase the revolutions on the side roll, or move your feet closer to the wall to create earlier recovery into the pins.

The launch angle is the trajectory of the ball across the lane after the release. It dictates when the ball will hit the wall. For bowlers who use little hook or when lanes are oily, use an out-to-in launch angle. Bowlers with a modest hook will want a launch angle that goes straight down the boards. An in-to-out launch angle is used by power players or when the lanes are drying out. The launch angle, in combination with the release strength, determines how strongly the ball rebounds off the wall.

Bowlers with weak releases need to contact the wall sooner (figure 12.8, path B). The ball will need the extra time to make it to the pocket. A bowler with a stronger release needs to just barely touch the wall or to contact the wall farther down the lane in order to keep the ball from hooking too soon (figure 12.8, path A). If the wall is soft—the dry part of the lane does not radically differ from the oily part—bowlers of all types will need to get the ball into the dry part sooner and keep it there longer to generate

181

enough friction for the ball to make the corner, meaning it hooks enough to bring the ball back to the strike pocket.

The three basic types of lane patterns are crown, block, and reverse. The crown condition (figure 12.9) is characterized by more oil near the middle of the lane, with a gradual tapering off toward the edges. Ideally, this condition should allow any style of player to be successful. A player with modest or little hook can move out and find drier boards from which to create ball reaction. Moving away from the center will create a better angle, while the drier boards will generate a stronger roll. Power players step inside and use the oil to either get the ball down the lane or control ball reaction. They need to touch only enough of the drier boards to make the ball hook back to the pocket.

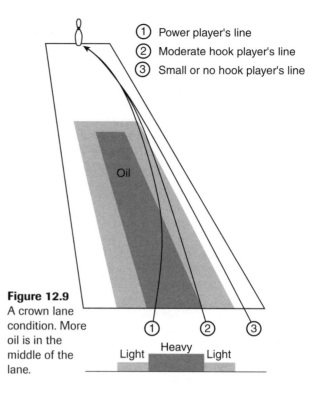

① Power player's line
② Moderate hook player's line
③ Small or no hook player's line

Figure 12.9
A crown lane condition. More oil is in the middle of the lane.

Misstep

You overreact to the crown lane condition by playing too close to the dry area for your release type. Or you underreact by playing too far away from the dry area.

Correction

For either error, adjust your feet, your target, or both until you find the ideal strike line.

When the lanes are blocked (or walled up), it is as if a large block of oil has been placed in the middle of the lane (figure 12.10). Any part of the lane outside or past the block is very dry. The block condition is like the crown condition on steroids. The middle is bulked up, and the outsides are trimmed down.

The block lane condition is the most common condition found in public centers. These centers modify the crown condition to create a favorable scoring environment. It is not unusual for a skilled bowler to average 20 or 30 pins higher on these lane conditions compared with what she would bowl on a flatter, more challenging lane with more evenly distributed oil.

A bowler can miss considerably to the inside and the ball will stay on line. If the bowler throws the ball inside, the oily part of the lane keeps it from hooking. The ball will hold the line all the way to the pins. If the bowler misses outside, the dry area of the lane guarantees a hook back

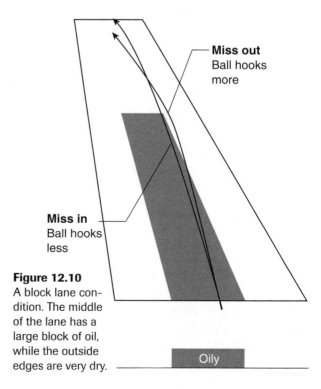

Miss out
Ball hooks more

Miss in
Ball hooks less

Figure 12.10
A block lane condition. The middle of the lane has a large block of oil, while the outside edges are very dry.

toward the pocket. The error margin is ludicrously large. The best strategy for a blocked lane is to play along the oil line. Reduce the ball's side roll, and control the arc off the dry part of the lane.

Although this lane condition favors many bowlers, unfortunately it also puts bowlers of some styles at a particular disadvantage. If you do not throw a hook, you cannot take advantage of the recovery area. A straight ball does just that—it goes straight, on dry lanes just as well as on oily lanes. A move out will create an angle, but the increase in angle will not be large enough to create an enhanced scoring environment. The bowler moving out to the dry part of the lane has other issues to deal with. A move out to the dry area will rob the ball of energy. When the ball hits the pins, it may not be rolling as strongly as it should.

It is not that the straight ball thrower will score any lower than normal; he can pretty much play the game the way he always does. He should just be cautious about getting too close to the heavy oil. The reduced angle that comes from throwing a straight ball to begin with combined with the extra skid and reduced roll from the heavy oil minimizes the straight ball thrower's strike potential. The real problem is that the average hook bowler will score much higher than his skills should dictate. The disparity is not created by any difference in skill level but primarily by the discrimination characteristics of the block lane condition.

Power players who hook the ball a lot also may struggle on a blocked lane as mentioned in figure 12.10 on page 182. The ball will tend to jump as soon as it touches the dry area, but a move into the oil provides too much skid. This condition often gives a power bowler an over- or underreaction from the ball. If she throws to the right, the ball overreacts on the dry and misses to the left. If she throws left, the ball skids on the heavy oil and misses to the right. For this style of bowler, very small adjustments on the lane create large variations in where the ball eventually ends up. It may be very frustrating for these bowlers to find just the right line to the strike pocket.

This style of bowler might be better off using a more conservative game when confronted

with these lane conditions. One strategy is to tone down the number of ball revolutions or side roll. After all, the lane has an obvious dry area from which the ball will hook quite easily. Why try so hard to make the ball hook?

The reverse (or reverse block) lane condition is bowling's version of a cruel joke. The middle of the lanes has less oil than the outside (figure 12.11). If the bowler throws his normal line, the ball may hook too much. When he moves in to adjust for the extra hook, the ball hooks even more. If he plays an outside line, the ball doesn't hook enough. If he moves farther out to adjust for the loss of angle, the ball hooks even less. None of the standard adjustments seem to work.

It is like bowling on top of a wall. Stray just a little to one side or the other and the ball falls off the edge. If the throw is just a little too far right, the ball ends up way right of the strike pocket. Throw the ball a little too far left, and it hooks way left of the headpin. Only one ball path will work for any given combination of release and speed. Misjudge either factor, or play the wrong part of the lane, and you won't score very well. The chance of getting the correct combination perfect on every throw of the ball is unlikely. All but the most highly skilled bowlers will be frustrated on these conditions.

The only satisfaction is that everybody is

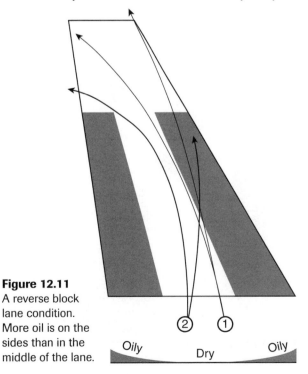

Figure 12.11
A reverse block lane condition. More oil is on the sides than in the middle of the lane.

competing under the same circumstances. When confronted with a seemingly impossible lane condition, keep your head. Play for a relatively straight line to the pocket. Nothing fancy! Try to leave yourself easy spares. A good spare-shooting strategy uses straight lines that mostly take lane conditions out of the equation. A good spare-shooting game, which helps minimize open frames, will allow you to average 170 to 180 even if you are not striking much.

On days when everybody is averaging more than 200, a score of 220 may not seem like much. In a situation where most bowlers are lucky to average 150, 170 games may make you a champion.

Reverse block patterns are rarely put on the lanes intentionally, but they may occur as a consequence of normal play. If the lane condition is fairly flat initially—the oil is evenly distributed from gutter to gutter—a reverse block may develop. Most bowlers like to use the second arrow as a target. That part of the lane develops a track, or dry area, first. As more and more players move their lines in to avoid the dry track, the track area expands. After enough games, little oil remains in the middle. Nobody has bowled on the outsides, so the oil remains relatively heavy there. A dry middle and oily outsides mean a reverse block.

Two common strategies are used to get around this uncommon problem. First, try moving way outside and pointing the ball through the oil into the pocket (figure 12.12a). Hope that the ball does not come out of the oil too soon and barrel through the nose (hit the center of the headpin) or stay on the oil too long and flag the headpin (miss it entirely).

It is a very touchy line to play. Point the ball off the corner, and throw a straight ball—no hook. Throw down the heaviest oil, trying for a back-end hook. Playing the outside line requires accuracy and precise speed control.

The other option is to try moving way inside and driving the ball through the dry area of the lane. Hope you can generate enough ball speed to allow the ball to hold the line. Chances are the angle will be so weak that you won't get a lot of strikes.

A power player might try to use the oil on the opposite side (figure 12.12b). Because there are fewer left-handed bowlers than there are right-handed bowlers, the left side of the lane doesn't change as frequently as the right side. A right-handed bowler might be able to play for a very late hook. Try to keep the ball in the oil for as long as possible.

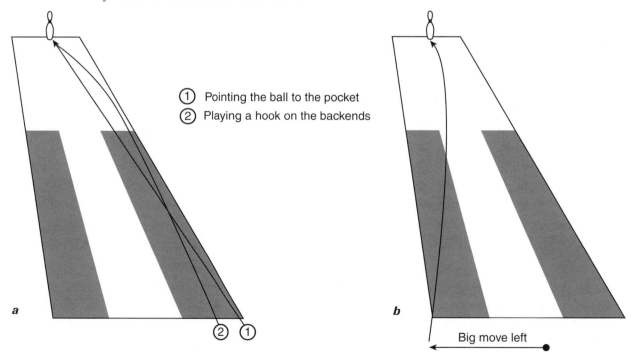

① Pointing the ball to the pocket
② Playing a hook on the backends

a   b

② ①   Big move left

Figure 12.12 *(a)* Move outside and try to force the ball through the oil into the strike pocket. *(b)* A right-handed power player might try moving to the left side of the lane because the left side doesn't change as much.

Sport Bowling

In the last few years, the ABC and WIBC approved a new series of lane conditions specifically designed to challenge bowlers. This new performance level, called *sport bowling*, includes a new sanctioning level for participants. For an additional sanctioning fee, bowlers may establish averages in leagues and tournaments using one of the approved sport conditions. The idea is to give bowlers the option of bowling on the more recreational conditions found in most bowling centers or stepping up to the challenge of the more difficult sport shots. A new awards program to recognize outstanding performance on the sport shots is available only to those who bowl in approved sport competitions. To qualify for these awards, the bowling center is required to take lane readings on a regular basis. This ensures that the oil pattern on the lanes meets the current guidelines for sport bowling.

Sport conditions require a more even distribution of oil. In its original conception, the most oily part of the lane could have no more than twice the depth of conditioner than the least oily part. Staying within this 2-to-1 conditioner ratio eliminates the steering effect that extreme variations in oil distribution can have on the ball's path.

A variety of sport patterns are in use. Some older centers that have wood lanes or synthetic overlays on top of wood are permitted to use a slightly different ratio. Depending on the amount of wear and tear the older lanes have been subjected to, a 2.5-to-1 or 3-to-1 ratio is permitted. The extra oil makes up for the damage older lanes may have experienced over the years.

In any case, the idea is to present a lane conditioning option for those bowlers who are no longer challenged by what the typical bowling center puts out on the lane. If the center you bowl at has a sport-sanctioned league, ask to see the graph. Currently, all bowling centers conducting sport-sanctioned competition are required to do a lane reading before *every day* of competition and forward the data to the USBC. This ensures that the sport standard of the competitive condition is maintained for every day of the competition.

Under the most challenging sport condition, there is no obvious line to play. Small areas of the lane allow for ball reaction, but they are bounded by areas that are more difficult. Finesse and accuracy is a premium on these shots. Most bowlers find that speed control is the critical factor for success. Variations in speed cause the bowler to overthrow or underthrow the line, creating a large variation in ball reaction. In general, no particular style of bowler is at an advantage. Scoring well is a matter of who plays her own game the best.

SUCCESS SUMMARY

This step was largely informative. There are no specific drills for lane conditions other than the drills you have already been introduced to in previous steps. The best advice is to bowl in as many different bowling centers as possible.

Challenge yourself to master as many lane conditions as you can. If you have only one bowling center in your area, then try to bowl at different times. Bowling early on a Sunday when there has been very little play will differ considerably from bowling late at night after the last league shift is finished. Bowl with different levels of competitors. A friendly couples league, which may not have very many serious bowlers, will present a different challenge than a serious scratch league, where many of the bowlers are using the best high-tech equipment they can get their hands on.

Keep notes every day you bowl. Keep track of days when you scored poorly because you were not bowling well as opposed to days when the lane conditions had you baffled. Recognize the difference between bowling well and scoring well.

Write down the details of a particular bowling center. What type of lane surface was it, wood or synthetic? How much oil and what kind of pattern? Did you bowl early or late in the day? What was the weather like? (Yes, temperature and humidity affect lane conditions.) What part of the lane were you playing? What ball did you throw? Were other people bowling with you? If so, did they affect the way the conditions changed?

If you have been conscientious in your practice, you should be developing the range of skills that will allow you to be successful under a variety of lane conditions. You should be confident in changing ball speed, moving your starting position on the lane, and looking at different visual targets. You should be able to throw the ball consistently, with the same kind of roll on every throw.

Develop versatility. Change the number of revolutions and the amount of side roll to create different types of hook. Can you throw the ball straight when you want to? Can you hook it more than you normally would?

Variations in lane conditions are what make bowling such a unique challenge. It is one of the few indoor sports where you do not know exactly what to expect on any given day. Bowlers must be aware of their own performances. Every subtle change of the ball's movement down the lane with each throw gives the observant bowler clues to the lane conditions on that day.

Recognize that lane conditions (and your scoring potential) will vary from day to day and from one bowling center to the next. Constantly practice in order to develop as consistent a physical game as you possibly can. Practice a variety of techniques—changing ball speed, release position, the shape of the swing—to create different ball movements.

Practice playing on various parts of the lane. Become comfortable with a deep inside line (inside the fourth arrow), an inside line between the third and fourth arrows, a track shot between the second and third arrows, an outside line between the first and second arrows, and a far outside line (outside the first arrow and up the edge of the gutter).

Work on your attention skills. Watch the way the ball rolls every time you throw it. Did it lose speed? Did it hook more or less than the previous shot? Did it roll over the intended target?

Watch other bowlers. If they are scoring very well, what can you learn from them? Ask yourself these questions: What part of the lanes are they playing? How are they throwing the ball? What is their style? What type of ball are they using?

If the other bowlers are not scoring well, what can you learn from that? Ask yourself these questions: What part of the lane is to be avoided? What aspects of their style are not particularly advantageous? Have they made errors in their equipment selection?

Once you have developed some skill at the game, you may want to involve yourself in the more competitive aspect of the sport. Bowling is a great social activity. There is enough downtime between shots for conversation and socializing. The competition does not have to be serious. You don't need to be bowling for a lot of money or representing your state or country in order to enjoy competition.

Besides the social aspect, competition gives you the opportunity to demonstrate your skills. There is nothing wrong with being proud of your achievements. If you have set goals for yourself and have reached them, you have every right to be pleased with yourself. But don't stop there!

Success in a competitive environment might be one of the goals you have set for yourself. Perhaps you relish the challenge of proving yourself against another athlete. Maybe you enjoy the camaraderie of teammates, people with similar interests and commitment to an activity.

Whatever your reasoning, you can find a competitive level that suits your needs. There are many competition formats, some more serious than others. The last step discusses the variety of bowling competitions and what to expect if you choose to take your game to that level.

You are getting better. You feel good about your game. It's time to put your skills to the test.

Bowling Competitively

After developing your bowling skills over time, you may find that you want to test your skills against other players. Competition can take many forms, from the friendly competition of a social gathering to the intensity of professional match play. Leagues are the most common form of organized bowling competition.

Let's state clearly, here and now, that not everybody aspires to a competitive status. Some people pursue prowess in an activity solely for the challenge itself, with no interest in matching skills with other participants. Others participate for the physical activity, and the fitness benefit may be their prime concern.

Physical activity presents opportunities for socializing, relieving stress, and developing physical fitness, along with the sense of self-satisfaction that comes from participating

and achieving goals. All of these have positive mental and physical health benefits. None of them have anything to do with a competitive environment, but they have a lot to do with quality-of-life issues.

For many athletes, though, it seems a natural progression of sport involvement to eventually compare their skills with another person's skills. Sometimes this happens in a very informal manner, what might be called a *pickup game*. At other times, this challenge of skills might take place in a specific venue, with rules and regulations outlining the format of the competition and the conduct of the competitors.

For those who cannot resist the urge to match skills, who constantly ask themselves, "Am I better than they are?" a variety of competitive formats are available.

BOWLING IN A LEAGUE

A league is a group of teams usually made up of two to five players that compete at regularly scheduled times. A schedule is posted in a conspicuous place or distributed to the team captains so that all players know whom they are bowling against and where. Most leagues have a formal organizational structure with someone in

charge of scheduling, collecting fees, establishing rules, and settling disputes.

All USBC-sanctioned leagues are required to have elected officers—president, vice president, secretary, treasurer—and a board of directors. The board of directors usually consists of league officers and team captains. A written set of league rules, or bylaws, outline organizational and financial responsibilities.

All sanctioned leagues—leagues whose participants have paid membership dues to the national organization—are given copies of the official USBC rule book. This brief manual covers almost all of the organizational and competitive concerns of the sport. Individual leagues are free to create their own rules to cover special circumstances.

All leagues make decisions about collecting fees, the type of competition allowed, how to handle absent bowlers, whether or not substitute bowlers are allowed, team or league sponsorship, length of the competitive season, and other matters. All leagues should have an organizational meeting a few weeks or more before the start of the season to iron out any disputes or confusion concerning the membership and organization of the league.

Qualification for league membership varies. Some leagues are purely social in nature, organized around the number and gender of team members. They could be all male, all female, mixed, or couples. Other leagues base membership on affiliation with specific groups such as civic organizations, churches, or businesses. If you are interested in joining a league, talk to the manager at your local bowling center. He or she will be able to describe the leagues available and should be able to provide you with contact information for the leagues you are interested in.

The league format determines certain aspects of competition, such as which team is the winner at the end of the day. Most leagues give a certain number of points for each game a team wins. Some also grant additional points for the team with the highest cumulative total.

Some leagues incorporate match play. The first bowler of one team's lineup tries to beat the first bowler on the other team, and so on down the lineup. Frequently these individual points are part of the total points a team can accumulate during the competition.

In the sample league scoring sheet shown in figure 13.1, Karen had the best day on the lanes. Although Betty is the best overall bowler (she has the lowest handicap) and had the second highest series, she actually contributed the least to the team's total score once the handicaps were considered. Betty's handicapped score was only 530, whereas Bob's handicapped score was 560, Jim's was 540, and Karen's was 573.

A league is no different from any other formal organization. It is expected that each member act in a manner that is respectful to both the sport of bowling and the other members of the league. No person's behavior has the right to take away from others' enjoyment of the sport.

Besides behaving in a respectable manner, participants need to fulfill other obligations to make the league run smoothly.

Bowling in a league is a personal commitment. Make time in your schedule to allow for regular attendance. It is unfair to your teammates if you consistently do not show up. If it is unavoidable that you miss an occasional league session, be sure to inform your team

Player	Handicap	Game 1	Game 2	Game 3	Total*
Bob	43	168	142	121	431
Betty	22	106	162	196	464
Jim	63	112	94	145	351
Karen	25	193	158	147	498
Team actual		579	556	609	1,744
Team handicap		153	153	153	459
Final team total		732	709	762	2,203

* To find an individual player's handicapped score, multiply the player's handicap by the number of games played and add that number to the player's total. For example, Bob's handicap is 43. Multiply 43 by 3 to get 129. Add 129 to his total of 431 to get his handicapped score of 560.

Figure 13.1 Sample league scoring sheet, including handicaps.

captain. The USBC rule book outlines some of the responsibilities of a team captain; the league may assign other responsibilities as well. One of the basic responsibilities is that a full team lineup be present on the day of competition. If you are not able to attend, both you and your team captain are responsible for finding a replacement. All leagues have strict guidelines dictating the use of substitutes. Make sure you know the rules for your particular league.

When organizing a team, make sure all the players are committed to bowling in that league. Try to select people who get along. Make sure the players are tolerant of and helpful to those teammates who have less skill.

Some leagues set limits on the types of teams allowed. They may require a specific combination of male and female participants. Others may set a limit based on average. This is called an average cap. The sum of all the individual averages cannot exceed the cap. If it does, the members of that team will not be allowed to bowl together. They must find another combination of bowlers whose total averages fit under the cap. The purpose of an average cap is to prevent the best bowlers from all bowling on the same team. An equitable cap forces the skill levels of the participants to be spread out.

Leagues are a financial obligation. Usually each team is responsible for each session's fees. If any one individual does not pay, the whole team may be held accountable. Every member is required to pay the league fee at every bowling session. A portion of that fee goes to the center to pay for the bowling (called *lineage)*, and the remainder goes toward league expenses such as secretary fees, the prize fund, the end-of-season awards or banquet, and so on.

A bowler who falls behind in league fee payment (who is in arrears) may be subject to a number of penalties:

- Prevented from bowling again until payments are caught up
- Made to forfeit all prize money or awards earned
- Removed from the team at the captain's discretion
- Sued by the league in a court of law
- Barred by the USBC from participation in all forms of sanctioned competition

PLAYING IN A TOURNAMENT

Another popular form of competition, tournaments differ from leagues in that they are not held as frequently and are usually on a larger scale. Tournaments have a variety of formats. Most require membership in the national sanctioning organization.

There is usually a tournament fee based on the type of tournament and the structure. Some tournaments offer multiple events, such as singles, doubles, and team, which may require separate fees. Some keep a separate prize fund for handicap and actual (scratch) events. Many tournaments expect you to have a sanctioned average from the previous year. If you do not have a previous sanctioned average, you may be assigned one.

Most inexperienced bowlers get their feet wet by bowling in local tournaments, which have a smaller field and usually use some manner of handicap system. This is a good place to start your tournament career. The competition is usually more relaxed, and there is a better chance of crossing lanes (being assigned to the same lanes) with people you know.

There are two types of match-play situations. In the round-robin format, each bowler or team bowls every other bowler or team at least once. If the round-robin schedule is properly conducted, each team will bowl every other team the same number of times. Each team will be bowled against once if only one cycle of the round-robin format is used. Some tournament formats award bonus pins for each match won. Some tournaments will conduct an extra round of bowling, called the *position round*. After all the teams have bowled each other, the team with the best win–loss record will bowl the team with the second-best record, third will bowl against fourth, fifth against sixth, and so on.

In an elimination format, players are seeded into a bracket. Sometimes the seeding is based on performance from a previous round of competition (called the *qualifying round),* and sometimes the seeding is purely random.

Another method of scoring used in tournaments is total pins. The total pinfall for an expressed number of games determines the winner. This is a common format for very large tournaments that have hundreds, perhaps thousands, of participants. The schedule may run for weeks or months.

Many tournaments have smaller events within the format. The most common are singles, doubles, and team events. Players can participate in any one of the smaller events, vying for that particular championship. If they bowl in all the scheduled events, the combined totals from all their games make them eligible for the all-events title. In many tournaments, the all-events champion is the most coveted title.

Almost all tournaments offer some kind of recognition for the champions. Money and trophies are the most common forms of recognition. In many smaller local tournaments, the financial reward is minimal. Many bowl in tournaments for the challenge. The praise they receive and the high regard in which their skills are held are reward enough.

If the tournament has a long history or a particularly strong reputation, competition results may appear in the local newspaper. Some local newspapers regularly publish results from league play and tournaments conducted in the area. These articles are likely to be in the sports or lifestyle sections.

Those on the professional tour participate in events with national recognition. Certain amateur tournaments have national recognition as well. The High Rollers, the Hoinke, the Louisville Derby Tournament, the Peterson in Chicago, and numerous others have been held for many years. A few of them have been conducted on an annual basis for more than 50 years. Some of these amateur tournaments have awarded $100,000 or more to the champion.

The men's (ABC) and women's (WIBC) national tournaments are held annually. Thousands of teams with tens of thousands of bowlers participate in these tournaments, which are conducted over a period of six or seven months. Based on the number of participants, not spectators, they are the largest regularly scheduled sporting events in the world. Champions of these events enjoy considerable enhancement to both their bank accounts and reputations.

SCORING FORMATS

In most competitions, each player bowls his or her own game, but there are alternative scoring formats.

Scotch Doubles

Scotch doubles is a popular social format, although leagues and tournaments rarely use this method of scoring. It is a fun way to get people to bowl together. Scotch doubles uses an alternating throw format. One person on the team throws the first ball. If any pins remain, his partner tries to make the spare.

In some versions of the game, the leadoff bowler remains the first bowler in every frame. If the leadoff bowler throws a strike, her partner doesn't play at all in that frame. In other versions of scotch doubles, bowlers alternate turns

on every throw, no matter what. If the leadoff player throws a strike, her partner throws the first ball in the next frame.

Baker System

The Baker system is named after Frank Baker, the ABC official who devised this scoring system. This is the truest form of team bowling, and it is a very challenging format. All levels of the sport, from high school bowling to Team USA, use Baker games as part of the regular competition format.

The Baker system is used at the Intercollegiate Bowling Championships as well. The sectional qualifiers are conducted exclusively using Baker games. The IBC sectional format consists of 16 Baker game blocks of four (for a total of 64 Baker games), conducted over a period of two days.

In the Baker format, all bowlers combine for one game. For a typical five-player team, bowlers one through five in the lineup bowl frames 1 through 5. After the 5th frame, the rotation starts over for frames 6 through 10. No bowler rolls more than 2 frames per game. Under the Baker system, one player cannot dominate the competition. One player cannot carry the team.

Unless all the team members are bowling well at the same time, it is difficult to produce high scores. The ABC has special awards available for teams bowling outstanding scores using a Baker format. One of the rarest feats in competitive bowling is a Baker 300, a perfect game bowled under the Baker format.

Handicap Scoring

When bowlers of unequal skill levels compete against each other, it is common for a handicap system to be used. Handicaps level the playing field, giving inexperienced bowlers a chance to compete. Because most league prizes do not involve large sums of money and many people participate solely for the camaraderie, it makes no sense to discourage new players. High averages get little handicap, while low averages get more. Success in a handicapped competition depends largely on whether a player bowls at or near his average.

The most common system for calculating handicaps begins with a base average. The base average is determined by either the tournament organizers or by the vote of the membership (for those bowling in a league.) The base is the number from which all other averages are subtracted.

Ideally, the base average should be higher than the averages of all the bowlers who are participating. A bowler who has an average higher than the base receives no handicap. However, a bowler whose average is higher than the base will always have an advantage. A handicap will bring the average of the lower-average bowler only up to the base. If the higher-average bowler bowls consistently over the base, then the higher-average bowler has a permanent advantage. The lower-average bowler will never catch the bowler whose average is higher than the base.

A bowler's handicap is calculated by using a specified percentage of the difference between a bowler's average and the base. The lower the percentage used, the more the advantage to the higher average. Every bowler must have an established average from which to compute the handicap. Some competitions specify how many games are needed to establish an average. The USBC uses a minimum of 21 games in the same league as the standard.

If a bowler does not have a verifiable average, she might be asked to use an average from a previous season. In some cases, the competition's rules committee will rate a bowler and assign an average to the player. For a new bowler in a league, often the games bowled on the first night in the league are used to establish an average.

As you can see from the worksheet in figure 13.2, the handicap increases as the percentage increases. Essentially, the larger the handicap,

Game	Score
1	128
2	136
3	142
4	94
5	103
6	167
7	119
Total	889

Step 1: Figure your average. For example, here is one player's scores for seven games:

Once you have the total score, divide by the number of games: 889 ÷ 7 = 127. This player's average would be 127. If you get a number with digits after the decimal, drop any numbers after the decimal point. Do not round up.

Step 2: Subtract your average from the base average. In our example, this player would subtract 127 from the base average of 200 to get a difference of 73.

Step 3: Multiply the difference by the percentage of the system. Common percentages are 80 percent, 90 percent, and 100 percent.

80-percent system: 73 x 0.8 = 58.4
90-percent system: 73 x 0.9 = 65.7
100-percent system: 73 x 1 = 73

Remember to drop any numbers after the decimal point. This player would have a 58 handicap under an 80-percent system, a 65 handicap under a 90-percent system, and a 73 handicap under a 100-percent system.

Figure 13.2 Sample handicap calculation using a base average of 200.

the greater the difference in skill level being made up by the handicap system. With a 100 percent system, all of the difference is made up. Using a percentage less than 100 percent for calculating handicap gives the advantage to the bowler who has a higher average.

In some competitions, no handicap is used. Totals are based on actual, or scratch, scores. These competitions are aimed largely at the bowler who has a higher average. If you are one of those bowlers who resent giving away pins to other bowlers through handicaps, then consider bowling in these types of competitions. Usually the terms *scratch league* or *classic league* are used to describe leagues geared to the higher-average bowler.

Although it evens the playing field, I see the 100 percent system as a disincentive toward improvement. A 190-average bowler who shoots a 190 game has demonstrated more skill than a 120-average bowler who rolls a 120 game. Under a 100 percent system, these bowlers would tie each other. If all it takes to equal a better bowler is to merely bowl your average, what is the incentive to work for a higher average? I have had the most success in my classes with a 90 percent system. Bowlers with higher averages have a slight advantage, inspiring students to keep improving, yet the difference is not so great that the less-experienced bowlers feel disadvantaged.

What do the handicap values stand for? Those are the number of pins added to each bowler's game. If a player is bowling on a team, those pins are added to the team's total for each game of the competition. On standard recap sheets, the handicap is listed in a separate column from the actual scores. The cumulative handicap for all the games bowled is added to the actual total to determine the final total.

Jackpot Bowling

Jackpot bowling exists in a variety of formats. In one format, the bowlers purchase tickets. The funds collected from the sale of the tickets go toward the jackpot. Each night one or more tickets are drawn. The person whose name is on the drawn ticket gets a chance at the jackpot.

This chance usually consists of throwing at a difficult spare or throwing a strike. If the bowler is successful, he wins the jackpot. If not, the jackpot rolls over to the next week and keeps growing until somebody finally wins it.

Another form of jackpot bowling consists of throwing strikes in predetermined frames for each game. In some bowling centers, you may notice a jackpot board. On this board, particular frames will be marked with a strike. These are the jackpot frames. Over the course of the night (usually a three-game series), the bowler must strike in all of the predetermined frames in order to win the jackpot. Some centers have a different jackpot board for higher-average bowlers than for lower-average bowlers. The higher-average board will specify more frames than the one for the lower-average bowlers.

Best Ball: Last Bowler Standing

In this simple elimination format, similar to a skins game, every bowler gets one throw at a full set of pins. All the bowlers who strike or tie for the highest pinfall stay in; everybody else is out. The bowlers throw only at a full set of pins. Remaining pins are swept off; spare shooting is not usually part of the game. If all remaining bowlers tie on a throw, then everybody stays in. Play continues until only one bowler is left.

Crazy Eights

This game is a test of shot consistency for players as they move from lane to lane. The goal is to knock down at least eight pins on the first throw. If you knock down eight pins, move on to the next lane.

In a short format of this game, as soon as a first ball scoring less than eight is thrown, that person is eliminated. The winner is the player who covers the highest number of lanes before throwing less than eight.

In a longer version that is suitable for a team practice, all bowlers start on the same lane. The goal is to make it to a predetermined lane, 8 or 10 lanes away. If a throw of less than eight occurs, the bowler must go back to the starting lane and start again. The winner is the one who makes it to the last lane first.

Black-Light Bowling

Black-light bowling is particularly popular among the younger generation. Many of the synthetic lanes are imprinted with images that are UV-light activated. When regular lights are turned off and black lights are turned on, these lane markings appear to glow. The concept has been taken to an extreme. Bowling balls, tables and seating, bowling shoes, carpeting, and so on are all being manufactured with materials that glow under black lights.

The phrase *Cosmic Bowling* is a registered trademark of the Brunswick Corporation. Only those using Brunswick's system are permitted to use the term *Cosmic Bowling* in the advertising for those events. AMF uses the term *Extreme Bowling* for those who use its proprietary system of lane markings and UV-sensitive equipment.

Events of this sort are purely social activities, and most have no real competitive structure. People are there solely for a good time. These activities usually feature loud music and may include laser lights and fog machines. Few leagues feature this atmosphere, and scoring well is not a priority for most of the participants.

SUCCESS SUMMARY

There are many forms of competition, some more formal, restrictive, or demanding than others. No matter what your social or competitive preferences, there is a competitive format out there for you. Do not worry about your skill level. Go out there to have fun, meet new people, make new friends, and enjoy the game.

If you wish to pursue the game to a high level, then by all means seek out stronger competition. Find out about leagues and tournaments in your area. Get to know some of the better bowlers in your local center. Pick their brains. Talk to them to find out what they do that has made them successful at this sport: what strategies they use in various situations, what their ball-selection process is, how they cope with the stress of intense competition. Bowl in as many bowling centers in as many competition formats as your time and financial resources allow.

If they are available in your area, take lessons. Some lessons are presented in a group format; other instructors offer private lessons. Check the credentials of the person offering the lessons. He should have taken coach's training classes. Check to see if the instructor is USA Bowling certified. If so, what level of certification does she have? If not, has the instructor gone through some other instructor-training regimen (Kegel Corporation, Dick Ritger's school)? Good bowlers don't always make good instructors.

Access as much information about the game as you can. Seek out a reputable pro shop. The pro-shop employees' knowledge of bowling equipment and how different types of equipment apply to your needs will be an important part of your development in the game.

Read! Many publications focus on the sport of bowling. From these sources, you will find information about equipment selection, lane conditions, and physical skill development. Take advantage of the wealth of information available to you from individuals as well as published sources.

Here are some good bowling periodicals:

- *American Bowler.* Published four times a year as a service to members of the USBC, the magazine includes articles on bowling instruction, tournament information, and other bowling-related activities.

- *Bowlers Journal International.* This is the oldest sport publication in the world. Published monthly by Luby Publications, it includes a wide variety of articles concerning professional and amateur events; interviews with the game's notables or influential personalities; and features on the history of the game, technological innovations, and promotional ideas.

- *Bowling This Month.* This monthly publication features articles aimed at the skilled participant. Some of the foremost instructors in the game frequently contribute articles. Featured articles include topics on sport psychology, physical fitness, ball technology and innovations, and skill development.

Bowling books are a wonderful source of skill instruction and bowling information. Here are some good books to read:

- *Bowling: Knowledge Is the Key* by Fred Borden. 1986. Bowling Green State University.
- *Right Down Your Alley* by Vesma Grinfelds. 1995. Wadsworth.
- *Par Bowling: The Challenge* by Thomas C. Kouros. 1993. Pin-Count Enterprises.
- *Revolutions* by Chip Zielke. 1995. Revolutions International.

Videos provide visual instruction and encouragement from some of the best instructors in bowling. Ebonite's *Bowl to Win* features former and current Team USA head coaches Fred Borden and Jeri Edwards. *The Perfect Strike Feeling* is a line of videos presenting the Dick Ritger system of skill development.

No matter what your skill level, you will find bowlers who are either worse off or better off than you are. Treat all your competitors with respect, and be tolerant of those with a different perspective on the game. Know and obey the rules. Have a sense of humor *and* a sense of humility. Demonstrating the qualities of good sportsmanship will make you a winner no matter what the final score may be.

Bowling is an amazing game—so simple in its concept, yet so subtle in its intricacies. The youngest child will find delight in it; the fiercest competitor will be challenged by it. It is an activity that can be a lifetime passion or a part-time pleasure. After reading this book and developing your skills in this sport, I hope you are heading more in the lifetime passion direction. Without a doubt, there will be pitfalls and frustrations along the way. The information provided in this book will help you work through these problems. Be patient! A good bowler is hiding inside all of us!

I hope you have found this book to be informative and useful. The concepts and practice drills presented provide a solid skill foundation for the sport of bowling. The rest is up to you.

I am convinced that with an informed viewpoint of the game, diligent practice, and a commitment to learning new techniques (don't be afraid of change), you will become as skilled a bowler as you ever desired.

Live well; bowl well. And may the pin gods smile on your efforts.

◧ About the Author

Douglas L. Wiedman maintains a continuing lectureship in bowling instruction for the department of health and kinesiology at Purdue University, where he has taught for 12 years. During this time, Purdue's bowling program has become one of the largest college-based instructional programs in the United States. Wiedman also coaches the Harrison High School bowling team in Lafayette, Indiana, where the boys team has won three sectional titles and was runner-up once under Wiedman's leadership. His 2003 and 2004 teams boasted top regional finishes and two semi-state final berths. In 2005, Wiedman's team appeared in the state finals.

Wiedman has 25 years of bowling experience, including 4 years on Purdue's intercollegiate team and 12 years as a member of the American Bowling Congress (ABC). In 2002, he earned Junior Olympic Gold Level II instructor certification, and he earned Team USA bronze level coaching certification in 2004. In August 2005, Wiedman completed the Silver level coaching course, attaining the second highest coaching certification offered by USA Bowling. Wiedman officially became an assistant coach to Purdue's intercollegiate team in the 2004-05 season, and he is a member of the National Collegiate Bowling Coaches Association (NCBCA).

Aside from bowling, in his spare time Wiedman enjoys playing tennis, reading, and attending his kids activities. He lives in West Lafayette, Indiana, with his wife, Beverly, and their three children.

STEPS TO SUCCESS SPORTS SERIES

The *Steps to Success Sports Series* is the most extensively researched and carefully developed set of books ever published for teaching and learning sports skills.

Each of the books offers a complete progression of skills, concepts, and strategies that are carefully sequenced to optimize learning for students, teaching for sport-specific instructors, and instructional program design techniques for future teachers.

The *Steps to Success Sports Series* includes:

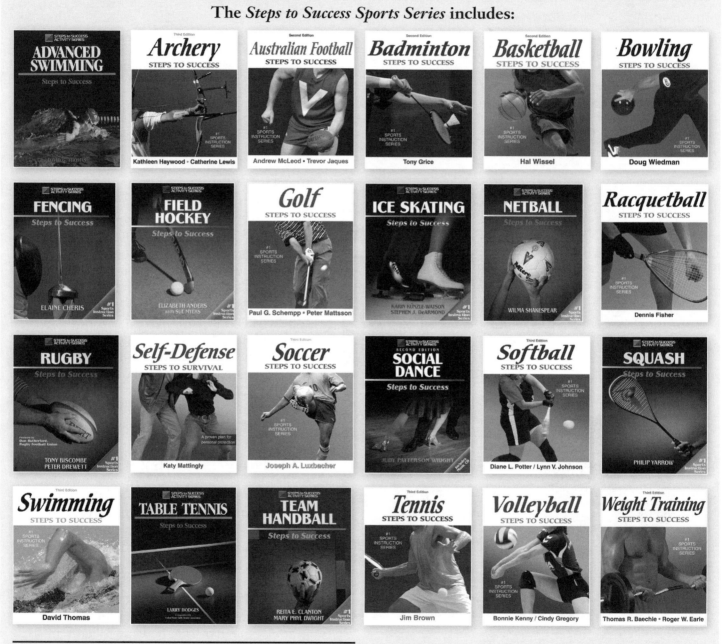

ADVANCED SWIMMING — Steps to Success — David Thomas

Archery — STEPS TO SUCCESS — Third Edition — Kathleen Haywood · Catherine Lewis

Australian Football — STEPS TO SUCCESS — Second Edition — Andrew McLeod · Trevor Jaques

Badminton — STEPS TO SUCCESS — Second Edition — Tony Grice

Basketball — STEPS TO SUCCESS — Second Edition — Hal Wissel

Bowling — STEPS TO SUCCESS — Doug Wiedman

FENCING — Steps to Success — ELAINE CHERIS

FIELD HOCKEY — Steps to Success — ELIZABETH ANDERS with SUE MYERS

Golf — STEPS TO SUCCESS — Paul G. Schempp · Peter Mattsson

ICE SKATING — Steps to Success — KARIN KÜNZLE-WATSON · STEPHEN J. DeARMOND

NETBALL — Steps to Success — WILMA SHAKESPEAR

Racquetball — STEPS TO SUCCESS — Dennis Fisher

RUGBY — Steps to Success — TONY BISCOMBE PETER DREWETT

Self-Defense — STEPS TO SURVIVAL — A proven plan for personal protection — Katy Mattingly

Soccer — STEPS TO SUCCESS — Joseph A. Luxbacher

SOCIAL DANCE — Steps to Success — SECOND EDITION — JUDY PATTERSON WRIGHT

Softball — STEPS TO SUCCESS — Diane L. Potter / Lynn V. Johnson

SQUASH — Steps to Success — PHILIP YARROW

Swimming — STEPS TO SUCCESS — Third Edition — David Thomas

TABLE TENNIS — Steps to Success — LARRY HODGES

TEAM HANDBALL — Steps to Success — REITA E. CLANTON MARY PHYL DWIGHT

Tennis — STEPS TO SUCCESS — Third Edition — Jim Brown

Volleyball — STEPS TO SUCCESS — Bonnie Kenny / Cindy Gregory

Weight Training — STEPS TO SUCCESS — Third Edition — Thomas R. Baechle · Roger W. Earle

To place your order, U.S. customers call
TOLL FREE **1-800-747-4457**
In Canada call 1-800-465-7301
In Australia call 08 8372 0999
In Europe call +44 (0) 113 255 5665
In New Zealand call 0064 9 448 1207
or visit **www.HumanKinetics.com/StepstoSuccess**

HUMAN KINETICS
The Premier Publisher for Sports & Fitness
P.O. Box 5076, Champaign, IL 61825-5076